The ideas of Galileo Galilei have had profound consequences for Western thought. In *Galileo Studies,* the distinguished scholar Stillman Drake presents his famous subject in a unique and insightful new light.

Historians of science have t cerned themselves with the medieval and modern thoug evolution of physics and astrc leo's time. Such an approac. obscure the elements of Galileo's work which were misconstrued or ignored by such later investigators as Bacon, Descartes, and Locke. A fictitious thinker is substituted for the real man.

D1540091

Stillman Drake's book offers a necessary complement to the historical approach, by focusing on the individuality of Galileo's creative work. With a view to placing the origins of modern science in better perspective, Drake examines Galileo's discoveries in isolation from a supposed continuity with the past and from analogies with later scientific developments. The aim is to see Galileo's work as he himself approached and evaluated it. Galileo's unique contributions are viewed against the intellectual backdrop of the age; and his scientific personality is revealed in his work with the telescope, his theory of the tides, and his dispute with the hidebound advocates of traditional science and philosophy.

Galileo's thought deserves study by anyone concerned with the right of free inquiry and the place of an individual in the search for truth. *Galileo Studies*—containing a wealth of information not readily available elsewhere—provides an essential source for an accurate assessment of this great scientific mind.

GALILEO STUDIES

Galileo Studies

Personality, Tradition, and Revolution

———

Stillman Drake

Ann Arbor
The University of Michigan Press

To Bernard Cohen and Marshall Clagett
—who encourage even dissenters—
this book is affectionately dedicated

Contents

Introduction

To hear it said that the Scientific Revolution was preceded by the Renaissance and followed by the Enlightenment would probably excite no emotional response in most of us; more likely, it would be received as a commonplace remark, and the only feeling it would generate would be surprise that anyone should bother to utter it. The same sentence spoken in a gathering of historians of ideas, however, might well provoke lively argument. That there ever was such a thing as the "Renaissance" is as dubious to many historians as the existence of the "Scientific Revolution" is to many others; nor is the "Enlightenment" historically separable from the Scientific Revolution by all those who recognize the existence of both.

This state of affairs is curious, since the contested phrases were originated by historians and not by laymen. Each was coined in order to have a convenient and expressive term by which we could refer to a prevailing set of attitudes toward the world as reflected in the characteristic writings of certain periods in European civilization. The word "Renaissance" conveyed the idea of a rebirth in a particularly happy double sense; that is, a discontinuity with the Middle Ages both by a reawakening of interest in classical antiquity and by a new interest in contemporary things. Abundant evidence can be found of such double rebirth shortly after the invention of printing. The fact that similar interests could be traced in earlier writings neither contradicted that evidence nor established those writings as characteristic of the earlier time. Likewise, the phrase "Scientific Revolution" expressed felicitously an overturn in age-old ways of viewing the physical universe beginning about the time of Galileo; the discovery of medieval anticipations of the new ways neither contradicted the evidence of seventeenth-century change nor established those anticipations as characteristic of their time. The word "Enlightenment" aptly denoted the effect of the rapid progress of physical science as seen by men who next sought the solution of social problems on an analogous pattern, with an optimism scarcely characteristic of any other epoch.

Yet these terms, invented by scholars for certain purposes which they served very well indeed, are now widely challenged if not rejected outright as misleading by historians. That they still serve their original purposes for the rest of us is no surprise; doubtless they will long continue to do so. The puzzle is why they have lost their utility for specialists. And the solution of that puzzle must lie in some change, not in the facts of history, but in the purposes and objectives of historians. Roughly speaking, where it was once the main purpose of historians to distinguish phases of European culture and to emphasize the characteristic differences between those phases, it has now become the principal objective to show how each supposedly different phase was but the superficial aspect of the consistent working of a few great underlying forces. For that purpose, any terminology that emphasizes differences merely tends to conceal the nature of the unitary underlying causes; it is therefore seen as misleading and as something to be attacked and destroyed.

In a word, historians have decided to be more philosophical; or rather, there is a strong movement among historians in that direction.

Nowhere is this movement more evident than among historians of science. A single example should suffice. Copernicus, once portrayed with strong emphasis on his break with past tradition, is now depicted as a timid follower of Ptolemy in the very form and structure of his book; as an adherent of Aristotelian physics and a believer in the Neoplatonic metaphysics of light; in short, as profoundly conservative. Neither portrayal does violence to any known facts; the contradiction between them exists only in a changing interpretation. The change is rather one in the fashionable style of caricature than a change from bad to good portrayal, or from good to better. The old style was to show each pioneer scientist as a revolutionary, acknowledging his debt to the past as little as possible and stressing the novelty of his me highly probable that the discussions of Zabarella, Ramus, and Bacon were widely influential in obtaining a hearing for the new sciences throughout Europe. It is to that phenomenon that historians of scientific ideas might properly address themselves. My objection is only to the implication, and sometimes the clear statement by them, that the influence was more than statistical; that it enables us to find the steps an individual such as Galileo must have taken, and the order in which he took them, toward a new physics. For those steps and their order, we should look primarily to his own writings, and utilize philosophical conjectures from a societal framework secondarily, to fill in any remaining gaps, and then only tentatively. For it is quite possible that any ideas Galileo had on method were formed latest of all in his life, and more as rationalizations of what he looked back upon than as chronicles of what started him out. There is some evidence to that effect in the absence of philosophical content in his early letters, compared with those of the years of his blindness.

It may be objected by the reader that psychological plausibility is hardly to be trusted as a criterion more than logical deduction from the works of many men over a long period. I think that this is true in one sense, and misunderstood in another. It is true that when we seek the broad evolution of the new physics from the thirteenth century to the eighteenth, we need not concern ourselves with the reconstruction of the thought of any one man, and indeed we should avoid the attempt. But when we seek to determine, if possible, the factors involved in some crucial step of the process taken (so far as we know) by a particular man, internal plausibility is precisely what we should concern ourselves with. Nor is psychological plausibility so vastly inferior a criterion in such researches as it is generally thought to be. This constitutes the misunderstanding to which I referred, and I shall endeavor to clear it up.

When we proceed by examining trends of philosophical thought over a long period of time, at the hands of many men, we feel quite safe because of the mass of material. We believe that we can discern a trend in some direction: toward greater use of mathematics, toward mysticism, toward naturalism, toward theology, and so on. But in fact, the number of philosophers whose works survive from any early period is rather small, scarcely a score in any one generation, and even these works are not all in agreement. So the assurance from quantity of material is not as strong as it seems. Next, we unconsciously select two or three works per generation that seem to be of particular interest, and in our selection we use (deliberately or inadvertently) our knowledge of what turned out later to be important to science. In this way it might happen that in a generation when seventeen philosophers whose works survive turned toward mysticism, and three toward a new and higher form of naturalism than known before, we would register a step toward science and ignore the stronger counter-movement. (In one sense, we should be right in doing so, but I shall not stop to amplify this.) I believe that "trends" made up of such patterns are seldom trends in the ordinary sense at all. So the use of logical deductions from a mass of material, after selection in the ordinary way, is not of outstanding superiority to all other possible criteria of truth.

The criterion of psychological plausibility in analyzing the path taken by a man whose writings fill twenty large volumes, on the other hand, is not demonstrably inferior to all other criteria. In the first place, we all possess a great deal of skill in judging other men's personalities—more than most of us possess in drawing rigorous logical deductions from masses of data. It is no good pretending that that skill should be set aside because it is sub-jective, unscientific, and inconclusive. It is no more so than the process I have just outlined in the preceding paragraph, a process that gets its appearance of logical objectivity only by a gracious custom of polite inattention to everything it really involves. But consider your own knowledge, right now, of my personality. You already know a good deal about it, even if you have never met me and have read no more than this introduction up to this point. If you have read other writings of mine, you know a good deal more; and when you have finished this book, you will know still more about my personality. I may even try to conceal it from you, and the chances are that you will be able to detect that also. If I write enough, discerning readers will get to know as much about me as many of my close friends do. Mistakes are possible, but they are not easy to make, for correctness in judging character is so im-portant to survival that we commence to learn it in infancy. Your judgment is not likely to be far wrong, even when you read what I write without consciously wondering about me personally.

If you were then to become interested, and reread what I have written with careful attention to my exact words, you would be able to discern a great deal more about me. In all this, psychological plausibility will be one of your chief criteria, though not the only available one. You could pretty well guess, if you wished, what sort of books I am likely to have read and what sort I consider worth reading; my main fields of interest and how I see them as related; the kinds of people I can put up with, and the kinds that can put up with me. If you were to compare notes with someone else who had attempted the same analysis, you would have a means of judging the accuracy of the method. Finally, if you got hold of my private correspondence, rather little of my personality would still be unknown to you. Especially if you had letters about me, written by others. But that is precisely our situation vis-à-vis Galileo, if we wish to take advantage of it.

There would be no point in anyone's wondering about my interests and my thoughts; but that is not the case with Galileo's. If physics was merely a part of philosophy when he went to school, it was no longer merely that when he died. Something happened to it during his lifetime, and he contributed much to its happening. It is unlikely that Galileo was outstandingly more brilliant than any of a hundred other men alive in his day, including at least a few professional philosophers. Yet they did nothing to change the status of physics. It seems to me evident that some part of the key to the change in physics is to be found in the particular assortment of interests that happened to appeal to Galileo—including philosophy, but by no means limited to it. Among his pupils and their pupils, some (like Castelli) contributed to physics but not mathematics; some (like Cavalieri) to mathematics but not physics; some (like Torricelli) contributed to both. This seems to me interesting. None, so far as I know, contributed anything at all to philosophy, at least not on purpose. This also seems interesting to me. If there are reasons for the differences, they might be found out by biographical investigations. The individual psychology of early scientists might be as useful a study as their joint restoration of Platonism, or initiation of philosophic positivism, or refinement of Aristotelianism, or whatever it turns out that they learned from or taught to philosophers. I hope to encourage others to undertake such studies by introducing them to these fragmentary essays about Galileo.

A permanent landmark in the prevailing approach to history of science was established by the *Etudes Galiléennes,* published by Alexandre Koyré thirty years ago. His goal was to analyze Galileo's thought and disclose his philosophical position by comparing selections from his scientific writings with those of his predecessors and contemporaries. The essays herein contained are concerned more with the scientific personality of Galileo than with his relation to philosophy. The reconstruction of Galileo's thought attempted here makes use chiefly of internal evidence and psychological plausibility; in Koyré's *Galilean Studies,* the criterion was mainly external evidence and logical deduction. The title chosen for the present volume is intended to suggest the complementary character of the two approaches. That our portrayals of Galileo's mind are widely different is to be expected. So is the fact that where Koyré's picture is essentially complete and definite, mine is sketchy and tentative; for ideas in general may be artfully arranged by logic, but there is no art to read a mind's construction in ideas. Koyré's Galileo, like Brecht's, is an actor in a larger drama written for him. Mine is himself a playwright with a great style.

Few of the essays presented here are entirely new. Many appeared in a series entitled "Galileo Gleanings," in various journals; others, in still more scattered places. Most were originally written without a specific theme in mind, but only to throw new light on disputed points, call attention to neglected documents, correct errors in translations, and the like. The selection, modification, combining and editing of previous articles were guided by several considerations. Primarily, the selected studies are intended to illustrate a theme that emerged from them as they accumulated—that insights into the history of ideas, however brilliant, still leave us in the dark with respect to the work of an individual as he himself approached it, performed it, regarded it, and evaluated it. After selecting these, some unnecessary technical material was deleted and some duplication of content was eliminated. It is believed that the result will be a collection of interest to the general reader and of use to the specialist as well, the originals being no longer uniformly accessible to all who are now interested in Galileo. Each essay is essentially self-contained and can be read separately, though this has been achieved at the cost of allowing some repetitions of material to remain. The reader of the entire collection (if any such there be) is asked to overlook those duplications, in the interest of readers whose concern with Galileo is of more reasonable proportions. Previously unpublished essays include some of a background or summary character, again with the general reader in mind. My recent studies of the sixteenth-century background of Galileo's science have been supported by grants from The Canada Council.

Acknowledgment is gratefully made to the editors of *Isis, Physis, Science, American Journal of Physics, British Journal for the History of Science, Journal of the History of Ideas,* and to the Johns Hopkins Press for permission to reprint material contained in this volume. Specific identification of publishers and articles used is made in the ensuing bibliography. Included are the titles of all my "Galileo Gleanings," whether or not reprinted; also the titles of the books most frequently cited in footnotes, together with the short title I have adopted for each in those notes.

I wish also to acknowledge the kindness of my colleague Trevor Levere in reading and commenting on the essays in their present form, and of Miss Susan Penfold and Miss Caroline Mac-Brien in preparing typescript for the press.

BIBLIOGRAPHY

Galileo Gleanings:
  I. "Some Unpublished Anecdotes of Galileo." *Isis,* 48 (1957), 393–97.
  II. "A Kind Word for Salusbury." *Isis,* 49 (1958), 26–33.
  III. "A Kind Word for Sizzi."[1] *Isis,* 49 (1958), 155–65.
  IV. "Bibliographical Notes." *Isis,* 49 (1958), 409–13.
  V. "The Earliest Version of Galileo's *Mechanics.*" *Osiris,* 13 (1958), 269–90.
  VI. "Galileo's First Telescopes at Padua and Venice."[2] *Isis,* 50 (1959), 245–54.
  VII. "An Unrecorded Manuscript Copy of Galileo's *Cosmography.*" *Physis,* 1 (1959), 294–306.
  VIII. "The Origin of Galileo's Book on Floating Bodies."[3] *Isis,* 51 (1960), 56–63.

IX. "An Unrecorded Copy of Galileo's *Use of the Compass.*" *Physis,* 2 (1960), 282–90.

X. "Origin and Fate of Galileo's Theory of Tides."[4] *Physis,* 3 (1961), 185–94.

XI (misnumbered XII). "Further Bibliographical Notes." *Physis,* 4 (1962), 33–38.

XII. "An Unpublished Letter of Galileo to Peiresc." *Isis,* 53 (1962), 201–11.

XIII. "An Unpublished Fragment Relating to the Telescope." *Physis,* 4 (1962), 342–44.

XIV. "Galileo and Girolamo Magagnati." *Physis,* 6 (1964), 269–86.

XV. "An Unpublished Letter, Possibly by Galileo." *Physis,* 8 (1966), 247–52.

XVI. "Semicircular Fall in the *Dialogue.*"[5] *Physis,* 10 (1968), 89–100.

XVII. "The Question of Circular Inertia."[6] *Physis,* 10 (1968), 282–98.

XVIII. "Galileo's 1604 Fragment on Falling Bodies."[7] *British Journal for the History of Science,* 4 (1969), 340–58.

XIX. "Uniform Acceleration, Space, and Time."[8] *BJHS,* 5 (1970), 21–43.

Other reprinted papers:

"Galileo and the Law of Inertia."[9] *American Journal of Physics,* 32 (1964), 601–8.

"The Accademia dei Lincei."[10] *Science,* 151 (1966), 1194–1200.

"The Concept of Inertia."[11] *Saggi su Galileo Galilei.* Florence, 1967.

"Mathematics, Astronomy, and Physics in the Work of Galileo."[12] *Art, Science and History in the Renaissance.* Edited by C. Singleton. Baltimore, 1968, pp. 305–30.

"Renaissance Music and Experimental Science."[13] *Journal of the History of Ideas* (Oct., 1970).

Short titles for works most frequently cited:

Opere	Le Opere di Galileo Galilei. Ristampa della Edizione Nazionale. 20 volumes. Florence, 1929–39.
Dialogue	Galileo Galilei. Dialogue Concerning the Two Chief World Systems. Translated by S. Drake. 2d rev. ed. Berkeley, 1967.
Discoveries	S. Drake. Discoveries and Opinions of Galileo. New York, 1957.
Bodies in Water	Galileo Galilei. Discourse on Bodies in Water. Translated by T. Salusbury. Urbana, 1960.

Controversy   S. Drake and C. D. O'Malley. *The Contro-versy on the Comets of 1618.* Philadel-phia, 1960.

Two New Sciences   Galileo Galilei. *Dialogues Concerning Two New Sciences.* Translated by H. Crew and A. De Salvio. New York, 1914.

Page references used are valid for all editions of the above works, except as to notes in the *Dialogue*.

Notes to Introduction

1. Revised for essay 9.
2. Revised for essay 7.
3. Combined in essay 8 with additions from Introduction to *Bodies in Water.*
4. Revised for essay 10.
5. Combined with revisions in essay 13.
6. See note 5.
7. Combined with revisions in essay 11.
8. See note 7.
9. Combined with revisions in essay 12.
10. Edited for essay 4.
11. See note 9.
12. Edited for essay 5.
13. Revised for essay 2.

Physics and Tradition
before Galileo

Until the present century, it was customary to regard the Middle Ages as a period essentially devoid of scientific contributions. The studies of Pierre Duhem, centered particularly on medieval manuscripts, led him to put forth the contrary thesis that the influence of medieval physical speculations on the origins of modern science was so great that it is possible to look upon science as having undergone a continual development and transformation from Greek antiquity to the present. Progress was at an uneven rate, in that view, but not discontinuous; the so-called Scientific Revolution of the seventeenth century belonged more properly to the thirteenth and fourteenth centuries, and its sources there lay still farther back.

Duhem's view offered an exciting program of research to historians of ideas that has been vigorously pursued in recent decades. Few, however, would adopt the same view today in the spirit in which it was first put forth. With respect to the sixteenth century, for example, it was definitely misleading. Having traced the threads of ancient and medieval mechanics in the notebooks of Leonardo da Vinci, Duhem tended to regard the sixteenth century as largely an epoch of plagiarism from the same sources that had been accessible to Leonardo, or from his notebooks. In fact, sixteenth-century writers on mechanics openly discussed and criticized their medieval predecessors, rejecting much contained in them in favor of the newly published methods and conclusions of Alexandrian and Greek mathematicians. At the same time, some of the physical concepts introduced in the Middle Ages came to be preferred over the orthodox Aristotelian explanations.

Whether we wish to look upon the history of science as continuous or discontinuous throughout the centuries depends more on philosophical prepossessions than it does on the record of ideas and events. Either approach is potentially fruitful of increased understanding, but not at the expense of the other. In any event, the historical understanding of each scientific advance benefits from the careful consideration of its immediate, as well as its remote, antecedents.

In approaching Galileo and the science ushered in by his work in the seventeenth century, therefore, it is good first to attempt to map out the development of physical thought in the sixteenth century. Among the writers of that period we can discern the survival or revival of several more or less conflicting and more or less complementary older traditions. Those traditions are seen in competition or in development in understandable ways, when we take the trouble to identify them and to trace their changing relations. Their various fortunes are related to the fates of manuscripts, the impact of printed books, the making of translations, and the individual prejudices, temperaments and idiosyncrasies of the men who favored or opposed them. If we are patient, we can frame some probable hypotheses concerning the scornful rejection of one tradition and the enthusiastic acceptance of another. Such hypotheses in turn can shed light on the apparently devious course of the emergence of a unified science of mechanics as the basis of a new physics.

In sketching a portrait of physical thought in the sixteenth century, I shall attach specific names to several traditions that have recognizably different temporal sources. Three of these traditions belong to antiquity, two to the Middle Ages, and one to no period and to every period.

The oldest tradition in point of time will be called the Aristotelian mechanical tradition, though it stems from a treatise that was not actually composed by Aristotle himself. Even during the sixteenth century, doubts about its authorship were raised. The treatise is known as *Questions of Mechanics,* and it seems to have been written not long after the death of Aristotle by one of his early successors as head of the Lyceum. There are reasons for calling the tradition in mechanics that derived from the *Questions* "Aristotelian," and employing a different term for the more general physical tradition embodied in medieval and sixteenth-century discussions of Aristotle's authentic writings. First, the ideas employed in the *Questions* definitely bear the stamp of Aristotle's own approach to causal explanation (in terms of motion) and to the subordinate place of mathematics in physics. Second, whatever the doubts entertained in the sixteenth century about the authenticity of the *Questions,* those who supported or attacked the ideas in it attributed them to Aristotle. And finally, the tradition inherited by sixteenth-century writers from commentaries on Aristotle's *Physics,* and still debated during that century among philosophers, may be more properly called Peripatetic than orthodox Aristotelian. The Peripatetic tradition, as I shall use that phrase, was more philosophical than scientific, and will be considered separately, after the recognizable mechanical traditions have been traced.

The *Questions of Mechanics* comprises thirty-five queries about balances and levers; oars, sails, and rudders; dental forceps and nutcrackers; about wheels and beds and vortices. Cabbages and kings are not included, but in their place there are mathematical paradoxes relating to motion and metaphysical speculations about the wonders of circles. The treatise is unsystematic, but it contains at least one central idea that was of great importance to the later development of mechanics. This is the idea that power is related to speed, so that a small force moving through a great distance can balance or overcome a large force moving in the same time through a smaller distance. In this way the lever was explained in terms of the arcs swept out by unequal radii. The reasoning was not mathematical, but causal. The Aristotelian tradition may be characterized as one in which force and motion caused all effects in mechanics, even that of equilibrium (in which no motion actually occurred).

Next in time came the Archimedean tradition, dating perhaps a century later. Euclid had meanwhile established geometry in a pattern of rigorous demonstration. Archimedes was able to apply Euclidean proofs to mechanical problems by the selection of suitable physical postulates. His book on the lever is lost, but those on the centers of gravity of plane figures and on the equilibrium of bodies in water have survived. The reasoning of Archimedes is purely mathematical; causal questions are not considered by him at all. His surviving books deal only with static problems. Force makes its appearance only in the form of weight, and speed is not considered.

The third tradition of antiquity was what I shall call the Alexandrian, represented by Hero of Alexandria, who flourished in the first century of our era, and by Pappus, who preserved a part of Hero's treatise on mechanics early in the fourth century. This tradition is characterized by the attempt to give a mathematical theory of the simple machines—the lever, pulley, windlass, wedge, and screw, and by the description of useful combinations of them.

In addition to his treatise on mechanics, Hero left some works on ingenious machinery worked by waterpower, steam, and compressed air, in a book called *Pneumatics;* another on automatic devices; and one on military machines. Those treatises, like the writings of Vitruvius on architecture, belong to what I shall call the technological tradition, which is rooted in antiquity but is not fixed to any date. It is a living and growing tradition, differing in each epoch, and preserved partly in writing but mostly in practice and oral instruction. As a part of the technological tradition, treatises were written on the balance and the steelyard as instruments in which precision was required for the weighing of commodities in trade, and on procedures for the determination of gold in alloys by weighing them in air and water, an essential technique in financial transactions.

The chief mechanical tradition that originated in the Middle Ages appears to have arisen in connection with some works, probably descended from the Alexandrian period, which belonged in the last-named sense to the technological tradition. Precise mathematical treatises on the theory of the balance and on hydrostatics, of which the earliest European copies belong to the beginning of the thirteenth century, show traces of their Greek or Arabic origin. Associated with those manuscripts are others, bearing the name of Jordanus Nemorarius, containing proofs for a variety of problems in statics. The tradition represented by these works, and the later commentaries on them, I shall call by the name of Jordanus. They constituted a discipline known in the later Middle Ages as the science of weights.

The Jordanus tradition has one thing in common with the Aristotelian tradition of antiquity: its proofs are based on dynamic assumptions, or rather on postulates concerning motion. But the medieval science of weights was entirely independent of the ancient *Questions of Mechanics,* of which no medieval Latin translation or commentary has ever been found. (The first known appearance of a translation and commentary on the *Questions* is in a printed book of the sixteenth century.) It is not difficult to find an ancient basis for the dynamic approach of Jordanus, but it is important to remember that the science of weights was a genuinely medieval creation, and not a lineal descendant of the older Aristotelian tradition in mechanics. The medieval writers were quite familiar with the *Physics* of Aristotle, in which nature is defined in terms of motion and motion is closely linked to weight. It was therefore natural for them to draw on Aristotle's ideas for the postulates of their science of weights, just as the writer of the *Questions of Mechanics* had done before them. But where the earlier writer applied the ideas in discursive style as causal explanations, Jordanus molded them into postulates from which he could draw mathematical deductions in more or less Euclidean form.

The Archimedean tradition was clearly reflected in that of Jordanus. Indeed, in one or two instances, theorems for which proofs were offered by Jordanus were genuine propositions of Archimedes, which had survived in the predecessor treatises with which Jordanus started, or in Archimedean fragments without proofs. But just as the Aristotelian and Jordanus traditions differed radically in form, so the Archimedean and Jordanus traditions differed radically in postulates. It is quite evident that Jordanus and the thirteenth-century writers on the science of weights did not have access to the authentic works of Archimedes. Their postulates, drawn from Aristotle's *Physics,* are usually inadequate to support their proofs, at least without a good deal of special pleading. We shall presently see the effect of this on some sixteenth-century writers.

When we look upon the Jordanus tradition as an attempted synthesis of the Aristotelian and Archimedean traditions, and as built around technological treatises on precision instruments needed for commerce and finance, we see at once the merits of the continuity theory of the history of science. But at the same time we must remember, as continuity historians frequently do not, that the medieval writers did not have access to the definitive works in what are here called the Aristotelian and Archimedean mechanical traditions. Paradoxical though it may sound, they used the genuine works of Aristotle and ignored the genuine works of Archimedes, but their mechanics, nevertheless, more closely resembled that of the geometrical Archimedean tradition than the discursive and causal Aristotelian tradition.

This situation resulted in a striking difference between the key idea used in the Jordanus proofs and its counterpart in the *Questions of Mechanics*. The medieval writers assumed that the product of weight and vertical displacement must be equal at the two ends of a connected system, such as the lever. The *Questions of Mechanics* linked speed and force rather than weight and distance, while it neglected the important distinction between vertical displacements and entire motions along the arcs of different circles. Hence the Jordanus tradition easily suggested the ideas of work and of static moment, while the Aristotelian tradition suggested rather the ideas of force and of virtual velocity. The two approaches were not brought together effectively until the time of Galileo, and I think it is more important to see what kept them apart than it is to gloss over the distinction between them, as continuity-historians are often tempted to do.

Among the things that kept the two approaches apart in the sixteenth century were first, certain basic attitudes toward mathematical rigor characteristic of the different traditions; second, the prevailing social separation of university-trained men from those who were advancing the practical arts; and finally, strange though it may seem, the revival of the genuine works of Archimedes in the mid-sixteenth century. These and related matters will become clearer as we proceed. Here I shall say only that it was probably a good thing that the medieval writers did not have access to the old Aristotelian *Questions of Mechanics,* for if they had had, they would very likely have allowed themselves to be dominated by it. Instead, they attempted to develop a new approach to the unification of statics and dynamics through mathematics.

For the present, we may limit our concern with the Peripatetic tradition to the theory of impetus. Orthodox Aristotelians required that every body in motion be in contact with a mover; for projectiles, the cause of continued motion was supposed to be the air, or any other medium through which motion took place. In place of that unsatisfactory conception, many Peripatetics conceived of "impetus" as a kind of force impressed on the body by the original mover and retained in the body, except insofar as it was destroyed by external resistance or by the conflict between this moving force and the natural motion of the body toward its proper place. This notion of impetus as the cause of motion was very widely held in the later Middle Ages, even by otherwise orthodox Aristotelians.

This extensive, if incomplete, list of traditions from the past assists in the study of physics in the sixteenth century, a period marked by the multiplication of printed books and a rapid rise in literacy. As the century opened, the Peripatetic philosophy of motion was already in print, but (except for the ideas of impetus) that tradition was the special heritage of university-trained men. Philosophy was an important part of every university curriculum, and it was usually taught by disputation in which commentaries on Aristotle, whether orthodox or not, were thoroughly discussed. Also widely accessible, though not through printed books, was the technological tradition. This was the special property of men engaged in the design and construction of buildings, machines, and mechanical devices; though literate, these men were usually not university-trained. But in 1500, neither the *Questions of Mechanics* nor the Archimedean mechanical works had yet appeared in printed form.

In Italy the development of mechanics by writers of the sixteenth century took place at the hands of at least two separate and distinct groups. Neither group took notice of the other except to make occasional criticisms. The group I shall describe first dwelt in northern Italy. Of its three most influential members, two had no formal education; all three were interested in practical mechanics and wrote chiefly on problems of motion and tended to treat static problems dynamically. The other group dwelt in east central Italy; its three chief representatives were all university-trained, wrote mainly on problems of equilibrium, and concerned themselves chiefly with classical science and mathematical rigor. Both groups, though isolated from one another, converged directly on Galileo, the former through his teacher of mathematics and the latter through his principal patron.

The north Italian group was founded by the first important writer on physical problems in the new century; he was born, appropriately, in 1500. He is known as Niccolò Tartaglia, though that may not have been his true name. The word *tartaglia* means "stutter," and appears to have been adopted from a nickname. During the sack of Brescia, his native city, by the French in 1512, Niccolò was taken by his mother into the church for sanctuary, but his tongue was damaged and his chin split by a sword cut, permanently impairing his speech. Without formal schooling, he became a great algebrist and earned a living by taking private pupils, first at Verona, and after 1534 at Venice.

Tartaglia's first book, published in 1537, was called the *New Science;* in it he attempted to analyze the trajectories of cannonballs. Behind the book lies an interesting story. At Verona, in 1531, an artilleryman had asked him the elevation at which a cannon would shoot farthest. Tartaglia gave him the correct angle of 45°, which became the subject of wagers among military experts, who believed this elevation to be too high. Those who backed Tartaglia won their bets at an experimental test. He went on to develop a theory of gunnery and was about to publish it when he reflected that it would be a most blameworthy thing to teach Christians how they could better slaughter one another. Considering his own childhood experience with the French, this seems remarkably objective on his part. But in 1537, when Venice feared a Turkish invasion, his moral scruples vanished, and he published the book in order that Christians might better slaughter infidels. From Tartaglia to the atom bomb, all that seems to have changed in the consciences of physicists is that patriotism has replaced religion.

It is interesting that in his theory of motion, the self-taught Tartaglia followed Aristotle rather than the later Peripatetic tradition. He did not mention impetus, but explained acceleration in animistic terms. Tartaglia analyzed trajectories in terms of natural and violent motion, assuming a straight path for the prevailing motion and a circular arc for the mixed motion. But he realized that mathematically the trajectory must be curved at every point, despite Aristotle. Nor can he have been entirely satisfied with Aristotle's idea that the air carried the projectile, for he clearly recognized the resistance of the air to motion. Tartaglia's invention of ballistics in this book called attention to the discrepancies between physical tradition and practice, but did little to resolve them.

His next contributions were made in 1543, a momentous year for science. In that year Copernicus published his book on the revolutions of the heavenly orbs, and Vesalius published his book on the structure of the human body. Both books invited decisive breaks with tradition. But in challenging Ptolemy's design of the universe and Galen's design of man, they left the Aristotelian interpretation of our immediate physical experience unchallenged. In that regard, two books published by Tartaglia in the same year were destined to be of lasting importance. The first was an Italian translation of Euclid's *Elements,* and the second, a medieval Latin translation of the two genuine works of Archimedes that dealt with statics and hydrostatics. Thus, for the first time, examples of the rigorous application of mathematics to physical problems passed into the public domain, and simultaneously the method of strict geometrical demonstration was put into the hands of engineers and artisans who knew no Greek or Latin.

In 1535 Tartaglia had developed a formula for the solution of certain cubic equations that enabled him to defeat a rival algebrist in a public challenge contest. This came to the ears of Girolamo Cardano, a physician, mathematician, and astrologer of Milan, who in 1539 managed to worm the formula out of Tartaglia under vows of secrecy. Tartaglia intended to make his discovery the crown jewel of a projected treatise on mathematics, which he postponed writing until his editions of Euclid and Archimedes were published. But in 1545 Cardano beat him to it by publishing a still more general treatment of cubic equations in a book of his own, with the lofty reason that the world was entitled to this knowledge. The high-minded action of Cardano has naturally resulted in our calling the method "Cardan's solution of the cubic," while Tartaglia's name is relegated to a footnote in algebra textbooks when it is mentioned at all.[1]

Tartaglia retaliated in 1546 by including at the end of a book called *Various Questions and Inventions* a full account of Cardano's correspondence (and other dealings) with him. In the same book, he set forth the science of weights as a discipline necessary for the correction of errors in the Aristotelian *Questions of Mechanics*. Cardano, not satisfied with having broken his word to Tartaglia, counterattacked in a series of polemics against him through the pen of a pupil, Ludovico Ferrari. As usual, the plagiarist charged his opponent with plagiarism; that is, Cardano accused Tartaglia of having stolen the medieval treatise of Jordanus. This charge is still repeated in current histories of science. But it is usually overlooked that in his Euclid of 1543, Tartaglia had already listed the science of weights as a recognized branch of mathematics and had named Jordanus as its founder. Also, substantial changes in axioms, postulates, and proofs were introduced by Tartaglia in his presentation of the science. It thus appears that Tartaglia considered the science of weights as in the public domain (an inferior version of Jordanus having been published in 1533), rather than that he tried to pass it off as his own invention. At any rate, it was largely through Tartaglia's efforts that all the main traditions in mechanics (except the Alexandrian) appeared in print by 1546, and of these all but the Archimedean works had appeared in Italian. This was partly remedied in 1551, when Tartaglia published an Italian translation of Archimedes on *Bodies in Water;* he also described the diving bell and a method of raising sunken vessels. This vernacular translation of the principle of Archimedes was soon to inspire the first direct attack on Aristotle's laws of falling bodies at the hands of a pupil of Tartaglia's.

Tartaglia died in 1557, while his extensive final treatise on mathematics was in press. Among his posthumous works were the first printed text of the best version of Jordanus, the text of a medieval work on hydrostatics, the first experimental table of specific gravities, and a complete Latin text of Archimedes on *Bodies in Water* from a medieval manuscript.

Tartaglia's algebrist rival, Girolamo Cardano, was born at Pavia in 1500. His father Fazio had been a friend of Leonardo da Vinci. Duhem believed that Cardano had examined Leonardo's manuscripts. If so, he made no discernible use of their mechanical sections in his main work on motion, the *Opus novum de proportionibus,* published at Basel in 1570. In that work Cardano's views are closely linked to the Peripatetic tradition of impetus, a concept that he adopted and extended. He did not advance beyond Tartaglia on projectiles, however; if anything, he fell behind him because of a conviction that violent and natural motions must actually impede one another. Like many of Cardano's ideas, this reflected his strong orthodoxy; for example, he explained acceleration in terms of pressure by the medium as it rushed in behind the body to prevent a vacuum.

Yet in other matters Cardano broke with tradition. He suggested a third class of motions, voluntary motions, in which a body rotated without changing place. (A similar abandonment of Aristotle's dichotomy of natural and violent motions later led Galileo to his inertial concept.) Cardano also stressed the fact that a ball on a horizontal plane would be moved by any force sufficient to overcome the resistance of the air, as was later demonstrated mathematically by Galileo. An important but neglected contribution by Cardano was his treatment of velocity as a ratio of space and time, an idea which could not be accepted widely as long as mathematicians were wedded to Euclid's theory of proportion; it had to await Descartes and analytic geometry. Cardano also thought of supported heavy bodies as having a kind of hidden motion, thus foreshadowing a potential energy concept.

Cardano, a university-trained man of wide interests, seems to have been familiar with all the traditions in mechanics and to have originated some useful ideas. But he did not attempt a systematic treatment of the subject, and nowhere does the Archimedean pattern of proof appear in his writings, either in its authentic or its medieval form.

The north Italian dynamic approach to mechanics found its greatest expositor in Giovanni Battista Benedetti, who was born at Venice in 1530. He was educated mostly by his father, and attended no university. He studied briefly under Tartaglia, probably about 1550. Benedetti learned only the first four books of Euclid's *Elements* under Tartaglia; he is explicit about this, and in terms that imply that he is only giving the devil his due.

Benedetti's first book, published in 1553, dealt with the solution of all Euclidean problems by means of a ruler and a compass of fixed setting.[2] To that book he prefaced a letter of dedication that is of great interest and importance to the history of physics, for it flatly rejected Aristotle's law that bodies fall with speeds proportional to their weights. Benedetti maintained that bodies of the same material must fall through the same medium with the same speed, regardless of their weights. In support of this, he offered a mathematical argument based on the principle of Archimedes and the assumption that nothing retards the fall of a body except the buoyancy of the medium. This was precisely the attack that Galileo at first adopted, many years later, against the same Aristotelian position.

The sudden appearance of this argument of Benedetti's may be reasonably traced to Tartaglia's publication, in 1551, of an Italian translation of Archimedes on *Bodies in Water*. Benedetti revealed his new theory of falling bodies orally to Gabriel de Guzman in the summer of 1552. Clearly it was newly arrived at, for he says in 1553 that he is publishing it in an otherwise inappropriate place, solely in order to prevent plagiarism. It excited wide interest and caused many discussions, some of his opponents declaring him to be wrong, and others arguing that his theory of fall did not really contradict Aristotle. So in 1554 Benedetti published a new version, with citations of the passages in Aristotle that it contradicted.[3] The new book was just off the press when he detected a flaw in his own argument, and a corrected edition appeared immediately afterward. This event had an amusing sequel.

In the winter of 1560, Benedetti gave some lectures at Rome on Aristotle's science. There he was heard by Girolamo Mei, who admired his independence of thought, and probably by Johannes Taisnier, one of the most barefaced plagiarists of all time, who published in 1562 at Cologne the exact text of Benedetti's second book as his own, along with some other thefts.[4] Ironies in this affair soon began to pile up. Taisnier had got hold of the uncorrected edition of Benedetti's book, and published it abroad. In that form it was read by Simon Stevin, the Flemish mathematician and engineer, who made the first recorded experimental test, establishing the fact of equal speed of fall. Stevin then criticized the related theory for its neglect of air resistance—the precise fault that Benedetti had long ago detected and corrected.[5] So Taisnier got the brunt of Stevin's criticism, not for stealing the idea, but for its scientific error. Benedetti escaped criticism for his initial error, but only because his authorship went unrecognized until a century after he had corrected that error.

In 1567 Benedetti moved to Turin, where he spent the balance of his life as engineer, mathematician, and court tutor in the service of the duke of Savoy. His chief work appeared there in 1585 under the title of *Various Mathematical and Physical Speculations*. In it appears not only his buoyancy theory of fall, but also a host of ideas important to physical science, as of course that theory is not. Benedetti recognized the rectilinear nature of impetus, though he applied it erroneously to account for the slowing of rotating bodies. He gave an explanation of acceleration in terms of the accumulation of impulses by a body retaining each impetus, an idea traceable to the Peripatetic tradition. He was strongly critical of Tartaglia and of Jordanus, as were all other writers whose work in mechanics came after the publication of the genuine works of Archimedes. Benedetti wrote a commentary on the *Questions of Mechanics* in which both his respect for Aristotle and his still higher regard for mathematical method are made evident.

The north Italian group of sixteenth-century writers ends with Benedetti. In the year of his death, 1590, the young Galileo was composing his first treatise on motion. After that time, motion ceased to be treated separately from statics, and a unified science of mechanics soon emerged. Statics, meanwhile, had been further developed mathematically in the central Italian school, founded by Federico Commandino, to which we may now turn.

Commandino was born at Urbino in 1509. His background and interests differed widely from those of his slightly older contemporary, Tartaglia. Commandino was first educated at Fano and Urbino by excellent tutors, from whom he learned Latin and Greek as well as mathematics. About 1530 he was taken to Rome by one of his tutors, and remained there for four years as secretary to Pope Clement VII. From Rome he went to the Universities of Padua and Ferrara, returning to Urbino with a medical degree about 1546. After a few years he abandoned medicine by reason of its "uncertainty," and devoted the rest of his life to mathematics.

An acquaintance with Marcello Cardinal Cervini, who had become Vatican librarian in 1548, determined his later career. Cervini wanted a reconstructed text of a work of Ptolemy's which existed only in a poor Latin translation. Commandino undertook to restore the text and thereafter applied himself for the rest of his life to the accurate translation and rehabilitation of ancient

Greek mathematical works, including those of Archimedes and of Pappus of Alexandria. His translations and commentaries far surpassed in scholarship any that had been made before, or that were made for a long time afterward. His Latin edition of the mathematical books of Archimedes was published in 1558, and that of Archimedes on hydrostatics in 1565, when Commandino also published an original contribution to mechanics. That treatise (on the centers of gravity of solid bodies, in the Archimedean style) was a first-rate production and was later a direct inspiration to Galileo, whose first original work in mathematics dealt with the same topic.

Commandino died in 1575, the year which saw publication of his Latin translation of Hero's *Pneumatics* and his Italian translation of Euclid, more accurate and scholarly than Tartaglia's. The curious indifference, or even hostility, of the two Italian groups toward each other is illustrated by the fact that in his long introduction to Euclid, Commandino did not even mention the existence of Tartaglia's previous Italian translation. Commandino's pupil, Guido Ubaldo, likewise ignored Tartaglia except to criticize him as a follower of Jordanus, while against Jordanus he directed very stern criticism, attacking the validity of his postulates and proofs and questioning whether he should even be considered a writer on mechanics for want of mathematical rigor.

Curiously enough, we do not find the same hostility on the part of the central Italian group toward the Aristotelian *Questions of Mechanics,* though it was even more lacking in mathematical rigor than Jordanus and utilized dynamic assumptions similar to his. This fact finds an explanation, at least partly, in a curious theory of the history of mechanics set forth by Guido Ubaldo and amplified by his pupil, Bernardino Baldi, who wrote a detailed commentary on the *Questions of Mechanics.*[6] The disdain of the central Italian writers for Jordanus and their admiration for Aristotle may be due partly to the fact that they were classic scholars and linguists before they were mathematicians, and began their studies in mechanics only after the authentic works of Archimedes were printed in Latin and in Greek in 1543 and 1544.

As to their theory of history, Guido Ubaldo and Bernardino Baldi declared that Aristotle, regarding mechanics as a subject belonging to both physics and mathematics, chose to disregard the mathematical part and to give only explanations drawn from his own physical principles. But Archimedes, they said, saw that the addition of mathematical proofs would render the subject clearer and make it productive of detailed conclusions. So where Aristotle was content to say that a greater circle overpowers a lesser, and therefore a heavier weight may be lifted by the same power on a shorter radius, Archimedes went on to show the exact ratios into which the lever should be divided by the fulcrum in a given case. Thus, they said, Archimedes followed faithfully in the footsteps of Aristotle with regard to physical principles and merely added to mechanics his exquisite mathematical proofs.

This curious theory—that Archimedes was inspired by Aristotle—enabled the central Italians to bypass the medieval writers entirely and to locate everything worthwhile in antiquity. In so doing, they expressed a viewpoint that flowered widely in the Renaissance. It is significant that Guido Ubaldo's stern rejection of the medieval traditions in mechanics arose not from a difference in program, which for him (as for Jordanus) was to reconcile Aristotle and Archimedes, but from a conviction that that program had been already carried out in antiquity and could be properly pursued in only one way. The Aristotelian tradition was not to be merged with the Archimedean, or grafted on to it, but was to be seen as its foundation. Perceiving that Archimedes had pursued a mathematically sounder course than Jordanus, they simply turned their backs on the medieval science of weights. In their return to the classics, they made it impossible for themselves to advance the science of mechanics as a whole, though they did improve the science of statics. In this sense the revival of the genuine works of Archimedes seems to have impeded for a time the progress of dynamics.

Guido Ubaldo, marquis del Monte, was born at Pesaro in 1545. He entered the University of Padua in 1564, the year Galileo was born. After leaving the university he studied mathematics under Commandino until the latter's death in 1575. Commandino had already translated into Latin the *Collections* of Pappus, which was later edited and published by Guido Ubaldo. From Pappus, the spokesman of the Alexandrian tradition, Guido Ubaldo drew (and improved on) the theory of simple machines, the last branch of ancient mechanics to appear in printed form.

He was thus able to publish in 1577 the first systematic treatise on mechanics.[7]

Guido Ubaldo's treatise opens with a very detailed analysis of the balance, entering into minute mathematical details and discussing at great length the purely theoretical point that the pans of a balance do not hang parallel, but converge toward the center of the earth. Guido Ubaldo's exaggerated concern for mathematical precision in statics probably explains his conviction that the rules of equilibrium are of no use to dynamics. The force necessary to sustain a weight *must* be less than that required to move it, and hence the latter defied mathematical analysis. So argued Guido Ubaldo, who maintained throughout his book a sharp distinction between mathematical theory and actual machines. Though he greatly improved the theory of pulley systems, neglected by medieval writers, his scorn of Jordanus prevented him from adopting the idea of conservation of work and even induced him to reject the correct medieval analysis of inclined planes. His belief that the work of Archimedes was based on and had superseded the Aristotelian *Questions of Mechanics* likewise blinded him to the principle of virtual velocities implicit in that treatise.

The revival of Archimedes and the growing anti-Aristotelian spirit of the late sixteenth century was by no means an unmixed blessing to the development of physics. An illustration of this outside Italy is offered by Simon Stevin, who in 1586 carried the logic of Guido Ubaldo one step further. Stevin's book was of momentous importance to physics, but his single-minded devotion to the Archimedean ideal made him completely reject the traditions in which dynamic ideas were applied to static problems. He stated this objection against Aristotle, perhaps sardonically, in an Aristotelian syllogism, thus:

> That which hangs still does not describe a circle;
> Two heavy bodies of equal effective weight, hang still;
> Therefore two heavy bodies of equal effective weight do not describe circles.[8]

Stevin's jibe was aimed at the very foundation of the *Questions of Mechanics.*

In fact, neither the pure Archimedean nor the pure Aristotelian tradition offered a sufficient basis for a unified mechanics, and since sixteenth-century mathematicians could not accept Jordanus, an impasse had been reached. It was in 1588 that Galileo entered the scene by sending to Guido Ubaldo, for comment, some theorems on centers of gravity. Guido Ubaldo at that very time had in press his own commentary on Archimedes and Commandino's translation of Pappus. It is said that in the same year, he was appointed inspector of forts in Tuscany. Whether or not this is true, he was sufficiently influential with the grand duke to secure for Galileo the chair of mathematics at the University of Pisa.

The old traditions tended to remain separated during the sixteenth century. How they were brought together in its closing years is a story in itself. A few remarks, however, will suggest why it was Galileo who ultimately broke the deadlock of separate traditions. As a university-trained man, Galileo was fully familiar with both the orthodox physics of Aristotle and the Peripatetic impetus tradition. His first teacher of mathematics was Ostilio Ricci, reputedly a pupil of the applied mathematician Tartaglia. Ricci put Galileo to the study of Euclid and Archimedes, and probably to that of Jordanus through Tartaglia's editions. Galileo's patron, Guido Ubaldo, encouraged his study of Archimedes and of the Alexandrian tradition in a Latin translation of Pappus. Thus every ingredient of former written tradition was borne in on Galileo by his teachers, his first patron, and his schooling. His own taste for the practical arts acquainted him with oral technological tradition. Few men, if any, had previously been in so good a position to know the strengths and weaknesses of every known approach to mechanics, and thus to see the need for their unification.

Galileo took the principle of static moment from Archimedes and the principle of virtual velocities from the *Questions of Mechanics*. He applied both to the theory of machines and then extended the idea of virtual velocities to hydrostatics. The same principle moved him toward a concept of minimal forces, for which he found a mathematical basis in the purely geometrical (nonmechanical) works of Archimedes, where indefinitely diminishing magnitudes were utilized for areas.

In the sixteenth century the problem of getting on with physics was not, as with us, the problem of fitting new data into a well-established explanatory model. Rather, it was the problem of reconciling several different explanatory models with a single set of widely observed and well-known data, when each model, though presented as complete, was in fact adaptable to some of those data only. Of the half-dozen previous traditions, no single one was entirely satisfactory. Historians who perceive that fact as Galileo perceived it will be in the best position to understand his achievement and to disentangle his contributions to physics from the contributions of his predecessors.

It remains to say something more about the Peripatetic tradition, which is widely believed to have been important to the progress of physics in Italy during the sixteenth century. That belief has its roots in the supposed transmission of a medieval mathematical analysis of certain philosophical problems of change, particularly change in place, or local motion. That analysis had developed the concept of acceleration, the mean-speed theorem, and various mathematical interpretations of Aristotle's rules relating motion, force, and resistance. There is no question that these topics are intimately related to the beginnings of modern physics. But the historical nature of that relation is still in dispute. The dispute seems destined to be perpetual, since it relates not to facts, but to their interpretation. In this argument some facts deserve more attention than they have received. They bear mainly on the dissemination and transmission of ideas, and on possible shifts of interest inside universities during the sixteenth century, especially in Italy.

Those of us who remain skeptical about the direct influence of medieval philosophy of motion on early modern science are fully aware that many printed books contained some relevant medieval texts. Those books replaced manuscripts that had circulated internationally from the thirteenth to the fifteenth century when they began to pass into printed form. The neglected facts to which I refer concern the distribution of those books, temporally and geographically, in the period up to 1600. To illustrate the problem, I have selected a number of medieval authors whose works seem to me particularly significant.

From 1475 to 1500, editions were printed in Italy of relevant works by Grosseteste, Burley, Bradwardine, Swineshead, and Heytesbury; by Buridan, Oresme, Marsilius of Inghen, Albert of Saxony, Marliani, and Gaetano de Thiene. Six of those works had been not only printed but reprinted by 1500. By 1525 six additional works by the same writers were in print, and six more reprintings had appeared. Thus in a period of fifty years, these medieval writers were represented by a book or a reprint every other year, on the average; in all, by at least seventeen books and ten reprints. That is certainly evidence of a lively interest in the medieval philosophy of motion up to 1525, the year in which publication of the Aristotelian *Questions of Mechanics* in Latin caused Renaissance mechanics in Italy to lose its medieval tint and begin to take on its modern tinge. Just as medieval statics in the Jordanus tradition dominated mechanics up to 1525, so the medieval philosophy of motion appears to have dominated physical speculation up to that year.

Now, printers do not venture on editions of books unless there is a market for them. It is reasonable to suppose that printers of the books in question looked largely to university men and to libraries for their market. Library copies might discourage further printings, and privately owned copies would appear from time to time in the used-book trade, so we should be cautious about assuming a loss of interest in the subject from a mere diminution in book production. But this hardly prepares us for what actually appears to have taken place. Thus far, I have found only one recorded edition in Italy of any of the significant books after 1525, and that was in 1536. From 1481 to 1500, at least one of these books was printed in all but four of the twenty years; from 1501 to 1520, at least one appeared in all but nine years; from 1521 to 1540, in but a single year. Thereafter, I find no further editions during the sixteenth century, at least in Italy.

A change in tone and emphasis in philosophical discussions of physics seems to have taken place in Italy along with the sharp decline in printing of books by medieval philosophers of motion and the almost simultaneous appearance of the first Latin editions of the *Questions of Mechanics*. The philosophy of motion is not closely connected with the study of mechanics; for one thing, philosophy belonged naturally within the universities, while mechanics found a new home outside them. Other events in publishing history also suggest that new interests in Italian academic circles may have supplanted the attempts to utilize mathematics in the philosophy of motion, to which little of significance had

been added from 1450 to 1525. In 1526 the first printed edition
of a postclassical commentary by Simplicius on Aristotle's *Physics*
appeared, to be reprinted in 1566 and 1587. It was followed in
1532 by the commentary of Themistius, and in 1535 by that
of Philoponus, which was reprinted in 1546, 1551, 1558, and
1569. Similarly, ancient commentaries on *De caelo* were printed
and reprinted in this period. Possibly those early commentaries
attracted the attention of scholars away from medieval writers; at
any rate, that would be in accord with a well-known tendency of
the Italian Renaissance. Another event is also suggestive; commentaries on Aristotle by living authors appeared in increasing
quantity after 1508, when Augustino Nifo's treatment of the
Physics was published. Similar writings of Achillini, Zimara,
Vallesius, and Vicomercati followed. Averroist disputes and the
relative merits of Plato and Aristotle seem to have attracted the
Italian printers, and may reflect a change in the philosophical
vogue among professors and students.

But if profound mathematical analyses of motion in the
abstract, developed by medieval physicists, had gone gradually
out of vogue in Italy between 1526 and 1580, giving way to an
interest there in classic commentators and contemporary writings
on the *Physics,* and to the textual study of Aristotle himself, this
was by no means the case elsewhere in Europe. Father William
Wallace has shown in several fascinating papers how the University of Paris served as a continuing center for Scotch, Dutch,
Spanish, and Portuguese exponents of the medieval philosophy
of motion.[9] Through the work of Mair, Dullaert, Celaya, Thomaz,
and others, he has shown the unbroken medieval ancestry of
Domingo de Soto's eventual statement in 1545 that actual free
fall exemplified uniform acceleration, implying velocities proportional to elapsed time, and making the mean-speed theorem applicable to falling bodies.

This puts us in a position to understand at last two puzzles
that have attended Soto's statement. The first puzzle is why the
connection between time and speed in acceleration was not applied
to actual falling bodies long before 1545. The second puzzle is
why that suggestion, reprinted half a dozen times in Spain, and
ultimately in 1582 at Venice, attracted no attention and was not

developed into the law of falling bodies, which first appears in Galileo's *Dialogue* of 1632.

The first puzzle is partly answered, in my view, precisely by the unbroken medieval ancestry of Soto's 1545 statement as shown by Father Wallace. It is, so to speak, only an accident that that statement was first made in the Renaissance; it could just as well have been made two centuries earlier. Indeed it is still not impossible that the same statement will be found in some medieval manuscript written long before 1545. At the risk of appearing facetious, I might say that so far as the history of physics is concerned, Soto's statement made in Spain in 1545 *was* made in the Middle Ages. There had been no Spanish printing of the pseudo-Aristotelian *Questions of Mechanics,* no Archimedean revival in Spain; there was no argument there over equal speed of fall, no attempt to analyze the path of a projectile, and no interest in centers of gravity. When Soto's book was reprinted at Venice, it could have been caught up in a whirlpool of ideas; there, a distinctive Renaissance mechanics was already a reality. But in Italy, if I am correct, the subject of Soto's book was already long out of fashion. In Spain, on the other hand, five editions of that book could float placidly on the smooth river of speculative philosophy, from which the new physics was not destined to emerge.

Perhaps neither puzzle is a real puzzle at all, seen in its proper context. The whole problem of Soto may owe its fascination for us to the modern context in which it was originally posed. We remark that Albert of Saxony related acceleration in free fall to space traversed, and that other philosophers related uniform acceleration to time elapsed. For us, it follows that either Albert was wrong, or actual acceleration in free fall is not uniform. Seeing a patent contradiction between the idea that velocity increases in proportion to time elapsed and the idea that it increases with the space traversed, we find it hard to accept the plain historical fact that this contradiction was not immediately apparent; we feel that it needs explanation.

Yet the contradiction was far from being apparent at first even to Galileo; for a long time, he thought he could derive mathematically from the latter idea some consequences of the former. Luckily, he recorded for us in dialogue form the frame of mind that once was his, and that probably had been normal for all his predecessors. In this, he makes his spokesman Salviati define uniform acceleration as increase of speed in proportion to time. The spokesman for common sense, Sagredo, does not reject this, but suggests that without *changing* the concept, it may be made *easier to grasp* by substituting proportionality to space traversed. It is evident that Sagredo considers space and time indifferently as measures of motion, and assumes that if an increasing speed may be made proportional to one of these measures, it must thereby be proportional to the other. Salviati denies the possibility of the suggested substitution. At this point, the Aristotelian spokesman Simplicio asserts his belief that space traversed will be found to measure actual acceleration. Even Simplicio, however (and this is usually overlooked), does not explicitly deny the alternative, that the same acceleration may be measured by time.[10] It is this open-mindedness, this assumption of compatibility, that we should attribute to Soto; otherwise we must either suppose him to have been unaware that other writers had put acceleration in free fall proportional to space traversed, or attribute to him a failure to weigh as alternatives things that he perceived to be mutually exclusive. Neither assumption, I think, is really tenable.

In any event, as I have said, the medieval philosophy of motion had been long out of fashion in Italy by the time Soto's book appeared there. For in Italy the transition from medieval to Renaissance physics had been effected by the exclusion of dynamic postulates from mechanics, and the more rigorous mathematization of statics, rather than by further mathematical discussions of motion within philosophy.

The very fact that no parallel transition had taken place in Spain vindicates the really interesting part of Duhem's thesis. Where the medieval philosophy of motion continued undisturbed by Renaissance classicism, eclecticism, and modernism, as it did at Paris and in Spain, it ultimately evolved a proposition capable of leading on to the mathematical analysis of an important natural phenomenon. I have no doubt that, in time, some later counterpart of the brilliant fourteenth-century mathematicians who developed the idea of uniform acceleration would have raised the question, by *dubitatio* and *responsio,* whether increase of local motion in proportion to elapsed time was really compatible with increase proportionate to distance traversed.

The question had only to be raised by a mathematician in order to be disposed of correctly and promptly. And just as it was only a historical accident that the connection between uniform acceleration and free fall was not suggested long before 1545, so it was only by accident that the critical question of conflict between proportionality of speed to time elapsed and to space traversed was in fact raised in a scientific investigation rather than in a philosophical context. The goal was certain to be reached sooner or later, and it could have been reached by either of those two roads. Perhaps it might have been reached by any of several other roads. Inasmuch as historians are primarily concerned with determining the road that was actually followed, their work has been impeded rather than assisted by philosophical emphasis on the first of these roads to have been opened, as if that road must necessarily have been followed to the end before any other trails were blazed.

Notes to Essay 1

1. Most scholars hold that the honor should go to Scipione del Ferro of Bologna, who had a solution similar to Tartaglia's as early as 1515. It was a knowledge of that fact that stimulated Tartaglia to seek the solution for himself, and his formula applied only to certain forms of equation. Since Tartaglia did not generalize it, and Cardano did, the customary name is justified. Del Ferro's solution has not survived; Ferrari and Cardano claimed to have seen it at Bologna after learning Tartaglia's formula, but their claim, used to justify publication, may be taken with a grain of salt.
2. *Resolutio omnium Euclidis problematum* (Venice, 1553); English translation of dedicatory letter in S. Drake and I. E. Drabkin, *Mechanics in Sixteenth-Century Italy* (Madison, 1969), pp. 147–53.
3. *Demonstratio proportionum motuum localium* (Venice, 1554); English translation in Drake and Drabkin, *op. cit.*, pp. 154–65.
4. *Opusculum perpetua memoria dignissimum* (Cologne, 1562); English

translation by Richard Eden, *A Very Necessary and Profitable Booke concerning Navigation* (London, 1578).

5. *The Principal Works of Simon Stevin,* ed. E. J. Dijksterhuis, vol. I (Amsterdam, 1955), p. 511.

6. *In mechanica Aristotelis problemata exercitationes* (Mainz, 1621); the book was composed before 1590 and published posthumously.

7. *Mechanicorum liber* (Pesaro, 1577); English translation, abridged, in Drake and Drabkin, *op. cit.,* pp. 241–328.

8. Stevin, *op. cit.,* pp. 507–9.

9. See especially "The Enigma of Domingo de Soto," *Isis,* 59, 4 (1968), 384–401, also "The Concept of Motion in the Sixteenth Century," *Proceedings of the American Catholic Philosophical Association* (Washington, 1967), and "The 'Calculatores' in Early Sixteenth-Century Physics," *British Journal for the History of Science,* 4 (1969), 221–32.

10. See essay 11.

2

Vincenzio Galilei and Galileo

Galileo's father, Vincenzio, was a professional musician who figured in the disputes over musical theory and the practices of musicians during the latter half of the sixteenth century. His role in those disputes, which were of vital importance in the transition from polyphony to harmony in the modern sense, was by no means a negligible one. Vincenzio's principal opponent, his former teacher Gioseffo Zarlino, gained a wider following and is better remembered by historians of music today. But that does not reduce the importance of Vincenzio's contribution, any more than the brief victory of Galileo's opponents over his "new science" detracted from the importance of that contribution. Moreover, I believe that there was an important connection between the disputes in which Vincenzio engaged and those that made Galileo famous. That connection has been neglected, if not overlooked, by historians of science.

Biographers of Galileo have noted some rather striking resemblances between the polemic style and the fundamental attitudes toward fact and theory of Vincenzio and his son. So far as I know, however, no one has remarked on the specific area in which their work overlapped; that is, on the treatment of the physics of sound by father and son in their published works. It is to that area that the present essay is directed. In order to clarify the issue to be discussed, it will be necessary first to review some points relating to the nature of the history of science and some principal lines of the development of musical theory and practice.

Historians of science are interested, among other things, in tracing back in unbroken lines those elements of thought that are still present in science today. This is by no means the only approach to a reconstruction of scientific history, but it is a useful

43

one. So far as physics is concerned, its present general pattern
may be traced back without difficulty to the work of Sir Isaac
Newton, who succeeded in welding together inseparably mathematics and physical experimentation. In the case of that fundamental branch of physics known as mechanics, it is fairly evident
that the Newtonian approach was already inherent in the work
of Galileo.

Attempts to find that same approach to mechanics before
Galileo, though numerous, are less convincing. The physics he
inherited can indeed be traced back through medieval Europe
to the Arabs, through them to the Greeks, back to Archimedes
and Aristotle and still further, until it is lost in the mists of prehistory. But before Galileo, physics seems to have been either
speculative—that is, based on general and casual rather than specific and purposeful observations, as with Aristotle—or else purely
mathematical, as in the work of Archimedes. At no time was
there any dearth of mathematical reasoning. But before Galileo,
the systematic appeal to experience in support of mathematical
laws seems to have been lacking. Hence, when we want to trace
modern physics as far back as we can go without a gap in time,
we are obliged to seek the earliest appearance of experiment in
its characteristically modern form.

Here, in order not to wander into interesting, but for the
present purpose irrelevant, inquiries, we may pause to define
experiment in its modern scientific sense. Experiment consists in
the deliberate manipulation of physical objects for the purpose
of confirming some exact rule that has been clearly formulated in
advance. The design of experiments to discover new mathematical
laws came after Galileo's time. The mere accumulation of observations unaccompanied by some previously formulated law to be
tested—a procedure that may be called the Baconian approach—
came much earlier, and belongs historically to craftsmanship
rather than science.

It is hard to believe that there was ever a time, and especially
a time as late as the sixteenth century, when men did not resort
to mechanical experiments to test physical laws. The simpler view
is often taken even by historians of science. There is a hidden
assumption carried in that view, however, that makes it of little
value in research. I shall try to illustrate this by an example.

It is natural enough to assume that the first physical experiments were connected with simple measurements, say the balancing of weights on a scale. Such assumptions are so plausible that they slip in unquestioned. It is thus that people reconstruct the invention of the wheel by imagining it to have evolved from the use of logs or rollers to move heavy objects. Fortunately for those who enjoy speculation, the invention of the wheel goes so far back in time that they need not fear contradiction, though neither can they adduce any positive evidence in favor of their unanimous conjecture. But mere speculation is not history. A historian who tries to discover the origin of scientific experimentation must present evidence. In unbroken succession, systematic experiment to confirm laws does not go very far back in time; not even as far back as the invention of printing, let alone of writing. Since it is not lost in prehistory, the historian may expect to see any assumption or conjecture that he may make about the origin of scientific experimentation challenged, and he is obliged to look for something that can be supported by some kind of recorded evidence.

With this in mind, let us look again at the idea that physical experimentation began in mechanics and was still practiced in the sixteenth century. A very simple and fundamental law in mechanics is the law of the lever. Of course, that law *may* have been discovered in antiquity by a Baconian accumulation of observations, but then again it may not. The law of the lever is a mathematical statement, adumbrated in the earliest known work on mechanics and first proved by Archimedes. Levers must have been long and widely used without their exact law having been known, just as that law may have been deduced by someone who never used a lever, let alone experimented with it. Archimedes certainly made no use of any kind of experimental evidence in his derivation of the law of the lever. I point this out not to imply that there was no scientific experimentation in antiquity, but to suggest that conjectures about its ancestral role in the science of mechanics, however plausible, may be quite misleading.

Obviously, the law relating distances and weights for the lever was both discovered and mathematically formulated so long ago that it would have been simply absurd to perform any experiments to verify it as late as the sixteenth century. Not only that, but the law of the lever is so simple and so far-reaching, once it is known, that there was little point in performing actual experiments to determine the laws of any of the other simple machines. They could be, and were, much more effectively discovered and demonstrated mathematically from the law of the lever. That, at least, was the attitude taken by writers on mechanics in the sixteenth century. Reliance on mathematical reasoning had by then driven out the feeling of need for experimentation that may once have existed. We shall see presently what the corresponding situation was in music. But first let me illustrate the situation in sixteenth-century mechanics, using a specific example.

Pappus of Alexandria, writing in the fourth century, had derived mathematically a law for the force required to drive or draw a heavy body up an inclined plane. His law was mistaken, because he had employed a false assumption; but his mathematical derivation was very ingenious and complicated, and it had the lovely aura of remote antiquity to recommend it to sixteenth-century mechanicians. From the theorem of Pappus, there easily followed a law for the equilibrium of bodies suspended on different inclined planes—also false, of course.

The correct law of equilibrium on inclined planes was stated in the thirteenth century by Jordanus Nemorarius, who did not know the work of Pappus. In 1546 Niccolò Tartaglia published this correct theorem, with some improvements in its medieval proof. Later writers were thus confronted with two different laws, each of which was accompanied by an attempted mathematical demonstration. If ever there was an occasion for experimental test, this was it; moreover, the deciding experiment would have been very easy to perform. But that is not what happened.

In 1570 Girolamo Cardano, who was certainly familiar with the correct medieval theorem and who in all probability also knew the work of Pappus, ignored them both and published a brand-new law for inclined planes, which had to be in error since the medieval theorem was correct. Seven years later Guido Ubaldo del Monte published the first comprehensive work on mechanics. An astute critic of his predecessors, he certainly knew the correct theorem of Jordanus and probably also knew the erroneous theorem of Cardano; yet he adopted in his own book the false (but ancient and elegant) theorem of Pappus. Three conflicting

laws would not all have found supporters in the sixteenth century
if the idea of experimentation in mechanics, to test a precon-
ceived mathematical rule, had been prevalent at that time.

Music and mechanics were more obviously closely related
sciences then than they are today. Both were in fact treated as
special branches of mathematics. In his preface to Euclid, Tartaglia
wrote:

> We know that all the other sciences, arts and disciplines
> need mathematics; not only the liberal arts, but all the mechanical
> arts as well. . . . And it is also certain that these mathematical
> sciences or disciplines are the nurses and mothers of the musical
> sciences, since it is with numbers and their properties, ratios, and
> proportions that we know the octave, or double ratio, to be made
> up of the ratios 4:3 and 3:2; and it is similarly that we know
> the former [that is, the interval of the fourth] to be composed
> of two tones and a minor semitone, while the latter [that is, the
> perfect fifth] is composed of three tones and a minor semitone.
> And thus the octave (or double) is composed of five tones and
> two minor semitones; that is, a comma less than six tones; and
> likewise we know a tone to be more than 8 commas and less
> than 9. Also, by virtue of those [mathematical] disciplines, we
> know it to be impossible to divide the tone, or any other super-
> particular ratio, into two equal [rational] parts [in geometric
> proportion], which our Euclid demonstrates in the eighth prop-
> osition of Book VIII.[1]

But if the sciences of music and mechanics in the mid-sixteenth century were alike in their purely mathematical character,
the relations of those two sciences to the arts that bore the same
names were totally different. Musical theorists were in possession
of mathematical rules that they believed must be very strictly followed in practice. It would be unthinkable for musicians to depart
from those rules, or the very basis of music would be destroyed.
Musical theorists, moreover, got a good deal of respectful attention from musical practitioners and even had a certain authority
over them. This was by no means the case with theorists in
mechanics. Musicians quite frequently studied under musical theorists, but engineers did not study under mechanical theoreticians.
And if there were any theorists of mechanics who believed that
their rules must be strictly followed in practice, this would have

been in the sense that failure to observe the rules would result in wasteful use of materials or in the collapse of buildings, not in the ruin of architecture.

There was a further difference between the arts of music and mechanics in the sixteenth century, a difference that has a bearing on the events which (in my opinion) led to the origin of experimental physics. Commencing about 1500, and quite markedly after 1550, musical practice began to change very rapidly, whereas mechanical practice did not. Those changes in musical practice brought about a real need to expand or alter musical theory, and with it a need for critical examination of its basis and its claims to correctness. No such need was felt by engineers. It was just as easy to test the mathematical rules of music experimentally as it would have been to test those of mechanics. Moreover, in music the tests could be carried out with a great deal more accuracy, for no available mechanical measurement came even close to the precision of the trained ear of a musician. That may very well still be true today, if we do not count electronic devices as mechanical.

It may be added that the only possible means of detecting errors in, and ultimately of overthrowing, the old musical theories was the appearance of experimental evidence against them. No exact analogy exists with the errors in theoretical mechanics, which were in fact corrected by the detection and elimination of certain false assumptions rather than by the study of actual practices among mechanics. One difference was that musical theories were not merely afflicted with a few errors, but were built on a false foundation.

This statement ought to be explained if we are to see how the role of experiment became central late in the sixteenth century, first in music and then in mechanics.

The heart of ancient musical doctrine was an arithmetical theory of proportion credited to the Pythagoreans. The very reason for existence of musical consonances and dissonances was ascribed to certain ratios. That is, the *cause* of consonance was thought to reside in the so-called sonorous numbers. According to the Pythagorean rule, the musical intervals of the octave, fifth and fourth were governed by the ratios 2:1, 3:2, and 4:3. Music owed the possibility of its existence to these three ratios, made up of the smallest integers. Here we have a marvelous example of the use and abuse of mathematics and experiment. Pythagoras was believed, preposterously, to have discovered these ratios as a result of his having noted, in good Baconian fashion, the different tones given out by hammers of different weight when struck on an anvil. However they obtained their simple ratios—most probably through observations of string-lengths—early theorists put those ratios in the place of any further experimentation and derived from them an elaborate theory of musical intonation. In time, the arithmetical theory was seen as transcending in authority its original source. The consequences were not serious for a very long time, but by the late sixteenth century it was no longer possible to maintain the ancient idea of three simple numerical ratios as the cause of all harmony, because of changes in musical practice.

Ancient Greek music, though it bore the name "harmony," was entirely innocent of harmony in its present musical sense. Singing was homophonic; when it was accompanied by instruments, the instruments appear to have been played in unison with the voice—or at most, in the octave. The fitting-together that was implied by the word "harmony" was not a fitting-together of different melodies or of parts sung simultaneously, as with us, but a fitting-together of succeeding notes so as to preserve consonance within the recognized modes, which differed in an essential way from our scales and keys. The limited range of the human voice, and the practice of remaining within the selected mode during a given song, made it possible to decide on the intervals that were to divide the octave without imposing severe limitations on the composition of music. By the thirteenth century, it seems, the simultaneous singing of two or three airs came into vogue, and thereafter much ingenuity was exercised in the composition and arrangement of motets in such a way that separate voices might interweave without clashing. The use of perfect fourths and fifths exclusively as chief accents, or points of repose, fitted in very nicely with this purpose, and the momentary appearance of imperfect consonances, as thirds and sixths were then regarded, did not disturb the ear so long as they were not carried to excess.

In time, however, deliberate violation of the ancient rules began to be attractive; the ears of singers and of listeners came to recognize a sort of general harmonic flow, though the form of composition remained polyphonic. Along with this came the development and multiplication of instruments, used at first to accompany voices, but later coming to be played together with or without voices. Instruments introduced a new element because, unlike voices, most instruments are incapable of producing whatever note the player desires with the exactitude of the trained voice. Lutes, recorders, and viols, for example, unlike trombones and the later violins, are limited to definite sets of notes by fretting or by the positions of windholes. Organ pipes emit specific notes that cannot be varied in pitch by the organist, just as the harp and most of the keyboard instruments are governed by fixed string-lengths. Inevitably, problems arose over the proper tuning of instruments, particularly when different kinds of instruments began to be played together, which brings us to the sixteenth century.

The fretting of early stringed instruments led quickly and naturally to tempered scales for them. Octaves simply must be in tune; even the untrained ear cannot tolerate much variation for the octave, which is heard instinctively much the same as unison. Combined intervals of fourth and fifth together must also make up the octave, and while it is nearly as easy to tune perfect fourths or fifths as it is perfect octaves, you cannot make several strings agree over a range of two or three octaves by tuning them in perfect fourths or fifths. There is that plaguey "comma" that Tartaglia mentioned, and it has to be divided up in some way. For lutes and viols, this was accomplished by tempering, usually by making each successive fret interval seventeen-eighteenths the length of the preceding interval, a formula attributed to Vincenzio Galilei. Organs seem to have been tuned by the mean-tone system from an early period, certainly before Galilei's time, rather than by a tempered scale. Recorders, on the other hand, were tuned in just intonation. But temperament, mean-tone tuning, and just intonation do not make use of precisely the same intervals.

The nature of the difficulty that gave rise to those various intervals is purely mathematical in a sense; the numbers 1, 2, 3 . . . are very useful for counting, but they do not form a continuum. Musical sounds do form a continuum, and hence the whole numbers, even when they are formed into fractions, have only a limited application to all possible musical sounds. Any set of fractions that will divide a given octave into seven different tones will obviously divide the next octave into seven analogous tones; but if we give them names in the ordinary way, those which bear the same names will not all be separated by an exact octave. As Tartaglia had remarked, and as the ancients knew, the ratio 2:1 for the octave and the ratio 3:2 for the fifth implied the ratio 9:8 for the whole tone between the fifth and the fourth. But no rational fraction could express the exact semitone. As Simon Stevin, Galileo's Flemish counterpart in physics, wrote, "The natural notes are not correctly hit off by such a division. And although the ancients perceived this fact, nevertheless they took this division to be correct and perfect and preferred to think that the defect was in our singing—which is as if one should say the sun may be wrong, but not the clock. They even considered the sweet and lovely sounds of the minor and major third and sixth, which sounded unpleasantly in their misdivided melodic line, to be wrong, the more so because a dislike for inappropriate numbers moved them to do so. But when Ptolemy afterwards wanted to amend this imperfection, he divided the syntonic diatonic in a different way, making a distinction between a major whole tone in the ratio 9:8 and a minor whole tone in the ratio 10:9—a difference that does not exist in nature, for it is obvious that all whole tones are sung as equal."[2]

Regarding musical pitch as a continuum, Stevin announced flatly that rational proportions had nothing whatever to do with music and declared that the proper division of the octave into equal semitones was governed by a clearly irrational quantity, the twelfth root of two. It is in this way that we tune pianos today; it enables us to play in all keys without seriously disturbing the ear in any key. Stevin's conclusion was obviously not experimental but purely mathematical; one might say that it only accidentally opened the door to modern harmony. I shall say no more about this here, except to add that Stevin gave a marvelous Renaissance explanation of the basic failure of the Greek approach when he wrote: ". . . the Greeks were of the most intelligent that Nature produces, but they lacked a good tool, that is, the Dutch language, without which in the most profound matters one can accomplish as little as a skilled carpenter without good tempered tools can carry on his trade."[3] Galileo was later to say that the book of

Nature was written in mathematics. It seems that for Stevin, the book of Mathematics was written in Dutch.

And so, at last, we come to the sixteenth-century controversy over musical tuning that created modern music, with experimental physics as a by-product. Defending the fortress were the champions of the mathematical theory of antiquity, which took sonorous number as the cause of concord and asserted that number must *govern* string-length, or placement of windholes, or the like. Besieging it were the partisans of the human ear, with its curious taste for pleasant sounds that goes along with—or at least then went along with—the composition and performance of music. They were in conflict, as Stevin observed, and with or without the Dutch language, the conflict had to be resolved. The question was which was to be master, numbers or sounds?

The conduct of the debate is instructive, because it is symbolic in many ways of all the debates that created the modern world, and of many that are still going on in it. For it was at once a battle of authority versus fredom; of theory versus practice; of purity versus beauty. Curiously enough, the issue was partly decided against the defenders of antiquity by the recovery of an ancient treatise that had been ignored by most theorists before the sixteenth century. Nothing helped a good cause in that century like the discovery that some ancient writer had already thought of it. Thus Copernicus was careful to mention some ancient writers who were said to have believed in the motion of the earth. It was of great help to musicians, in their struggle for emancipation from the syntonic diatonic tuning of Ptolemy, to be able to cite the view of Aristoxenus that when all was said and done, the ear of the musician must prevail.

Paradoxically, the struggle to free and broaden music in our own time is a complete reversal of the struggle that freed and broadened it in the seventeenth century. Electronic computer music has much in common with the program of those conservatives who fought to preserve the mathematical beauty of sonorous number and superparticular ratios against the mere pleasure' of the human ear. The argument of Gioseffo Zarlino, roughly paraphrased for its philosophical content, was that there could be only one correct tuning, established by the mystic properties of numbers, and if that tuning put limitations on instrumental music, then so much the worse for the instruments. The voice must govern instruments, and the voice was in turn governed by divine proportions of numbers. It is amusing to me that the argument for the divine right of theory, used in the sixteenth century to confine music within bounds, can be used in the twentieth to support the abandonment of all bounds, and with them all mere sensory criteria for music. "Theory before pleasure," once conservative, is now avant-garde.

I might add that if, as I am now inclined to believe, music was the father of modern physical science and mathematics was its mother, we may be about to witness the devastating culmination of a monumental Oedipus complex. I hope not, inasmuch as I am personally no less fond of both parents than I am of their child. I should not be at all distressed to see science wedded to mathematics, but not at the cost of its first destroying music, and later blinding itself entirely, driven by guilt and grief. But as the world goes, I should be less astonished than would Galileo, who started the courtship if he did not officiate at the wedding.

On purely theoretical grounds, Zarlino advocated the extension of the Pythagorean ratios up to the number 6, from the ancient 4. This would allow as consonances, in addition to the fourth and fifth, the major sixth as 5:3, the major third as 5:4, and the minor third as 6:5. He was also willing to allow the minor sixth as 8:5, but that finished the list; no other consonances were admissible. The number 6 was, after all, the first perfect number— that is, the lowest number that was equal to the sum of its factors. With that magical addition, the sonorous numbers could safely be extended to accommodate thirds and sixths, but no further. Zarlino's *Harmonical Institutions,* published in 1558, did away with all rivals of the syntonic diatonic tuning, including equal temperament and the mean-tone system, as theoretically unjustifiable. His treatise on composition thus still limited music to polyphony, though that was given somewhat larger range. Method had been perfected. Mathematical music theory was saved by the *senario,* as Zarlino called his six-based ratio system. But harmony was stillborn if that system prevailed.

About five years later Zarlino's scheme was subjected to criticism by Giovanni Battista Benedetti, Galileo's most important Italian precursor. Benedetti's achievements in the physics of music are contained in two letters written to Cipriano da Rore at Venice, probably in 1563, the year before Galileo was born. Benedetti showed, by means of examples, that a strict adherence by singers to Zarlino's ratios for consonances could result in a considerable change of pitch within a few bars. Benedetti argued from this that singers must in fact make use of some kind of tempered scale in order to preserve even the most elemental musical orthodoxy that relates the closing to the opening tone.[4]

Next, Benedetti proceeded to examine the fundamental problem from the standpoint of physics. Instead of relating pitch and consonance directly to numbers, that is to string-lengths and their ratios, he related them to rates of vibration of the source of sound. Consonance, he asserted, was heard when air waves produced by different notes concurred or recurred frequently together; dissonance, when the air waves joined together infrequently. Thus, strings vibrating in the ratio 2:1 would concur on every other vibration; in the ratio 3:2, on every sixth vibration, and so on. The direct cause of consonance was thus related by Benedetti to a physical phenomenon, which in turn bore a relation to certain numbers; numbers as such were no longer regarded by Benedetti as the cause of the phenomenon of consonance. The cause was a physical phenomenon, for which he suggested an index formed by multiplying together the terms of the interval-ratio. The smaller this product, the greater the consonance. Viewed in this light, consonance and dissonance were not two separate and contradictory qualities of sounds, but rather they were terms in a continuous series without sharp divisions. In Benedetti's index, the traditionally abhorred subminor fifth with the ratio 7:5 was in fact a better consonance than the minor sixth with the ratio 8:5 (which Zarlino himself had allowed, even though it lay outside his *senario*). Obviously, Benedetti offered not just a further modification of the old theory, but a fundamental attack on the very basis of that theory.

Yet Benedetti's results were in an important sense only a small start toward the modern physical science of musical acoustics. His brief writings on music did not remove mathematics from musical theory; they merely changed its role. For his contemporaries, as for the ancients, numbers were the cause of harmonious sound in a totally different way from which Benedetti saw them as related to that cause. They regarded numbers as ruling the nature

of sound; Benedetti formulated a physical theory of sound that
was capable of explaining the association of certain numbers or
ratios with certain tonal effects. Since Benedetti himself was not a
musician, he did not concern himself with the possibility or desira-
bility of expanding the range of acceptable tonal effects. This
would soon come.

What Benedetti contributed was a new explanation of known
effects rather than a basis for the exploration of new ground. Thus
to the question, "Why is the fifth more harmonious than the
major third?" the traditional answer was of this form: "Because
the ratio 3:2 contains two sonorous numbers, and the ratio 5:4
does not." Zarlino's reply might have been: "The ancients were
mistaken; both are equally harmonious, for all numbers within
the *senario* are sonorous numbers. But since sonorous numbers are
the cause of harmony, the slightest departure in practice from the
approved ratios must be avoided, or dissonance will result." Benedetti's reply would have been, "Because harmony proceeds from
coincidence of air-pulses, which occurs with every sixth vibration
for the fifth, and only with every twentieth for the major third."
But to the question, "What can we do to widen the scope of
harmonious music?" no one gave an answer. To Benedetti's opponents, the question was unthinkable; and to Benedetti, the first
man who might have been able to answer, the question happened
not to occur. For he was a theorist and not a practicing musician.

Zarlino, who opposed any systematic tempering of the vocal
scales, never heard of Benedetti's demonstration that this was practically necessary, and that the *senario* could no more govern consonance than could sonorous number.

Benedetti's letters were not published until 1585, but Zarlino
was opposed in print by his former pupil, Vincenzio Galilei. In
1578 Galilei sent to Zarlino a discourse in which the departures
of practicing musicians from the tuning recommended by Zarlino
were stated and defended; there was no escape from a tempered
scale in the music of the late sixteenth century. Zarlino paid no
attention, other than to discourage the printing of his former
pupil's book at Venice. It nevertheless appeared, much expanded,
at Florence in 1581. Galilei, who had long followed Zarlino's
teaching, began to question it only after he had learned from
Girolamo Mei, the best informed man in Italy on ancient music,

that among the ancients themselves there had been musicians who
questioned the absolute authority of mathematical theory over
sense. It was Mei who invited Galilei to put to actual test certain
doctrines of the old theory. The result was Galilei's abandonment
of Zarlino's teaching, and along with it the whole mathematical
mystique of antiquity.

Zarlino, far from accepting the new view, counterattacked
in 1588 with his final book on music theory, the *Sopplementi
Armoniche*. Though he did not mention Galilei by name, he
quoted from his book and identified him as a former pupil. Galilei
lost no time in replying; in 1589 he published a little volume
which he dedicated, with obvious sarcasm, to Zarlino. The first
part of this book is merely polemical and personal, but the balance contains something of great interest with respect to the beginnings of experimental physics.

Galilei was outspokenly against the acceptance of authority
in matters that can be investigated directly. He did not even
accept the idea that some musical intervals were "natural," or that
any were consonant by reason of their being capable of representation by simple proportions. Any sound was as natural as any
other. Whether it pleased the ear was quite another matter, and
the way to determine this was to use the ear, not the number
system. Zarlino had extolled the human voice as the greatest
musical instrument, being the natural one, and concluded that
musical instruments, as artificial devices, were bound by the laws
of the natural instrument. Galilei replied that instruments had
nothing to do with the voice and made no attempt to imitate it;
they were devised for certain purposes, and their excellence depended solely on how well they served those purposes. Mathematics had no power over the senses, which in turn were the
final criterion of excellence in colors, tastes, smells, and sounds.

For a tuning system, Galilei advocated an approximate equal
temperament as determined by the trained ear. Stevin, about the
same time, had gone still further; he simply declared that ratios
and proportions had nothing whatever to do with music, and that
the proper and ideal intervals were those given by the irrational
twelfth root of two. These come to much the same thing in practice.

It is in Galilei's final refutation of Zarlino that we first find the specific experimental contradiction of sonorous number as the cause of consonance. Not only did Galilei assert that he had reached his conclusion by experiment, but it is hardly conceivable that it could have been reached in any other way than by a test designed for the purpose. Galilei confirmed that the ratios 2:1, 3:2, 4:3 will give octaves, fifths and fourths for strings of like material and equal tension having lengths in these ratios, or for columns of air having similar lengths. But he added that if the lengths are equal and the tensions are varied, the weights required to produce tensions giving the same intervals are inversely as the squares of the length-ratios. He remarked further that cubes instead of squares would be involved where sound production was related to volume.[5] This meant that the ratio 3:2 was no more "naturally" related to the interval of the fifth than was the ratio 4:9 or even 8:27—ratios which were simple abominations to the musical numerologists of his time, who took sonorous number as the underlying cause of harmony. These experiments and conclusions he extended in further unpublished treatises.

The manuscripts of Vincenzio passed to his son Galileo on his death in 1590. Many years later, in his last great book on physics, Galileo incorporated his father's ideas in his own discussion of the physics of sound. More important, Galileo's inspiration to use experiments in mechanics was probably connected with Vincenzio's musical experimentation. Galileo left the University of Pisa without a degree in 1585. During the ensuing four years he lived mainly in Florence, giving some private instruction in mathematics and commencing researches that obtained for him the chair of mathematics at Pisa in 1589. Now it was precisely during those years, and particularly in 1588–89, that Vincenzio Galilei carried out many of the experiments in refutation of Pythagorean music theory, including some that he never published but that survive in manuscripts among Galileo's papers. It seems to me very likely that Galileo was directly involved in the experiments of his father, some of which he described many years later in his *Two New Sciences*. Galileo was an accomplished amateur musician, instructed by his father, and as a young mathematician he could hardly have remained indifferent to what his father was doing in the measurement of tuned strings of varying length, tension, and diameter and the examination of Pythagorean musical

numerology. Thus the conception of experimental verification for
mathematical laws in physics, which is first illustrated in Galileo's
books, seems to me likely to have been directly inspired by his
father's work during those years in which he had just left the
university and was developing his own mathematical skills.

If we consider the nature of Galilei's musical experiments,
this probability is increased. The experiment to determine the
weights that must be used to stretch similar strings to given
pitches is not particularly difficult, but however it is carried out,
the observer can hardly escape the phenomena of the pendulum.
If one suspends two strings of equal length and size, weighting
one with four times the weight attached to the other, then even
without attempting to elicit a tone, say by plucking, the strings
and their weights are almost certain to be set in at least a slight
swinging motion. The pendulum effect would likewise be observable if parallel strings were stretched over a flat bed, weights
being applied to their free ends hanging over a terminal bridge,
as on the monochord. The application of different weights to these
relatively short vertical strings would likewise set them swinging
and would invite attention to some relationship between the
lengths and periods of oscillation.

Galileo's discussion of musical acoustics in the *Two New
Sciences* follows immediately after, and is connected with, his discussion of pendulums. This fact tends to support the idea that
the two were connected in his mind, perhaps through their early
association in experiments he had observed. In any case, what
Galileo as a physicist had to say about music suggests a theory
of consonance that no one appears to have taken up again in all
the voluminous discussions of that topic that ensued. His discussion is interesting; it begins as follows:

> The explanations hitherto given by those learned in music
> impress me as insufficiently conclusive. They tell us that the
> octave involves the ratio 2:1, and the fifth involves the ratio
> 3:2, because if the open string be sounded and afterwards the
> bridge is placed in the middle, one hears the octave; and if the
> bridge is placed at one-third the length of the string, the fifth is
> given. . . . This explanation does not impress me as sufficient
> to establish 2:1 and 3:2 as the natural ratios of octave and fifth,
> . . . for there are three different ways to sharpen the pitch of the

string; namely, by shortening its length, or by stretching it tighter, or by reducing its diameter.[6]

After discussing the resulting ratios, he stated that "The ratio associated with a musical interval is not immediately determined by the length, size, or tension of the strings, but rather by their frequencies of vibration; that is, by the number of pulses of air that strike the eardrum and cause it to vibrate. . . . Unpleasant sensation arises, I think, from the discordant vibrations of two notes that strike the ear out of proportion."[7]

Galileo's clue to the consideration of frequencies of vibration came first from his observation that when a glass containing water is set in vibration by rubbing its rim, waves are seen in the surface of the water; and when the note suddenly jumps an octave, as often happens, the distances between waves is cut in half. He was enabled to carry out further investigation by an accidental observation, which he described as follows:

> As I was scraping a brass plate with a sharp iron chisel to remove some spots from it . . . once or twice during many strokes, I heard the plate emit a rather strong and clear note, and noticed a long row of fine streaks, parallel and uniformly distant from one another. Scraping with the chisel repeatedly, I noticed that it was only when the plate emitted a sound that marks were left on it. Repeating the act and making the stroke now faster and now slower, the sound was now higher and now lower. . . . I also observed among the strings of a spinet two which were in unison with two of the notes produced by the scraping, and found them to be separated by the interval of a perfect fifth. Upon measuring the distance between the markings produced by the two scrapings, I found that the space which contained 45 of one set contained 30 of the other, which is the ratio assigned to the fifth.[8]

Galileo's remark that unpleasant sound occurs when vibrations reach the ear "out of proportion" is too general to suggest any specific answer to the question, how does the *ear* know proportions?—a question that has been subjected to discussion over and over again since his day. But Galileo proceeded to give an analysis that does suggest a specific kind of answer, and one that seems never to have been pursued by others. It is not ever likely to be pursued, now that the work of Helmholtz has established our knowledge of partials as related to fundamental vibrations. But Galileo's idea is so interesting, and so picturesquely interpreted from mathematics into sensation, that it is worth bringing to attention.

Considering the interval of the fifth, Galileo represents the amplitude of vibration of two strings whose lengths are in the ratio of 3:2. Dividing these by the common unit of measure, he marks three equal spaces for the travel of one string and two for the other. He then supposes that a pulse is emitted only when each string reverses its direction. Investigating the pattern of sounds for equal time-intervals, if we suppose for purposes of illustration that the interval is C-G, Galileo finds this succession: CG, silence, G, C, G, silence, CG. . . . The same pattern is then repeated cyclically as long as the two strings vibrate. Obviously, for intervals other than the fifth, the patterns of silences separating the single tones from one another and from simultaneous occurrences of both tones are radically changed. It is to these proportions that Galileo alluded when he spoke of vibrations reaching the ear "out of proportion"; that is, to the time pattern of single sounds, double sounds, and silences. This *kind* of proposed explanation of consonance was quite novel, and here is what one of Galileo's interlocutors replied to it:

> I must express to you the great pleasure I have in hearing such a complete explanation of phenomena with regard to which I have so long been in darkness. Now I understand why unison does not differ from a single tone; I understand why the octave is the principal harmony, so like unison as often to be mistaken for it, and yet having a place with the harmonies. It resembles unison because in unison all the pulsations occur together, just as those of the lower string in the octave are always accompanied by those of the upper string, but between the latter there is interposed a solitary pulse, occurring at equal intervals and in such a manner as to produce no disturbance. The result is that such a harmony is rather too bland and lacks fire. The fifth, however, is characterized by its displaced beats; that is, by the interposition of two solitary beats of the upper string and one solitary beat of the lower string between each pair of simultaneous pulses; these three solitary pulses are moreover separated by intervals of time equal to half the interval which separates each pair of simultaneous beats from the solitary beats of the upper

string. Thus the effect of the fifth is to produce a tickling of the eardrum so that its gentleness is modified by sprightliness, giving the impression simultaneously of a gentle kiss and of a bite.[9]

The theory of sensation implied in this passage is consonant with Galileo's famed distinction between what have come to be called "primary" and "secondary" qualities, in *The Assayer*. For the first time, sensations of tone are reduced to temporal patterns of toneless pulses of air. It is implied that we would hear as two tones, separated by the interval of a fifth, any pattern in which, during equal time intervals, there reached the ear a pulse of double strength, no pulse, three single pulses, and no pulse, followed by the same cycle again and again. The quality of pitch is removed from the sounding string and placed in the sensitive being; to the string, the air, and the eardrum are left only mechanical motions, devoid of tonal properties.

It is hardly necessary to dwell on the inadequacies of this analysis; what is important is the method of segregating the mathematical aspects of acoustic problems from their psychological aspects, a method that Galileo had previously illustrated by a discussion of heat as a physical phenomenon and heat as sensation. Against those who regard Galileo as the advocate of a Platonic scheme in which the real world is but a poor copy of some mathematical ideal world, it must be noted that along with his analytical suggestion of toneless pulses, he introduces tickling, kisses, and bites as of equal importance in understanding the real world that interested him. Nature had written a book in the language of mathematics; those who knew the language could put it on paper; but Galileo was still concerned in all his discussions with the real world, and not—as were his philosophical opponents of all sects, Aristotelian or Platonic—merely with one on paper.

Notes to Essay 2

1. *Euclide . . . diligentemente rassettato . . . per . . . Nicolò Tartalea* (Venice, 1569), p. 3. The prefatory address in the first edition (1543) is less specific about the ratios and even declares that the interval of the fourth is dissonant.

2. *The Principal Works of Simon Stevin,* vol. V (Amsterdam, 1966), pp. 432–33.

3. Stevin, *loc. cit.,* p. 433.

4. Benedetti's achievement was discussed by Claude Palisca in an essay to which I am indebted for my knowledge of it; see "Scientific Empiricism in Musical Thought," *Seventeenth Century Science and the Arts,* ed. H. H. Rhys (Princeton, 1961), pp. 104–10.

5. Vincenzio Galilei, *Discorso intorno all'opere di Gioseffo Zarlino* (Florence, 1589; reprinted ed., Milan, 1933), pp. 104–5.

6. *Two New Sciences,* pp. 99–100.

7. *Two New Sciences,* p. 103.

8. *Two New Sciences,* pp. 101–2.

9. *Two New Sciences,* pp. 106–7.

3

The Scientific Personality
of Galileo

Whether the role of Galileo in the history of science was that of a truly great innovator or that of the coordinator of various ideas transmitted by his predecessors, there is a perfectly real sense in which his role was unique. This becomes clear when we consider that the epoch in which he lived was that of the first organization of physical science as a recognized separate discipline. Before the time of Galileo, physics was a part—an integral part—of philosophy as a whole. After his time, it began to have a life of its own. To some degree, at least, this meant the creation of new activities. To a much greater degree, however, it meant the severing of previously existing pursuits from their traditional accompaniments and their regrouping into more fruitful and more readily recognizable coherent patterns.

The creator of a truly new field of human activity (if such a thing can be conceived) might well expect to remain its leader, at peace with the world, until such time as his supremacy might be challenged from within the new field. But a man who attempts to reorganize old activities, endowing them with different methods, purposes, and affiliations, must expect swift and powerful opposition. Such was the situation of Galileo; his conception of physical science threatened the authority of the universities as well as that of the churches. Though he was personally defeated by their joint and powerful opposition, his initial leadership helped to establish science as a still more powerful force in society. Universities in time became the greatest champions of this new force, while the churches (more gradually) have withdrawn at least their avowed hostility to it.

To historians of ideas falls the task of discovering the predecessors of Galileo. Social historians undertake to explain his success in terms of large-scale forces at work in religion, education, politics, and economics. No less interesting, and possibly no less important a task remains to the biographer: the task of discovering those facets of Galileo's character that played a part in the formation of interests and the style he adopted in their pursuit. There were personal factors that induced him to make an open breach with established traditions, enabled him to influence others to support him, and helped him to avoid errors that might have been disastrous to his cause. Taken together, they constitute what I shall call his "scientific personality," borrowing the phrase of the late Professor Leonardo Olschki. They are probably as significant to an understanding of his intellectual influence as are the much more widely studied aspects of his direct scientific work.

The origin of modern physical science is no longer portrayed as the revolutionary product of the geniuses of Galileo and Newton, but as the outgrowth of innumerable bits of knowledge, pieced gradually together. The history of science is seen as a continuous process with occasional bursts of unusual energy related to general social changes. Thus Albert Einstein wrote in his foreword to a translation of Galileo's *Dialogue:*

> It may well be that . . . the fetters of an obsolete intellectual tradition would not have held much longer, with or without Galileo. . . . Our age takes a more sceptical view of the role of the individual, . . . for the extensive specialization . . . of knowledge lets the individual appear "replaceable" as it were, like a part of a mass-produced machine.[1]

In describing science as it stands today, there is much to be said for that view. By and large, needed technical and theoretical advances seem to come forth as if extruded by a kind of social pressure, in a historically logical sequence. This makes it appear that the names of particular men associated with them are mere accidental sounds, having no real place in the history of science, where they are preserved only through custom and courtesy. In no field of endeavor today is it more difficult for a man to leave the imprint of his personality than in science. One might say that it is in the very nature of science to exclude the subjective, and the personal along with it. So there is some justification for a theory of the history of science in which progress is made to appear impersonal and inevitable. But from this, it is all too easy to assume in retrospect that when the accumulation of knowledge in physics had grown large enough to warrant the creation of a separate field of study, almost anyone might have inaugurated and successfully led it.

I am distrustful of any theory which tends to make the origin of an idea, or of a field of science, appear as inevitable as its subsequent progress. Perhaps the introduction here of the word "origin" begs the question, in the view of the historians of ideas. But my point is that even if it were true that modern scientists are now like parts of a mass-produced machine (which is at least debatable), that would be a result of the standardization of scientific information and the ease of communication that exists among modern scientists. Surely it would be stretching things too far to apply the same reasoning to the epoch of Galileo. Granted that the romanticizing of an individual may result in a distortion of historical facts, it is equally true that the depersonalization of past scientists may diminish one's historical understanding. To me, at least, the history of modern physical science without the personality of Galileo is *Hamlet* without the Prince of Denmark. It is a tale told by a computer, purged indeed of sound and fury, but signifying little.

Einstein's recognition of the present historical emphasis on societies rather than individuals does not mean that he himself saw things entirely that way. Einstein described Galileo (in the same foreword) as: "A man who possessed the passionate will, the intelligence, and the courage to stand up as the representative of rational thinking against the host of those who, relying on the ignorance of the people and the indolence of teachers in priestly and scholarly garb, maintained and defended their positions of authority. His unusual literary gift enabled him to address the educated man of his age in such clear and convincing language as to overcome the anthropocentric and myth-ridden thinking of his contemporaries."[2]

That succinct description points up some of Galileo's personal traits which appear to me to have played as important a role in the establishment of modern science as did his physical and astronomical discoveries. Perhaps the history of science, meaning by that a proper account of those past events which have some evident connection with significant components of present-day science, needs to have at least three dimensions: first, an ideological dimension, that is, the study of fundamentally significant scientific ideas in their various historical forms and relationships; second, a sociological dimension, given by the study of the societies in which those ideas were put forth, whether they prospered or vanished at the time; and finally, a personal dimension, a study of the men who put them forth, especially those who ultimately established the place of those ideas in the body of science. No one questions the importance of the ideological and sociological dimensions of the history of science; certainly I do not. They are indeed of paramount importance in understanding the growth of modern science. But the personal dimension of human thought or action, often neglected now, throws an equal light upon its origin.

The interest and importance of the scientific personality of Galileo was first stressed by Leonardo Olschki in 1942, the tercentenary of Galileo's death. His paper opened up a large field for study; and having borrowed its title, I propose to develop certain themes stated in the following words by Professor Olschki: "Galileo's intellectual independence was not merely a theoretical one . . . but a ripening scientific conscience of an unmistakably personal character. The explanation of fundamental human accomplishments as individual approaches, or as strokes of genius, may not satisfy the determinist tendencies of evolutionary historians; but there is no better way of doing justice to an outstanding personality, or of understanding his intellectual traits."[3]

There is another justification: Galileo's personality was an essential ingredient in his scientific leadership, and therefore it cannot be neglected in a full comprehension of that scientific revolution in thought which distinguishes the seventeenth century from those which had gone before. I have in mind two quite separate aspects of Galileo's personality. One of them is his rather pugnacious disposition, as a result of which he engaged in numerous disputes which helped to overthrow tradition and vindicate his scientific position. The other, which I shall discuss first, is a certain aspect of Galileo's general temperament that parallels in a curious way the essential structure of modern physical science.

Modern physical science, despite its admirable precision, is by no means a body of inalterable doctrine. Rather, it is a continually changing system of knowledge arrived at by a process of successive approximation; never entirely accurate, and never to be completed. Aristotelian physics, which prevailed up to the time of Galileo, was a body of inalterable doctrine—and that is precisely what was wrong with it. Galileo was temperamentally opposed to the idea that any fixed doctrine would ever succeed in describing the real physical world which he saw changing about him. He used to say that Aristotle, if he were to come back to life, would be the first to recognize new knowledge and disavow the doctrinaire position of the Peripatetics. Were he but to look through the telescope, Galileo said, Aristotle would promptly withdraw the astronomical dogmas that he had created and to which his disciples were stubbornly clinging in his name. Galileo doubted that complete knowledge of anything could be achieved by human beings, and he declared that the more deeply one investigated any subject, the more one came to realize the extent of one's own ignorance. That theme he illustrated by a parable, in *The Assayer,* about a man who began by believing that he knew the cause of sound; proceeding to investigate the many and various sources of sound, he gradually relinquished his original dogmatic confidence, and ultimately admitted that there might be an infinity of sources still unknown to him.

In speaking of physical science as a method of successive approximations, I mean generally that the progress of science may be characterized as the finding first of some rule that fits a great many data rather well; next, finding that there are other related data which it fits badly, or seems not to fit at all. Those are in turn brought in by modifying the rule or replacing it by another, and the process goes on indefinitely. Now, in that kind of process, two quite different kinds of temperament have turned out to be extremely useful. One is that of a man who delights in observing things, notes resemblances and relationships among them, and forms generalizations without being unduly disturbed by apparent exceptions or anomalies. Such a personality is obviously valuable in the original discovery and formulation of laws that fit many phenomena tolerably well. The other general temperament useful to the progress of science is that of a man who frets and worries over any unexplained deviation from a rule, and who may even prefer no rule at all over one that does not always work with mathematical precision. Of course, both these attitudes are present to some extent in every scientist, but one or the other is likely to predominate. In their extreme forms, the two conflicting temperaments are related in a way to those which today characterize the theoretical physicist as opposed to the experimental physicist; and as we know, in extreme cases such men are likely not to speak highly of one another's work, though they both recognize grudgingly that they work on the same team.

In Galileo's day there was no such profession as that of physicist. The role of the theoretical physicist was played by the philosopher. By temperament and tradition, the philosopher liked to generalize and was not unduly perturbed by apparent anomalies; indeed, he welcomed them as things to explain, or at any rate to explain away. The role of the experimental physicist, to the extent that it was played at all, fell to craftsmen, artisans, and mechanics. But philosophers and mechanics did not work on the same team, nor was there any apparent reason why they should. Consequently there was a highly developed branch of philosophy, called physics, which bore only a loose verbal relationship to reality; and there was a highly developed technology, which was generally not even noticed by philosophers, let alone integrated with their physics. Philosophers knew how physical objects ought to behave, and cared relatively little if they didn't always seem to behave that way; craftsmen knew how objects behaved, and cared relatively little for theoretical explanations. Though both were deeply concerned (each in his own way) with precision, neither habitually associated that with mathematics.

Galileo's temperament was about as evenly balanced between the two extremes I have mentioned as it is possible to conceive. He liked to observe relations and generalize about them, though unexplained deviations from theory did bother him. He lived among professors, but he enjoyed discussing technical practices with artisans, and he liked to tinker. He saw mathematics as a common ground of the two demands for precision, and conceived of departures from mathematical regularity in terms of a mercantile analogy set forth in the *Dialogue:*

> . . . what happens in the concrete . . . happens the same way in the abstract. It would indeed be surprising if computations made in abstract numbers did not thereafter correspond to

actual gold and silver coins and merchandise. Do you know what does happen, Simplicio? Just as the accountant who wants his calculations to deal with sugar, silk and wool must subtract the boxes, bales, and other packings, so the mathematical physicist, when he wants to recognize in the concrete the effects which he has proved in the abstract, must deduct the material hindrances; and if he is able to do that, I assure you that matters are in no less agreement than for arithmetical computations. The sources of errors, then, lie not in abstractness or concreteness, not in geometry or physics, but in a calculator who does not know how to make a true accounting.[4]

Thus Galileo maintained his belief in mathematical laws, but without feeling that he should abstain from generalizing in the quest for perfection. His attitude toward theorizing is clear from his writing. He thought it highly creditable to Copernicus that the apparent absence of great changes in magnitude by the planet Venus did not induce the Polish astronomer to abandon his theory, from which such changes would be expected, but that despite their absence, he kept to the theory and left the apparent anomaly to be explained later—as it eventually was, by Galileo's telescopic observation of the phases of Venus.

It was certainly helpful, if not absolutely necessary to the birth of modern physical science, that someone should formulate mathematical laws without waiting for their precise confirmation, and at the same time refrain from merely speculating, as all philosophers had previously done. Indeed, it may have been the nice balance in Galileo between the two extremes of temperament that made possible his new conception of physics. If so, that conception may represent, in its origins, a personal characteristic rather than an intellectual achievement.

That such a balance between temperaments was rare in his day is shown by two contemporary examples. Marin Mersenne, who represents the extreme of the critical temperament, was much distressed that his careful experiments with falling bodies departed from the mathematical laws confidently announced by Galileo. Mersenne, left to himself, would probably never have discovered the law of falling bodies; yet he quickly became a valuable part of the newly forming scientific team when that was done. On the other hand, René Descartes, in whom a predilection for generalization predominated strongly over concern for precise observation, went far astray in his formulation of general physical laws such as the laws of impact. In attempting to advance physics as a coherent mathematical structure, Descartes adopted laws that were not in fact valid.

It is true that in his published works Galileo often claimed for his scientific laws a precise accordance with experimental results that they did not have. Thus, with regard to the uniform period of oscillations of a given pendulum, he asserted that the size of arc did not matter, whereas in fact it does; and with respect to the verification of the law relating spaces traversed to the squares of elapsed times, he asserted that he had obtained precise correspondence in hundreds of trials on inclined planes, which is rather unlikely. Because of such exaggerations it has been suggested that Galileo made few actual experiments or careful observations, and that his traditional place as founder of experimental physics is therefore undeserved. It is at least as likely that in the case of the inclined plane, he observed the discrepancies and attributed them to "material hindrances," outweighed in his mind by the general plausibility and utility of his laws—much as the apparent anomaly of the magnitudes of Venus was outweighed for Copernicus by the general coherence of his astronomical theory. Moreover, many of Galileo's exaggerations in such matters as the pendulum may be regarded as literary devices, designed to excite the interest and wonder of his lay readers, rather than as attempts to conceal discrepancies from fellow scientists, whom he urged to make similar observations for themselves. That is, his exaggerations probably often constituted the popularizing and not the sober content of his writings. Both elements were essential to his task. Galileo's preference for Italian over Latin even in scientific writing, his generous use of commonplace phenomena to illustrate for his readers the principles of physics, and his clarity of style, had much to do with the spread of interest in the new science.

This leads me naturally back to that more familiar general aspect of Galileo's personality which was an essential ingredient in his scientific success—his willingness and ability to fight for his ideas. No doubt Galileo's most striking personal characteristic was his refusal to accept authority as a substitute for direct personal inquiry and observation. That refusal went counter to the whole social pattern of his time, and not only with respect to the Church. All political and most social institutions of his day were authoritarian in structure. Even in the universities, the primary centers of intellectual life, the authority of ancient writers was sedulously preserved. Only a born fighter could hope to change such well-established traditions.

Galileo's refusal to accept authority as a substitute for direct inquiry belonged specifically to his scientific outlook and did not extend to a defiance of authority in other fields. While he rejected dogma in physics, as symbolized by Aristotle, he did not combat it in politics or religion. On the contrary, he remained a good Catholic even through the ordeal of his trial by the Inquisition, and he remained always a loyal subject of the grand duke of Tuscany, despite the fact that that worthy did not overexert himself to protect Galileo's interests. A superficial evaluation of those facts might suggest that Galileo lacked the full courage of his convictions; that he sought the protection of some powerful authorities in order to fight against others. But that is very dubious. Galileo was not given to defiance on principle, and he saw the enormous difference between direct inquiry where it may significantly be made and its counterfeit in other fields. Here is a passage from the *Dialogue* in which he replied to a defense of Aristotle's physics:

> If what we are dicussing were a point of law or of the humanities, in which neither true nor false exists, one might trust in subtlety of mind and readiness of tongue and the comparative expertness of writers, expecting him who excelled in those qualities to make his arguments the most plausible; and one might judge that to be correct. But in the physical sciences, where conclusions are true and necessary and have nothing to do with human preferences, one must take care not to place oneself in the defence of error; for here, a thousand Demostheneses and a thousand Aristotles would be left in the lurch by any average man who happened to hit on the truth for himself.[5]

Galileo urged his church not to exert its authority against freedom in scientific matters, but he never questioned its right or its power to do so, nor did he sympathize with the demands of Protestants for the right of free inquiry in matters of faith. His

plea for a sharp distinction between scientific and theological questions may seem to us now a purely intellectual achievement, necessary for the establishment of science in the modern sense; but
that is because we are not compelled to view the question of the
earth's motion, for example, as a dreadfully complicated question,
with reason pulling in one direction and all our deeper feelings
pulling in the other. Galileo's resolution of that problem was an
expression of his personality even more than it was a product of
his intelligence. It is an evidence of that "ripening scientific conscience" of which Professor Olschki spoke. That kind of conscience
was new, and Galileo had to forge it in the smithy of his own
soul under the heat of internal conflicts. We may now take the
demands of objective truth for granted, but we should not suppose them to have been always clearly perceived, at least so far
as science is concerned.

But Galileo's earliest conflicts with authority had nothing to
do with religion. They were directed against the philosophers at
the University of Pisa. Shortly after his appointment there as professor of mathematics in 1589, Galileo composed a formal treatise
on motion. Its theme was that the physics of Aristotle was completely untenable, that physics must be established on the principles of mathematics, and that it must be in accordance with
actual observation. Critiques of Aristotle were nothing new; in
fact, they made up the bulk of the philosophical literature of the
period. But Galileo's method of attack had an element of novelty.
Where conventional philosophers, in whose province physics still
lay, cited authorities for virtually every opinion they put forth,
Galileo appealed directly to reason and observation. When he did
cite an authority, as in presenting his early (but mistaken) theory
of acceleration in falling bodies, he made it clear that he had first
independently arrived at his theory, believing it to be original,
and only later found it attributed by Alexander of Aphrodisias to
Hipparchus. A conventional writer would first have cited Alexander
and Hipparchus, and only then have added his own new reasons
in support of ancient authority.

Had Galileo published his anti-Aristotelian theory of motion,
it would certainly have gained him a reputation as early as 1590;
for in spite of its errors it was original and highly creditable by
standards of the time. But though Galileo polished the work, in

the end he did not publish it; we know of it only because he preserved its various manuscript versions throughout his life, as many
of us have preserved some youthful production of which we are
privately proud, though we know it does not merit publication. Considering the personal advantages that Galileo stood to gain from
public notice at the age of twenty-six, in his first and poorly paid
academic position, it is necessary to account in some way for his
having withheld his treatise from the press. Here, I think, enters
another conspicuous trait in Galileo's scientific personality, namely,
prudence. I do not mean caution on the part of a young professor
against offending his more powerful colleagues; that would indeed
be an un-Galilean trait. What I mean is scientific prudence, an
attitude well summarized by Galileo in 1613 in his book on sunspots, where he says:

> I am quite content to be last and to come forth with a
> correct idea, rather than get ahead of other people and later be
> compelled to retract what might have been said sooner, indeed,
> but with less consideration.[6]

Before his treatise on motion was fully completed, Galileo
realized that even though his first ideas in physics were superior
to those of Aristotle, they accorded in some respects no better with
actual observation. He attributed some of the discrepancies to properties of matter—what we have heard him call "material hindrances"—friction, the yielding of surfaces, and the impossibility
of achieving perfect flatness. But his predicted speeds of descent
along inclined planes departed too far from observed events to
be thus accounted for. Scientific prudence restrained him from
publication of his results, and scientific curiosity kept him working
at them until they were finally corrected and published, nearly
half a century later.

Galileo's scientific prudence is further illustrated by his delay
in supporting openly the Copernican theory. He personally preferred that theory as early as 1597, but the first time he endorsed
it in print was in 1610, and then only mildly, his unequivocal
support being withheld until 1613. Some writers attribute his long
delay to fear of criticism, a trait not elsewhere conspicuous in
Galileo; others, to intellectual dishonesty, a charge too preposterous
to be taken seriously. Such characterizations of Galileo's delay are

no better founded than it would be to call Charles Darwin cowardly or dishonest for his having taken so long to publish his theory of evolution. The fact is that until 1610, when Galileo had discovered the satellites of Jupiter, and 1613, when he had seen the phases of Venus and carefully observed the motions of sunspots, he had no personal direct evidence on which to decide between the theories of Ptolemy and Copernicus, those theories being mathematically equivalent—as Galileo's foes still take a perverse joy in pointing out when they are criticizing him not for his long delay, but for his ultimate commitment. It is significant that as soon as Galileo had what he considered to be ocular proof that Ptolemy was wrong, he spoke out openly for Copernicus.

Galileo's rejection of authority as a substitute for direct inquiry or observation had its counterpart in his respect for sensory evidence and his willingness to abide by the verdict of observation or experiment. Galileo was by habit an unusually keen observer, and he rarely gave unequivocal support to a theory for which he did not have some direct sensory evidence of his own, but he was perfectly aware that the senses themselves are not infallible.

In any event, Galileo came out openly for Copernicus as soon as he had *what he considered* to be ocular proof that Ptolemy was wrong. In recent years it has been much debated whether Galileo had any right as a scientist to conclude in favor of Copernicus on the basis of the evidence in his possession. I think it is evident that whatever a better scientist might have done, Galileo did what a born leader would do. Intellectual boldness as well as intellectual prudence has a role in the progress of science. Either may be called for by the existing state of knowledge and the conditions favoring its advance. The crucial point is not whether Galileo had or did not have evidence decisively in favor of Copernicus; it is how he behaved when he considered that he did have such evidence. His words and actions in that and analogous instances are the means by which we may observe the "ripening scientific conscience" of which Professor Olschki spoke.

A mature scientific conscience must exhibit both a positive and a negative aspect. On the positive side, it will drive a man to put forward, at whatever personal hazard, any scientific idea or discovery in his possession, and to oppose resolutely any forces that would act to suppress it. On the negative side, it will inhibit a man from imposing on others with purported facts or observations, or with interpretations or theories known by him to be defective, even though he may have the power to persuade others to accept them. Now these intimate and personal drives can justly be appraised only by a careful study of a scientist's whole behavior, by everything he did and wrote, as well as by what his friends and enemies wrote about him. Galileo's ripening scientific conscience coincided in time with the beginnings of modern physical science; it was therefore put to unprecedented tests and accordingly offers a peculiarly interesting field for research. Ultimately it drove him to risk his own personal comfort and even his safety in a battle against overwhelming odds, which of course he lost. Throughout his life, it restrained him from publishing conjectures that would have gained for him a fleeting prestige; and not only when he was a young professor, as I have already indicated, but also in later life, when his established reputation would have enabled him to impose on less well-informed men by means of specious arguments.

Not only impassioned writers like Arthur Koestler, but some serious students as well, see in Galileo's propaganda for Copernicus certain arguments which they consider unsound and some which they believe that he himself knew, or should have known, to be unsound. Two frequently cited instances of this alleged blindness or duplicity are his argument for the earth's motion drawn from the seasonal variations in the paths of sunspots and his theory of the causes of the tides. To examine these in detail now would lead me too far from matters directly related to Galileo's scientific personality; my analysis of those arguments may be read in some of the ensuing essays.[7] What is relevant here is that Galileo's published views on those two subjects were not in contradiction with any facts known to him, nor were the convictions he expressed concerning them in any way insincere or deceptive. Indeed, the caliber of the men who were his friends and pupils, the extent of his influence over them, and the many avowals of admiration and respect for him in their letters and their publications make it most improbable that deception or insincerity existed in any of his scientific teachings or his writings.

On the other hand, Galileo was by no means above utilizing the prejudices of his opponents to neutralize their opposition. Personally, I find that amusing, and not at all the same thing morally as it would have been to impose on them with specious scientific arguments or authoritative assertions. For instance, in arguing for the circular motion of the earth, Galileo resorted in the opening pages of the *Dialogue* to the use of Aristotelian doctrines concerning circular motion in general. Those pages are often interpreted as showing that Galileo had been unable to shake off entirely the old bonds of metaphysical tradition. But since he knew his opponents to be vulnerable to such arguments, why should he not hoist them with their own petard?

Galileo's maturing scientific conscience had to contend with his personal ambition, and there is no doubt that Galileo was an ambitious man. An example often cited is his exploitation of the telescope as a means of improving his academic and financial position at Padua through his presentation of the instrument to the Venetian Senate. He then promptly used his advancement at Padua as a basis for negotiating a still better post at the Tuscan Court, with the same salary and with freedom from all teaching duties. (This use of an improvement in research instrumentation as a means of escape from teaching may constitute a previously unnoticed scientific priority for Galileo.) Nevertheless, as Professor Olschki long ago pointed out, Galileo's resignation from the university after his first telescopic discoveries was the move of a man who could no longer conscientiously teach the old doctrines.

Galileo's ambition was doubtless a factor in his writing of that early treatise on motion that has been mentioned previously. He appears to have wanted to remove physics from the jurisdiction of philosophers in the university and add it to his own department of mathematics. As a step in that direction, he undertook to overthrow the authority of Aristotle in physics. In that sense, one might say that any valuable new ideas arrived at during the composition of the treatise arose basically from Galileo's personal ambition and his temperamental distaste for Aristotle's dogmatic physics. One such idea in particular that turned out to be of enormous importance to the development of physics was the first germ of the concept of inertia. The origin of that concept is universally treated by historians as something quite independent of the personality of any man. To historians of ideas, it was the end product of a long series of philosophical speculations about the motion of projectiles, beginning no later than the sixth century. To sociological historians, it may appear as an inevitable result of the invention of gunpowder and the military, economic, and political consequences of artillery. Either or both of those views may be correct, but are nevertheless misleading to the extent that they purport to explain the actual manner in which the concept of inertia historically happened to come into being. How it came to be accepted and developed is another matter. As to Galileo's first clue in the matter, ambition and pugnacity played a larger role than philosophical speculation or the invention of artillery.[8]

Galileo was a controversial figure in his own day; he is still a controversial figure in ours. That in itself implies a vivid personality. Of its many facets, I have dwelt on those which seem particularly significant to an understanding of his success in organizing, amplifying, and gaining adherents to the study of physical science. There were, of course, other traits of Galileo's personality that contributed to his leadership. One was his gregarious nature, which allowed him to move among widely diverse groups—churchmen, courtiers, craftsmen, artists, and men of the world—with the result that he could draw from many fields ideas and methods useful to science, and then explain his discoveries and opinions in language and examples familiar to any reader. I have already mentioned his preference for Italian over Latin, even in scientific writing; that aided in breaking the hold of tradition on physics and astronomy, and at the same time excited the interest of many people who would otherwise have been excluded from reading his works. Correlated with this was his amusing, witty, and often sarcastic style, almost conversational in its ease of comprehension. His fondness for communication made him a voluminous correspondent and an active participant in scientific and literary academies, which greatly aided in the dissemination of scientific information. He was an outstanding teacher, as admitted even by his enemies, and that means that he could change the course of other men's thinking. Yet, as a teacher, he knew how difficult a task that was. In the *Dialogue* of 1632, when Galileo, at the age of sixty-eight, had spent a lifetime trying to destroy the authority of Aristotle in sciences, he ruefully remarked:

> There is no danger that a multitude of great, subtle and wise philosophers will allow themselves to be overcome by one or two of us who bluster a bit. . . . It is vanity to imagine that

one can introduce a new philosophy by refuting some one author. It is necessary rather to teach the reform of the human mind, and to render it capable of distinguishing truth from falsehood, which only God can do.[9]

Notes to Essay 3

1. *Dialogue,* pp. vii–viii.
2. *Dialogue,* p. vii.
3. L. Olschki, "The Scientific Personality of Galileo," *Bulletin of the History of Medicine,* 12 (1942), 262.
4. *Dialogue,* pp. 207–8.
5. *Dialogue,* pp. 53–54.
6. *Discoveries,* p. 90.
7. See essays 9 and 10.
8. See essay 12.
9. *Dialogue,* p. 57.

4

The Accademia dei Lincei

Logically, on a priori grounds, one might expect the first scientific society to have been founded by early modern scientists as they awakened to the need for mutual communication and mutual defense of their interests.

But that does not appear to have been the case. Instead, half a dozen years before the first startling discoveries and theories of modern science were published by Galileo and Kepler, and scarcely a dozen years before the first onslaught of established authority against freedom of scientific research and publication, a society prepared to further science and protect its interests was founded by four nonscientists. If we attempt to explain this by saying that social conditions favorable to the rise of modern science must have prevailed at that time, then we should expect such an organization to have had rather an easy time getting under way. But in fact, from its very foundation, it was subjected to relentless persecution. Nor did it survive by virtue of its size or the prestige of its members. For seven years, before it attracted to membership any widely recognized scientist, it consisted of but four members, all under thirty years of age. The founder was a young nobleman, but his three associates lacked even social prestige. Six months after the society was founded at Rome, only one member remained there; the other three were dispersed over a wide area.

On any reasonable grounds, the Lincean Academy should have collapsed. Yet it survived to carry out the essential purposes of a scientific society at a crucial period which saw the birth of modern science and its initial battle for survival. The fact that this pioneer scientific society was founded in the very city in which that battle was destined to be centered makes the whole affair, if not a miracle, at least a very interesting and curious set of historical coincidences.

The Lincean Academy was a forerunner of modern scientific societies, if not the first such society. For comparison, and because one man belonged in turn to both, I shall briefly describe its only rival for the title of "first" among scientific academies which is deemed worthy of mention in the eleventh edition of the *Encyclopaedia Britannica.*

Giambattista della Porta, author of a celebrated, often published, and widely translated book on *Natural Magic,* founded at Naples some time before 1589 (the *Britannica* asserts that the year was 1560) an *Academia Secretorum Naturae* which used to meet at his house to investigate and experiment concerning curiosities of nature. No one was admitted to the group who had not offered some remarkable and little-known information useful either to the health of the body or to the science of mechanics. Porta's academicians called themselves the *Otiosi,* or idle men, after a pleasant custom then prevalent in Italy of selecting humorously derogatory names for societies engaged in the pursuit of various studies. Thus, for example, one famous academy bore the name of *Umidi,* or the moistures; another academy was the *Scomposti,* which may mean the disorganized, the confused, or the abashed men; and the very learned academy at Florence which in 1612 gave Italy (and the world) its first compendious vernacular dictionary was (and still is) called the *Accademia della Crusca,* or academy of chaff.

There is no record of the actual accomplishments of Porta's *Otiosi* apart from occasional allusions to it in his books. It is said to have been dissolved on order of Pope Paul V, after Porta had been called to Rome to answer charges of the practice of magic, including divination and the making of poisons, although Porta was personally exonerated from these charges. The academy at Naples was strictly local in membership, sponsored no publications, and appears to have had no other distinguished member than Porta. Devoted essentially to satisfying the curiosity of its own members, it was a private and virtually a secret society. In contrast the *Accademia dei Lincei,* founded at Rome in 1603, from the outset declared its intention not merely of studying the phenomena of nature but of attempting new discoveries and publishing them to the world. Its fundamental aspirations are to be found in the

Praescriptiones, or declaration of principles, drafted in 1604–5 and published in 1624:

> The Lincean Academy desires as its members philosophers who are eager for real knowledge, and who will give themselves to the study of nature, and especially to mathematics; at the same time, it will not neglect the ornaments of elegant literature and philology, which, like graceful garments, adorn the whole body of science. . . . It is not within the Lincean plan to find leisure for recitations and debates; meetings will be neither frequent nor lengthy, and chiefly for the transaction of necessary business of the academy; but those who wish to enjoy such exercises will not be hindered in any way, so long as they perform them as incidental studies, decently and quietly, and not as vain promises and professions of how much they are about to accomplish. For there is ample philosophical employment for everyone by himself, particularly if pains are taken in the observation of natural phenomena and the book of nature which is always at hand; this is, the heavens and the earth. . . . Let members add to their names the title of Lincean, which has been chosen as a caution and a constant stimulus, especially when they write on any literary subject, or in their private letters to associates, and in general when any work is wisely and well performed. . . . The Linceans will pass over in silence all political controversies and every kind of quarrels and wordy disputes, especially gratuitous ones which give occasion to deceit, unfriendliness and hatred, as men who desire peace and seek to preserve their studies from molestation and would avoid any sort of disturbance. And if anyone by command of his superiors or some other requirement shall be reduced to the handling of such questions, let those be printed without the name of Lincean, since they are alien to physical and mathematical science and hence to the objects of the Academy.[1]

These principles alone establish the Lincean Academy as the forerunner of modern scientific societies, many of which have adopted strikingly similar rules for their conduct and that of their members. The very modernity and wisdom of the objectives stated must give rise to the question how these can have been incorporated, by a youth of eighteen, into the constitution of the very first organization of its kind. In reply it may be said first that the founder was obviously no ordinary youth, and second, that although there was indeed no predecessor scientific academy from which he could draw the wisdom embodied in his principles, there were in Italy plenty of literary, artistic, humanistic, and forensic academies, some of which were conspicuously given to florid declamation and empty debate—to what Galileo later called the "lovely flowers of rhetoric that are followed by no fruit at all."[2] The Lincean academicians, with their precocious interest in the physical and mathematical sciences, had no wish to emulate such examples.

Though the Lincean Academy at the time of its founding took quite seriously the lofty principles of its constitution, it also had some human foibles, to be expected in a group of young men who were close personal friends. It adopted, for example, much of the paraphernalia associated with romantically conceived organizations such as those founded for patriotic causes. Each original member took a secret name, a symbolic emblem, and a motto; all were sworn to brotherhood; the society had an emblem and a patron saint; it gave a diploma and a ring evidencing membership; and it had a secret cipher for the transmission of information about activities of the society and personal news of its members.

The founder of the Lincean Academy, and its leading spirit at all times, was Federico Cesi, second marquis of Monticelli. His special name in the society was *Celivago,* or heaven-wanderer, and his emblem was an eagle illuminated by the sun and holding in its claws a terrestrial globe. Cesi was official head of the academy from its founding until his death in 1630; he was also its sole source of financial support and its undaunted preserver during many years of persecution and adversity.

Most colorful of the charter members was a Dutch physician, Johannes Eck, who was known in the Academy as *l'Illuminato,* or the enlightened one. His emblem was that of the moon at quarter, illuminated by a triangle from the sun. Eck was the most learned member of the society, from whom the others expected to receive instruction; he was also the member whose presence nearly brought about the early dissolution of the organization, as will be explained presently.

Third of the founding members was Francesco Stelluti, who was known as *Tardigrado* or the slow one; his emblem was the planet Saturn, slowest moving of the planets known at the time. This was not intended as a reflection on his intellect but as a symbol of the idea that the surest way to knowledge is that of a slow and measured tread. Stelluti's special talent lay in the direction of editing, criticizing, and commenting on the works of others.

Anastasio de Filiis completed the original group. He was known as *l'Eclissato,* the eclipsed one—his emblem being that of the moon darkened by the interposed earth hiding it from the sun. In his case, the symbol was literally intended, for de Filiis was the least educated of the members, lacking even a knowledge of Latin. That was a real handicap at the time, especially in astronomy and mathematics, when few men had defied tradition by writing scientific works in the common language. De Filiis, who died in 1608, was dependent on his colleagues for scientific information; when he despaired of progress, Cesi encouraged him by pointing out in his letters that close observation of the things about him, especially plants and animals, would open to him more real knowledge than could be found in any book.

By 1610, when the Academy added its first new member, it had abandoned the mystical notion of sworn brotherhood and the romantic idea of assigning special names and symbolic emblems to its members. The emblem of the society itself was retained; this was a lynx, destroying with its claws the infernal Cerberus while turning its eyes to the sky, representing the crushing of ignorance by true knowledge. The name of the lynx was adopted by the society because of the fabled acuteness of vision of that animal, then still to be found in parts of Italy. It is worth noting that the emblem of the lynx was used on the title page of the Neapolitan edition of an expanded version of Porta's *Natural Magic* published in 1589.

The Academy was formally established on 17 August 1603 and held its meetings at the palace of the Cesi family in Rome. Two cardinal principles adopted at once were that each member should give instruction to the others in some science, and that each must hold some active office in the society. Eck was first assigned to teach astronomy and the philosophy of Plato; later, to propound experiments relating to natural history and medicine. Cesi was assigned another course in philosophy, presumably Aristotelian, and was made responsible for providing books, instruments, and equipment needed by the Academy. Stelluti was appointed to give a course in geometry and to explain the uses of mathematical instruments and mechanical devices, as well as to give practical meaning to Eck's theoretical instruction by making astronomical observations and calculations. De Filiis was to lecture on history and was made secretary of the society. Five lectures were to be given on each of three days of the week, two lectures by Eck and one each by the other members. But this rigorous program, begun late in October of 1603, was doomed soon to be abandoned.

Eck, who had come to Italy from Daventer in Holland, studied medicine at the University of Perugia and began his practice in Italy. In June 1603 he was imprisoned as the result of the death of a pharmacist whom he had reprimanded on several occasions and who in turn had waylaid and assaulted him. The evidence now shows clearly that Eck's mortal wounding of the pharmacist was entirely in self-defense. Nevertheless Eck, being then a friendless foreigner in Rome, was still languishing in prison when the matter came to the attention of young Cesi. Eck was released through the mediation of Cesi and Stelluti, after which he was invited to live for a time with Cesi. It appears that the presence of this well-educated physician, who also had a good knowledge of astronomy and a deep interest in botany, inspired in Cesi the idea of a mutual-instruction society which promptly became the *Accademia dei Lincei*. For the first few years of its existence, an elaborate record was kept of its activities and tribulations; this record, entitled *Linceografia*, is preserved in manuscript and provides the source for much of what follows.

Cesi's father was hostile to the Academy from the very beginning, perhaps partly because he considered intensive study a most inappropriate form of behavior for a young nobleman in Rome at the epoch, but principally out of distrust and fear of Johannes Eck, whom he regarded as little better than a pardoned murderer. As a physician, Eck would know how to make poisons, a subject on which the elder Cesi tried twice to draw him out; it was one which was calculated to make any Italian aristocrat apprehensive at that time. The marquis was also disturbed by the general air of secrecy, sworn brotherhood, and mystery which prevailed among his young son and the three older associates who began to frequent his palace. No doubt Cesi's father associated these things with some nefarious political plot, and one may imagine that he would consider patently absurd the pretense that only the study of science concerned the young men.

After an unsuccessful attempt to persuade his son to break off with Eck, the father attempted to have the Dutch physician imprisoned again, first by civil and then by ecclesiastical authorities. Though all these maneuvers failed, the situation had become so unpleasant that at the beginning of May 1604 Eck left Rome in the custody of two escorts provided by Cesi's father. Shortly thereafter, Stelluti returned to his home in Fabriano, and de Filiis left Rome for his home in Terni. Stelluti appears from the correspondence to have had a series of personal troubles, probably financial, and de Filiis despaired of ever acquiring the kind of knowledge that was expected of members, now that he was isolated from the others.

At this point, the odds against continuance of the Lincean Academy were enormous. But neither Cesi nor Eck would abandon the project of creating a significant scientific society. Eck proceeded from Rome to Siena, Florence, Milan, and Turin, in each city meeting with scholars and telling them of the Academy. To Cesi at Rome he forwarded accounts of his travels, his meetings, and the observations he had made of the flora and fauna of the Italian provinces and the other lands through which he passed, which included France, England, Scotland, and Ireland. When he finally arrived back in Holland, he became involved in a religious controversy, upholding the Catholic side, and for this he was exiled. After a sojourn in Norway, Sweden, and Denmark, he was allowed to return to Daventer, but stayed only a short time and then journeyed on to Germany, Poland, and Austria. At the court of Rudolf II in Prague, he met Johannes Kepler and Francis Tengnagel, to whom he spoke of the Lincean Academy. He wrote to Cesi recommending that they be elected members, but nothing came of it; it is probable that Cesi hesitated to admit any Protestants to his society, which was having trouble enough at Rome already. Eck observed the nova of 1604 and sent to Cesi a short treatise on it, which Cesi published at Rome in 1605; this was the first publication sponsored by the Lincean Academy. Eck also sent or described several other books he had composed, some of which survive in manuscript in the archives of the Academy.

Meanwhile Cesi, left alone at Rome, steadfastly refused to

enter into the social life of the city as his father demanded. Instead, he held the Academy together by correspondence and composed further plans for its organization and expansion. He visited Naples for a few months, where he met Porta. Porta was then an old man, but he took a great interest in Cesi and dedicated to him his next two books. Some correspondence between Porta and Cesi from this period survives; one letter of particular interest will be mentioned below. At Naples Cesi also met Ferrante Imperato, a distinguished botanist, in whose possession he saw a manuscript copy of a very important work on the natural history of Mexico, plans for the publication of which occupied the Academy intermittently over a long period of years.

Early in 1606 Eck returned to Italy and even ventured to come to Rome despite Cesi's warnings of possible trouble. For a time all went well, and Cesi began to hope that the period of persecution of the Academy had ended. But it soon began again from the same quarter, and Eck resumed his peregrinations, writing from Madrid in June 1608 and proceeding from there through France, England, and Belgium. Eck returned to Rome for the last time in 1614, but by that time his many struggles had unbalanced his mind, and he did not long continue his activity in the Lincean Academy.

Membership in the society had declined to three in 1608 as the result of the death of de Filiis at Naples. In 1610 the first new member was added, and this was none other than Porta himself. Cesi had long before drawn up an elaborate plan for the establishment of houses of study by the Lincean Academy in various cities of the world, a plan similar to the project proposed a few years later in England by Francis Bacon. Negotiations were undertaken to establish the first of these branch academies at Naples, and Cesi hoped that Porta might be induced to contribute to it his valuable library. This scheme did not materialize, though Naples became in the ensuing years a principal center of Lincean activity.

The Academy now had four members again: two in Rome, one in Naples, and the other abroad. Cesi was in frequent correspondence with all the others, and in 1609, shortly before Galileo produced his first telescope at Padua and took it to Venice, Cesi had heard rumors of the Dutch invention and wrote to Porta about it. Cesi's letter is lost, but Porta's answer survives; in it he told Cesi that the instrument was a mere toy which he himself had long known about, and of which he drew a rough illustration in his letter. Galileo is not mentioned in any of the surviving correspondence on the Lincean Academy up to this time, and there is no reason to think that any of its members had ever heard of him until after the publication of his first telescopic discoveries early in 1610. It is interesting that in September of that year, Stelluti wrote to his brother as follows:

> I believe by now you have seen Galileo, that is, his *Sidereus Nuncius,* and the great things he says. But now Kepler, a pupil of Tycho's, has written against him, and there has come from Venice one of his books for Father Clavius, saying that he (Galileo) claims to be the author of the instrument, whereas more than thirty years ago Giovanni Battista della Porta wrote about it in his *Natural Magic,* and hinted at it also in his book on *Optical Refraction.* So poor old Galileo is cut down; but meanwhile the Grand Duke has given him 800 piasters, and the Venetian government has increased his salary.[3]

The interest of this first mention of Galileo by a member of the Lincean Academy lies in its unfriendly tone, circulating as it did a somewhat confused version of the facts. Kepler's book, the *Conversation with the Sidereal Messenger,* was anything but hostile to Galileo. The grand duke had indeed employed Galileo, who had moved to Florence, but that contradicted the idea that he was still employed by the Venetian government at the University of Padua. Moreover, Galileo had not claimed the invention of the telescope, which he attributed to a Fleming. Stelluti's letter is dated from Rome; it is clear that he had not himself seen Kepler's book, which he believed to have been published at Venice, but his first instinct was to support the implied priority of a fellow Lincean to this important invention.

In the spring of 1611, after his prodigious success with the improvement and the astronomical application of the telescope, Galileo journeyed to Rome to exhibit his discoveries and to secure support, if possible, from the Jesuits there against a number of professional astronomers and university professors who declared his claimed discoveries to be a fraud or an illusion of the lenses of his instrument. His visit was an enormous success, and while he was there, on 14 April 1611, Cesi held a banquet in his honor. Among those present were Johann Faber, Antonio Persio, John Demisiani, and Johann Schreck (or Terrentius), all of whom were elected members of the Lincean Academy within a short time thereafter. At this banquet the name "telescope" was given to Galileo's instrument, probably at the suggestion of the Greek scholar Demisiani, but possibly at Cesi's instigation. On 25 April Galileo was elected a member of the Lincean Academy, becoming its fifth living member and the second member who enjoyed a wide scientific reputation at the time, Porta having been the first.

Here let us pause to speculate on the question of what attraction Galileo found in the Lincean Academy. He had personally met but a single member, Cesi, and the Academy as such was not yet widely known. On the other hand, Galileo himself was already a celebrity, having risen to international fame with the publication of his *Starry Messenger* only a year before. At Rome he had been feted by the Jesuit mathematicians of the Collegio Romano, entertained by cardinals, and received by the Pope himself (the same Pope Paul V who had closed Porta's academy at Naples and who was later to order Galileo's silence on the Copernican theory). Galileo was a distinguished figure at the Tuscan court, as well as having a wide acquaintance and high reputation in the universities of Pisa and of Pauda.

It is not immediately apparent why a man of such prominence was quick to lend his name to a small and struggling academy at Rome; it is still less obvious, at least on the surface, why it was that from that time forth Galileo took great pride in the title of Lincean, employing it in his correspondence and on the title pages of most of his books. Because the Lincean Academy later became very famous, because it subsequently elected to membership several men distinguished in science, and because it is closely associated in the minds of historians with the name of Galileo, his original association with the Academy is widely taken for granted as a natural occurrence. It seems to me, however, that this involves a sort of circular reasoning, for it was only after Galileo's election that the Lincean Academy became large and prominent. Nor can it be said that Galileo was a joiner by nature; if he had been seeking honor by membership, there were several more distinguished academies at Florence, such as the Crusca and the Florentine

Academy, that would have been more appropriate for that purpose.

Galileo's alacrity in joining the Lincean Academy might, of course, be accounted for by the charm of Cesi's personality, but that alone seems to me an insufficient reason. Perhaps a clue to an adequate explanation may be found in something already mentioned —namely, that four other persons present at the banquet given by Cesi in Galileo's honor were shortly afterwards elected to membership. When one considers that in the first eight years of the Academy's troubled existence, only one new member had been added, whereas five were added in 1611 and ten more in 1612, it begins to appear that the famous banquet at Rome marked a turning point in the policies of Cesi, who was always in complete control of the Academy's affairs. But if that is so, it can only have been because of his conversations with Galileo during the visit to Rome, for the other men mentioned were by no means newcomers to Cesi's acquaintance.

In the summer of 1610 Galileo, after twenty years as a professor, had left the universities to accept a court position. It is not improbable that by 1611 he was already feeling the effects of the break in communication with other scholars which resulted from his departure from the University of Padua. He was also experiencing the open hostility of the official scholarly world to the reception of his discoveries and ideas. He was probably not anxious to reestablish communication with his former associates at the universities, even if that had been practicable; yet he was aware of the need for some avenue of communication with men who were truly interested in new scientific ideas and who had no commitment to the official doctrines of professional educators. The famous banquet introduced him to Cesi, a truly extraordinary organizer of marked intelligence and genuine interest in science, and also to a group of congenial scholars outside the universities. Persio was attached to the retinue of Cardinal Cesi; Faber was a physician of German origin; Demisiani, a Greek, was mathematician to Cardinal Gonzaga; and Schreck was a Fleming of great scientific ability, then unattached, but soon to join the Jesuit missionaries to the Far East. These are the banqueters who were elected to the Academy soon after Galileo.

In striking support of my assumption that university channels at the time were useless to the new science, it may be mentioned that the only two university professors known to have been present at the banquet were the only two guests who were never elected to the Academy. They were Francesco Pifferi, mathematician at the University of Siena and author of a commentary on Sacrobosco's *Sphere,* and Julius Caesar La Galla, professor of logic at the Sapienza in Rome, leader of the Peripatetic philosophers of the city, and author in 1612 of a wretched book on lunar astronomy which consisted chiefly in the deprecation of Galileo's discoveries and had the sole redeeming feature of being the first printed book to use the word "telescope."

I conjecture that either at the banquet of 14 April 1611 or in immediately subsequent conversations, Cesi recounted to Galileo and to some or all of the others, the principles of, and his plans for, the Academy; and that in reply, Galileo not only gave his endorsement but added some suggestions that would strengthen the organization in the interests of the new science as he saw it. It is only a conjecture, but it seems to fit in rather well with what is known. Five members including Galileo were added in 1611, doubling the society; ten more were added in 1612, doubling it again. Among the new members, other than those already mentioned, were the Roman mathematician Luca Valerio, with whom Galileo had been in correspondence for some time and whom he later referred to as "the Archimedes of our age"; Mark Welser, an influential amateur of science; and Fabio Colonna, a naturalist of the first rank. Another indication of the accelerated activity of the Academy is that the entire surviving correspondence of the Linceans up to the evening of Cesi's banquet for Galileo consists of 60 letters written over a period of seven or eight years, from July 1603 to February 1611. For the single year from April 1611 to April 1612, 55 letters survive, of which 22 were either to or from Galileo. By the end of 1615, a total of 422 letters concerning the Academy and its affairs had been written, counting only those which still survive.

The speed, scope, and effectiveness of the Academy as a means of transmitting scientific news may be illustrated by a single example. Four days after the banquet, Mark Welser wrote from Augsburg to Johann Faber thanking him for a description of that event. In May 1611, writing to Paolo Gualdo, an old friend of Galileo's at Padua, Welser in turn supplied information about the banquet to him, Gualdo having meanwhile sent other information to Welser concerning the honors received by Galileo on his Roman visit. Thus the news of the meeting was transmitted from Rome to Padua via Augsburg within a month.

Galileo commenced an active correspondence with Cesi immediately upon his return to Florence. Galileo's first letter is lost, but Cesi's reply, dated 23 July 1611, asks for a copy of Galileo's long letter written at the request of Cardinal Joyeuse in defense of his account of the lunar mountains, and tells Galileo that Cesi has urged La Galla to show him his treatise on the same subject. He reports that Porta has read and ridiculed Francesco Sizzi's attack on Galileo, the first to introduce theological arguments. Thus news and gossip of scientific interest began immediately to flow through Cesi to and from leaders of science. In August 1611 Cesi reports to Galileo on the arguments to be brought against him by the Peripatetics and urges him to publish a supplement to his *Starry Messenger,* mentioning the phases of Venus and the appearances of Saturn in order to protect his scientific priority. In September he tells Galileo that the Academy's publication of the book on Mexican plants has been begun; Galileo had seen the manuscripts at Cesi's house in Rome. In Cesi's next letter he mentions the phenomenon of light storage and reemission in a species of pyrites known as Bolognese stone, long of interest to Galileo, and gives further news of attacks being prepared against him. And so the correspondence grew, month after month, between Rome, Florence, Augsburg, Naples, and Acquasparta, Cesi's country home.

Meanwhile, Galileo had become involved in a dispute at Florence against the Aristotelians over the nature of floating bodies. To Cesi he sent, in May 1612, a copy of his book on hydrostatics which had grown out of that controversy. Earlier in the year, Mark Welser had sent to Johann Faber at Rome a copy of the letters on sunspots, which Welser had published for the Jesuit Christopher Scheiner, and expressed his desire to hear Galileo's comments on them. These eventually reached Galileo, who replied to them at great length in three letters written during 1612. Though the letters were addressed to Welser, copies were sent to Cesi, and Cesi undertook to publish them under the auspices of the Academy at Rome in 1613. The dissemination of Galileo's views on sunspots with this sponsorship was not an unmixed blessing, because the

Academy prefixed an introduction by Angelo de Filiis (brother of Anastasio) in which Galileo's claim to priority in the discovery of sunspots was strongly argued. This led ultimately to a serious dispute between Scheiner and Galileo that had disastrous consequences. As the sunspot letters were being edited for publication, Galileo corresponded with Cesi concerning corrections and revisions and sought his assistance in clearing certain touchy philosophical and theological points with authorities at Rome.

Brushing aside a multitude of interesting letters which show the intense activity of the Academy in the years 1612–14, we come to the period in which Galileo and his followers were first subjected to serious opposition in Church quarters. Up to that time, Galileo's noisy opponents had been chiefly professors, whose contentions he had been more than able to combat by himself. Trouble from the Church, however, was a different matter, and Galileo quickly availed himself of his Lincean colleagues at Rome, as well as other friends there, to assess the extent of the threat. When Cesi, ill in Acquasparta, heard that an open attack on Galileo had been made from the pulpit in Florence, he wrote at once to commiserate with Galileo, saying that:

> These enemies of knowledge who take it upon themselves to distract you from your heroic and useful inventions and works are of that group of perfidious and rabid men that are never to be quieted, nor is there in fact any better way to defeat them than by ignoring them.[4]

He went on to counsel caution on Galileo's part, saying that in his opinion, if Copernicus had had to consult the Congregation of the Index, his great book would never have been published. He gave Galileo a good deal of specific advice on the handling of the matter both at Florence and at Rome, where Cesi was well acquainted with the officials and with procedures.

Two months later, in March 1615, Cesi wrote from Rome to tell Galileo that a Carmelite friar had published a book reconciling Copernicus with the Bible. In the same letter Cesi remarked, "The writer reputes all of us to be Copernicans, which is not so, as we profess ourselves at one only in the freedom to philosophize about physical matters."[5] The Academy took that position officially a little later, when the subject was still more dangerous as a result of the Church's edict suppressing the Copernican theory. This came about in 1616, when Galileo was at Rome and had been instructed to desist from holding or defending the Copernican system. Luca Valerio then protested to the Academy against the activities and beliefs of his illustrious colleague, but the Linceans instead took formal action to censure Valerio and to declare their support of freedom in scientific thought. This is not the place to enlarge on the events surrounding what has been called "the first trial of Galileo," but the loyalty of the Academy to him in his battle for freedom from authority was unflinching and extremely helpful.

While at Rome in 1616, Galileo debated the Copernican theory publicly at the home of Virginio Cesarini, a young man of letters who subsequently became a member of the Academy. After the Church edict, Galileo had to lie low for several years, but in 1619 he became involved in a dispute about comets, first indirectly and then openly, taking sides against the mathematician of the Jesuit college in Rome. His most famous polemic, *The Assayer,* was written in the form of a letter to Cesarini, and was published at Rome in 1623 under the auspices of the Lincean Academy. This was a ticklish undertaking, the target of attack being a Jesuit, and Galileo himself having been warned to tread carefully in dealing with astronomical questions. There is no doubt that he benefited greatly by the careful reading and editing given to his sarcastic masterpiece by his Lincean colleagues at Rome. Indeed, the book would probably not have been written had it not been for the urging he received from those colleagues not to leave unanswered the attack his Jesuit adversary had published against him. To them we owe the existence of what is in effect an outline of Galileo's ideas about proper scientific reasoning and investigation.

The academicians were also responsible for the dedication of *The Assayer* to the new pope, who appointed Cesarini to a post at the papal court. Urban VIII, long friendly toward Galileo, gave him permission to write his *Dialogue Concerning the Two Chief World Systems,* provided that it gave equal treatment to Ptolemy and Copernicus. This book also was planned to be published at Rome by the Lincean Academy, but the arrangement was terminated by the sudden death of Cesi in 1630, at the age of forty-five. Without Cesi, the Academy had neither funds nor stable organization. The end of the Lincean Academy coincided with the decline of Galileo's fortunes, just as its beginning had been auspicious for their rise. The publication of his *Dialogue* at Florence brought about a storm of controversy and resulted in his summons to Rome for trial by the Inquisition. Whether the support of Cesi and an active Lincean Academy might have prevented this can never be known, but the change of place of publication after the securing of a license to print at Rome was at least one of the factors in the debacle. And certainly the existence of the Lincean Academy during Galileo's most active period of public life was a principal factor in his success.

Notes to Essay 4

1. Quoted with some modification from [J. E. Drinkwater-Bethune], *Life of Galileo* (London, 1829), p. 37.
2. *Discoveries,* p. 238.
3. *Opere,* X, 430.
4. *Opere,* XII, 128–29.
5. *Opere,* XII, 150.

5

The Effectiveness of Galileo's Work

Until the present century it was customary to call Galileo the founder of modern physical science. Ancient science was thought of as having ended with the decline of Greek civilization, and no real contribution to scientific thought was known to have been made during the long ensuing period to the late Renaissance. The seemingly abrupt emergence of many recognizably modern scientific concepts early in the seventeenth century thus appeared to have been a true revolution in human thought. In that scientific revolution, Galileo appeared as the prime mover. The persecution that he suffered as a result of his active propagation of new ideas lent color to the idea that his had been a totally new and revolutionary kind of science.

As historians of ideas gave more careful attention to the treatment of scientific questions in medieval and early Renaissance times, the traditional role that had rather romantically been assigned to Galileo was critically reexamined. Many early anticipations of modern science or its fundamental concepts were found in manuscript commentaries on the philosophy of Aristotle and in treatises on statics forming what is known as the medieval science of weights. Anti-Aristotelian traditions were shown to have existed perennially in the universities, particularly those of Oxford, Paris, and Padua—traditions which had long been obscured by an overwhelming ascendancy of the Peripatetic philosophy in the official curricula at most times. Study of works by such men as Philoponus, Jordanus Nemorarius, Thomas Bradwardine, Walter Burley, Robert Grosseteste, Nicole Oresme, and Jean Buridan, coupled with evidence that their writings had circulated widely among scholars, first in manuscript and later in printed form, suggested that modern science was not suddenly born with Galileo, but simply emerged

95

about that time after a long period of incubation. Many scholars now question whether it is proper to speak of a scientific revolution as having occurred in the late Renaissance or at any other time, and believe that it would be more accurate to characterize the emergence of modern science as a gradual event in a continuous process of thought which has merely shown periods of slower and of more rapid development.

Though much may be said for this sophisticated modern viewpoint, it does tend to obscure a striking historical fact which the older, more naïve conception recognized and at least attempted to explain. The fact is that man's attitude toward the world about him and his control of natural phenomena have altered more in the four centuries that have elapsed since the birth of Galileo than in as many millennia before that time. No matter how many of the fundamental ideas underlying modern science were in some sense anticipated by his medieval predecessors, their insights had no marked effect on the pursuits of other men as did those of Galileo. Whether or not one wishes to call his undoubted effectiveness "revolutionary" is a matter of taste; but whatever one calls it, the manner in which it is to be explained is still deserving of serious study.

The principal sources of Galileo's effectiveness, as I see them, were intimately related to the temper of the time in which he lived. But in saying that, I do not mean that the emergence of a Galileo at that period was in any way inevitable. Such social-deterministic views are coming to be more and more widely held, but to me they seem too smug, implying as they do that we now know so much that we can retroactively predict the appearance of a genius, or perceive that the spirit of an age is bound to produce one.

Reflecting on what I know of Galileo's contemporaries, I find it hard to select one who could have filled his place. Those who took up his work did not hesitate to credit him with having placed them on the path to further achievement. Those who opposed his work rarely even understood what Galileo was telling them, despite his clarity of expression; hence I think it unlikely that they would have found out the same things for themselves. Two of his great contemporaries, Kepler and Descartes, each excelled him in one field—Kepler in astronomy and Descartes in mathematics—but they were both woefully deficient as physicists. And this leads me to the first point that I wish to make in explanation of Galileo's effectiveness.

Galileo was born into a world that already had a highly developed and technically advanced mathematical astronomy, but it had no coherent mathematical physics and no physical astronomy at all.[1] It was Galileo who, by consistently applying mathematics to physics and physics to astronomy, first brought mathematics, physics, and astronomy together in a truly significant and fruitful way. The three disciplines had always been looked upon as essentially separate; Galileo revealed their triply paired relationships and thereby opened new fields of investigation to men of widely divergent interests and abilities. Mathematical astronomy, mathematical physics, and physical astronomy have ever since constituted an inseparable triad of sciences at the very base of modern physical science. Therein, I think, lies the primary explanation of Galileo's effectiveness.

The inner unity of mathematics, astronomy, and physics is more often implied than overtly stated in the work of Galileo. It is to me doubtful whether a philosophical theory of that unity would have sufficed to produce the effects here under consideration. A contrary view may be taken by those historians who see in Galileo's work little more than a loyal carrying out of the philosophical program of Plato, through showing that geometry indeed governs the physical universe. But there are difficulties with that view. Galileo did not acknowledge any leadership but that of Archimedes; he spent most of his life trying to persuade people not to swear by the words of any master; his notion of the instrumental role of geometry in understanding nature is quite different from that of Plato; and eminent Platonists of the time were much better informed in that philosophy than Galileo, yet had no discernible influence on the study of physical science.

In any event Galileo, not content with a general statement from outside science concerning the relationship of mathematics, astronomy, and physics, set forth particulars within each pairing of those sciences which established their interconnections. And that suggests a second source of his effectiveness: he was an acknowledged expert in each of the three separate disciplines. In view of the recognized merit of his own contributions to each of them, it was evident that he knew what he was talking about, even when what he said appeared paradoxical or absurd. Astronomers were drawn to his physics by his eminence in astronomy; mathematicians took up his mechanics because he was a respected professor of mathematics.

One may contrast the case of Galileo with that of his contemporary Francis Bacon, who likewise formulated a program for the reform of knowledge. That program included three basic ideas which are also found in Galileo's works; namely, recognition of the inadequacy of traditional knowledge, an understanding of the obstacles standing in the way of any departure from it, and the suggestion of methods by which real advances in knowledge might be made. But Bacon, unlike Galileo, was no expert in mathematics or science; hence, though he could discern the goal and suggest a path, he did not actually lead others along that path to the goal. As he himself wrote in a letter to Dr. Playfere: "I have only taken upon me to ring a bell to call other wits together."[2] Bacon's program stressed the accumulation of observational data, a valuable antidote to authority and a most useful procedure in the natural sciences. But it did not clearly open a new path to physical science, as did the bringing together of mathematics, astronomy, and physics. Bacon's bell served its purpose; but—at least so far as physical science was concerned—when the wits assembled, it was in Galileo's study.

Of course, to be an expert in as many as three separate fields was not uncommon for men of the Renaissance. That is the way in which Galileo's effectiveness was closely related to the temper of his time. But to be an expert in each of the three disciplines now under discussion was not a likely combination at his time for reasons which will presently appear. It was not unusual in 1600 to be an expert in mathematics, astronomy, and music, for example, or in astronomy, physics, and metaphysics. But Galileo's expertness in mathematics, astronomy, and physics was exceptional, and in certain curious ways was largely accidental. Indeed I believe that it was only gradually that Galileo himself fully discerned the essential interrelationships of his deepest interests. Eventually he did so, and as a result he became a critic and a reformer of, as well as a contributor to, science; that is, a man with a definitely formulated program for the study of natural phenomena, not just a versatile technical specialist. That, in my opinion, was the third source of his effectiveness.

Certain personal traits of Galileo's also contributed to his effectiveness. They have been discussed in a preceding essay; here it will be remarked only that his concern for precision was sufficient to protect him from indulging in rash conjectures, but not so great as to hinder him from declaring certain kinds of observed discrepancies or apparent contradictions to be irrelevant or negligible. This is essential in a discoverer of truly fundamental laws, just as an inflexible and uncompromising precision is necessary for their refinement and extension. It is interesting that most of Galileo's scientific contemporaries tended to fret over detail, which fitted them admirably for the next step in physical science, but made it hard for them to perceive and formulate its first mathematical laws. The exception is Kepler, and it is interesting that his contribution was essentially mathematical rather than physical in the modern sense.

Let us next examine the origin and development of Galileo's program for the reform of physical science, beginning with the period of his life immediately before his full comprehension of the magnitude of his task. In so doing we shall be better able to see how his work contrasted with that of his predecessors and what traditions and prejudices he was obliged to break down.

For a period of more than twenty years, from 1589 to 1610, Galileo was a professor of mathematics, first at the University of Pisa and then at Padua. No record remains of his lectures at Pisa. At Padua, however, records show his assigned subjects for various years.

> 1593—*leget Sphaeram et Euclidem.*
> 1594—*leget quintum librum Euclidis et theoricas planetarum.*
> 1598—*leget Euclidis Elementa et Mechanicas Aristotelis Quaestiones.*
> 1599—*Leget Sphaeram et Euclidem.*
> 1603—*leget librum De sphera et librum Elementorum Euclidis.*
> 1604—*leget theoricem planetarum.*

By *librum De sphera,* in the entry for 1603, we may assume that the text of Sacrobosco was meant and that the same text was explained in 1593 and 1599.[3] The syllabus of Galileo's public lectures on that subject is preserved in five closely corresponding copies in manuscript, one of which was published in 1656 by Urbano D'Aviso as the *Trattato della Sfera di Galileo Galilei.* Apart from its clarity of style, it differs little from dozens of similar treatises of the epoch.

Galileo's lectures on Euclid's *Elements* probably likewise represented merely the usual course in geometry; if he wrote a syllabus for them, it has been lost. The fifth book of Euclid, however, was of particular interest to Galileo, and we have what is probably an edited version of his course of 1594 in a book published by Vincenzio Viviani in 1674 under the title, "The fifth book of Euclid or the universal science of proportion explained by the teaching of Galileo, arranged in a new order." Galileo's special interest in the theory of proportion had an important bearing on his method of applying mathematics to physics, but it is unlikely that such applications were discussed in his public lectures at Padua.

There is strong reason to believe that Galileo also wrote a syllabus for his course on the treatise *Questions of Mechanics,* then attributed to Aristotle though now ascribed to one of his disciples.[4] That syllabus, now lost, must not be confused with Galileo's own treatise *On Mechanics,* drafted about 1593 and successively revised, which seems to have been used by Galileo in his private lessons to special pupils. At the end of that treatise and in a letter written in 1610, Galileo refers specifically to another work on questions of mechanics.

The basis of Galileo's lectures on planetary theory is conjectural, as again no syllabus has survived. Probably they constituted an exposition of Ptolemy's *Almagest,* for Galileo once mentioned that he had composed a commentary on Ptolemy about 1590, which he intended to publish. It is improbable that his public lectures included an exposition of the Copernican theory, though the heliocentric theory was probably mentioned in passing —as it was, contrary to the assertion of many modern historians, in his lectures on the sphere.[5]

In short, Galileo's public teaching had the general characteristics of most courses offered in mathematics at any leading university around 1600. Even at the enlightened University of Padua, Galileo appears to have departed only to a small degree from conventional routine instruction. In the six years for which we have a definite record, he lectured in only one term on anything that might today be considered as related to physics—and even that course was designed as a commentary on an ancient treatise.

Physics at that time belonged to philosophy rather than mathematics and was taught in universities by philosophers as an exposition of Aristotle's *Physica.* Such a course was probably taken by Galileo as a student at Pisa under Francesco Buonamico or Girolamo Borro. Since the chair of mathematics at Pisa was vacant during most of Galileo's student days, his only formal instruction in astronomy was probably associated with philosophy rather than with mathematics. From the so-called *Juvenilia* preserved among his papers, it appears that he heard the lectures of Buonamico on Aristotle's *De caelo,* a purely speculative treatment of astronomy devoid not only of what we should call physics, but even of the mathematical theory of astronomical calculation which had long since been brought to an impressive degree of accuracy.

It should be remembered that the entire tradition in professional astronomy up to that time was essentially technical rather than scientific. The task of astronomers was to improve the methods of describing and calculating the observed positions and motions of heavenly bodies, rather than to explain such motions physically. That tradition found strong support in the Aristotelian philosophy, which made a fundamental distinction between terrestrial and celestial matter and motions. Such a distinction had long been incorporated into Christian theology. Thus astronomy, like physics, had evolved along two distinct paths in formal education. The philosophical part of each science remained quite foreign to the mathematical part in the minds of even the best-educated men. Astronomical calculations, moreover, which fell to the mathematicians, remained strictly kinematic. The science of dynamics had not yet been born, and even if terrestrial dynamics had existed, it would not have been applied to astronomy so long as celestial objects were regarded as pure lights constituted of quintessential material. But not even terrestrial dynamics existed; such a science was effectively precluded in scholarly circles by Aristotle's dictum that every body moved must be in contact with a separate mover. With respect to physics, all that was traditionally open to mathematical treatment was a single branch of mechanics; namely, statics.

Even in his earliest studies, however, Galileo defied Aristotle and attempted to expand the applications of mathematics to physics. Since his achievements along that line gave him the first essential clue to his wider program, we should consider some ways in which his approach differed from those of his predecessors. This bears directly on the effectiveness of his work. An excellent example is provided by comparing his treatment of a celebrated theorem in statics with the analyses of the same proposition by the best medieval writer on statics, Jordanus Nemorarius, and by an older contemporary of Galileo, Simon Stevin. Here is the theorem of Jordanus:

IF TWO WEIGHTS DESCEND ALONG DIVERSELY INCLINED PLANES, AND IF THE INCLINATIONS ARE DIRECTLY PROPORTIONAL TO THE WEIGHTS, THEN THEY WILL BE OF EQUAL FORCE IN DE-SCENDING.

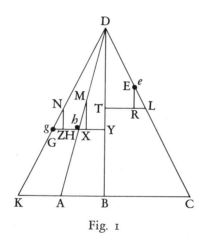

Fig. 1

Let there be a line ABC parallel to the horizon, and let BD be erected vertically to it; and from D draw the lines DA and DC, with DC the more oblique. I then mean by proportion of inclinations, not the ratio of the angles, but of the lines taken to where a horizontal line cuts off an equal segment of the vertical.

Let the weight e be on DC, and the weight h on DA, and let e be to h as DC is to DA. I say that those weights are of the same force in this position.

For let DK be a line of the same obliquity as DC, and let there be on it a weight *g*, equal to *e*. If then it is possible, suppose that *e* descends to L and draws *h* up to M. Now let GN be equal to HM, which is equal to EL. Draw a perpendicular on DB through G to H and Y, and another from L, which will be TL. On GHY erect the perpendiculars NZ and MX, and on LT erect the perpendicular ER.

Then since the proportion of NZ to NG is that of DY to DG, and hence as that of DB to DK; and since likewise MX is to MH as DB is to DA, MX is to NZ as DK is to DA; that is, as the weight *g* is to the weight *h*.

But because *e* does not suffice to lift *g* to N, it will not suffice to lift *h* to M. Therefore they will remain as they are.[6]

In this demonstration the physical element is, as you see, brought in as an afterthought to the geometry, by main force as it were. That the weights *e* and *g* are in equilibrium perhaps requires no proof; but the relation of that fact to the situation of the weight *h* does demand some further explanation than a mere reiteration of the theorem itself. The theorem happens to be true, but what Jordanus has to say in support of it does not afford any hint of a method by which other physical theorems might be developed.

Next, let us consider the ingenious treatment given to the same proposition by Simon Stevin in 1586. Here the previous situation is reversed; geometry is eliminated in favor of pure mechanical intuition. Here is a paraphrase of Stevin's proof of the theorem:

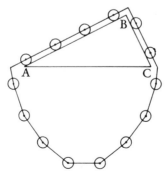

Fig. 2

Imagine a circular necklace of equal-spaced heavy balls, draped over two diversely inclined planes. (See Fig. 2.) The chain will not move, there being no more reason for it to rotate in one direction than the other. Now, the bottom part of the chain is perfectly symmetrical, so it cannot affect the balancing. Cut it off, and the remainder of the chain will still not move. But since the total weight now resting on either plane is in proportion to the length of that plane, such weights are in equilibrium.[7]

Stevin's physical reasoning is superb, but the theorem remains isolated. No further physical application of the method suggests itself, this time because geometry is left out. In the attempted proof by Jordanus, geometry ruled and physics was left out.

Galileo's way of merging geometry and physics became apparent in his proof of the same theorem in his early treatise on motion, dating from 1590. The method itself suggested to him not only many corollaries, but successive improvements of the proof itself and further physical implications of it. Here is Galileo's original proof:

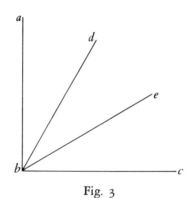

Fig. 3

    . . . A heavy body tends downward with as much force as is necessary to lift it up. . . . If, then, we can find with how much less force the heavy body can be drawn up on the line *bd* than on the line *ba,* we will have found with how much greater force the same heavy body descends on line *ab* than on line *db.* . . . We shall know how much less force is required to draw the body upward on *bd* than on *be* as soon as we find out how much greater will be the weight of that body on the plane . . . along *bd* than on the plane along *be.*

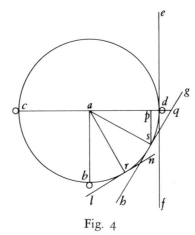

Fig. 4

Let us proceed then to investigate that weight. Consider a balance *cd*, with center *a*, having at point *c* a weight equal to another weight at point *d*. Now, if we suppose that the line *ad* moves toward *b*, pivoting about the fixed point *a*, then the descent of the body *at the initial point d* will be as if on the line *ef*. Therefore the descent of the body on line *ef* will be a consequence of the weight of the body at point *d*. Again, when the body is at *s*, its descent *at the initial point s* will be as if on line *gh*, and hence its motion on *gh* will be a consequence of its weight at point *s*. . . .

Now it is clear that the body exerts less force at point *s* than at *d*. For the weight at point *d* just balances the weight at point *c*, since the distances *ca* and *ad* are equal. But the weight at point *s* does not balance that at *c*. For if a line is drawn from point *s* perpendicular to *cd*, the weight at *s*, as compared to the weight at *c*, is as if it were suspended from *p*. But a weight at *p* exerts less force than at *c*, since the distance *pa* is less than the distance *ac*. . . . It is obvious, then, that the body will descend on line *ef* with greater force than on line *gh*. . . .

But with how much greater force it moves on *ef* than on *gh* will be made clear as follows. Extend line *ad* beyond the circle to meet line *gh* at point *q*. Now since the body descends on line *ef* more readily than on *gh* in the same ratio as the body is heavier at point *d* than at point *s*, and since it is heavier at *d* than at *s* in proportion as line *da* is longer than *ap*, it follows that the body will descend on line *ef* more readily than on *gh* in proportion as line *da* is longer than *pa*. . . . And as *da* is to *pa,* so *qs* is to *sp;* that is, as the length of the oblique descent is to the vertical drop. And it is clear that the same weight can be drawn up an inclined plane with less force than vertically in proportion as the vertical ascent is shorter than the oblique. Consequently the same heavy body will descend vertically with greater force than on an inclined plane in proportion as the length of the descent is greater than the vertical fall. . . .[8]

First, note the physical rule stated at the outset, that the downward tendency is measured by the upward resistance, suggesting Newton's law of action and reaction; this device was repeatedly used by Galileo as a step to mathematical analysis in physics. Next, you see how the entire demonstration constitutes a reduction of the problem of equilibrium on inclined planes to the lever, which in itself removes the theorem from the isolation in which it stood before. Galileo applied the idea of virtual displacements as Jordanus had intended to do; but unlike Jordanus, Galileo assumed that the force acting on a body at the initial point of movement alone would determine its mode of descent along a given plane. In place of the macroscopic intervals geometrically equated by Jordanus, Galileo's method assumes a determinate tendency to motion at a point, or along an infinitesimally small distance.

That form of analysis is all the more noteworthy if we recall that when Galileo composed this first demonstration, he still believed that the motion of descent was essentially uniform and that acceleration was only an accidental and temporary effect. Probably his words were governed by physical intuition that the force of descent or tendency to move is not the same for a body at rest as for one already in motion, or his choice of terminology may have been governed by his feeling for mathematical precision of statement. In any event, his choice of a correct form of expression at the outset helped him later to discover, and perhaps even led him directly to, the essential and fundamental role of acceleration in free fall.

A further significant feature of Galileo's analysis here is that he made vertical motion the common measure of all motions on various inclined planes, instead of attempting a direct comparison of different planes as Jordanus and Stevin had done. That approach enhanced the fruitfulness of his demonstration by suggesting to him several corollaries and later helped him to generalize correctly when comparing the inclined plane to other simple machines.

But when Galileo framed the foregoing demonstration, he was attempting to analyze the *speeds* of bodies on inclined planes. He mistakenly supposed the speed for any plane to be constant and to be related to the force or effective weight that he had correctly analyzed. Because of that misapprehension, several corollaries he deduced from his theorem were illusory. But it is characteristic of scientific reasoning, especially when mathematics is applied, that errors and inconsistencies are readily detected and may even aid in the discovery of truth. Galileo himself often pointed this out in his writings. In the present instance, he deduced the ratios of speeds that would hold under his assumption for a given body on different planes and observed that those ratios were contradicted by experiment. Very likely it was that troublesome fact that caused him to withhold from publication his early treatise on motion. He also deduced that a body on a horizontal plane could be moved, at least in theory, by a force smaller than any previously assigned force. This terminology is arresting—it is that of an Archimedean concept in pure mathematics, later to become the foundation of the theory of limits, applied here for perhaps the first time to a purely physical concept. The fruitfulness of that application of mathematics to physics was enormous; in Galileo's hands it led quickly to a limited inertial concept and to the first bridge between statics and dynamics. But let us now examine Galileo's development of the same theorem in his next composition, his treatise *On Mechanics*.

Consider the circle AJC and in it the diameter ABC with center B, and two weights at the extremities A and C, so that the line AC being a lever or balance, movable about the center B, the weight C will be sustained by the weight A. Now if we imagine the arm of the balance as bent downward along the line BF . . . then the moment of the weight C will no longer be equal to the moment of the weight A, since the distance of the point F from the perpendicular line BJ has been diminished.

Now if we draw from the point F a perpendicular to BC, which is FK, the moment of the weight at F will be as if it were hung from the line KB; and as the distance KB is made smaller with respect to the distance BA, the moment of the weight F is accordingly diminished from the moment of weight A. Likewise, as the weight inclines more, as along the line BL, its moment will go on diminishing, and it will be as if it were hung from the distance BM along the line ML, in which point L it may be

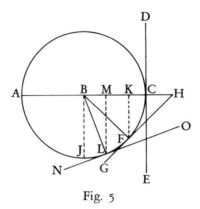

Fig. 5

sustained by a weight placed at A that is as much less than itself as the distance BA is greater than the distance BM.

You see, then, how the weight placed at the end of the line BC, inclining downward along the circumference CFLJ, comes gradually to diminish its moment and its impetus to go downward, being sustained more and more by the lines BF and BL. But to consider this heavy body as descending and sustained now less and now more by the radii BF and BL, and as constrained to travel along the circumference CFL, is not different from imagining the circumference CFLJ to be a surface of the same curvature placed under the same movable body, so that this body, being supported upon it, would be constrained to descend along it. For in either case the movable body traces the same path, and it does not matter whether it is suspended from the center B and sustained by the radius of the circle, or whether that support is removed and the body is supported by and travels upon the circumference CFLJ. Whence we may undoubtedly affirm that the heavy body descending from the point C along the circumference CFLJ, its moment of descent *at the first point* C is total and integral, since it is in no way supported by the (corresponding) circumference; and at this first point C it has no disposition to move differently from what it would freely do in the perpendicular tangent line DCE. But if the movable body is located at the point F, then its heaviness is partly sustained by the circular path placed under it, and its moment downward is diminished in that proportion by which the line BK is exceeded by the line BC. Now when the movable body is at F, *at the first point of its motion* it is as if it were on an inclined plane according with the tangent line GFH,

since the tilt of the circumference at the point F does not differ
from the tilt of the tangent FG, apart from the insensible angle
of contact. . . .[9]

The balance of this revised demonstration need not detain
us here; it suffices to note how fruitful Galileo's approach had
already been for him. By his original restriction of virtual motions
to the initial point, he was led to perceive on the one hand the
analogy between a series of tangential tendencies and the motion
of a pendulum; and on the other hand, the analogy between those
tendencies and the descent of a body along a circular path supported from below. From that, he arrived at a number of new
and interesting corollaries concerning descent along arcs and
chords of circles, and wrote to Guido Ubaldo del Monte about
these in 1602. Probably it was in the course of those investigations that he was led to his discovery that the spaces traversed
in free fall, whether vertical, inclined, or tangential, were proportional to the squares of the times of descent. That conclusion
was communicated to Paolo Sarpi in 1604, though at that time
Galileo had not yet satisfactorily defined uniform acceleration or
derived his result correctly from fundamental assumptions. The
patient ordering of his definitions, assumptions, theorems, and
observations took many years and will be reconstructed in a later
essay. Enough has now been said to illustrate the novelty and
effectiveness of Galileo's method in applying mathematics to the
problems of mechanics.

Galileo's assigned university courses gave him little or no
scope for the communication of his researches in mathematical
physics. He went on with them, but one might say that he did so
almost despite his official position rather than in pursuance of it.
From a letter written to him by Luca Valerio, a Roman mathematician best known for his work on centers of gravity, it is evident that by June 1609 Galileo had selected two fundamental
propositions on which he was prepared to found the science of
mechanics. But in that same month, his attention was diverted
from that project by news of the telescope, and his energies were
applied immediately to its improvement and to the astronomical
discoveries which soon made him famous throughout Europe.

Galileo's sudden celebrity quickly suggested to him a way in
which he might free himself from routine teaching and find time

to write and publish the books which had been evolving in his mind. It was mainly for that purpose that, after twenty years of university teaching, he applied for a court position with the grand duke of Tuscany. In making his application he included a significant and unusual request: ". . . As to the title of my position," he wrote, "I desire that in addition to the title of 'mathematician,' his Highness will annex that of 'philosopher,' for I may claim to have studied for a greater number of years in philosophy than months in pure mathematics."[10]

To the historian, Galileo's request is striking in two respects: first, because he sought the unusual title of court philosopher, and second, because he *did not* seek the customary title of court astronomer. That title was not uncommon in Europe at that time. Johannes Kepler, for example, was imperial astronomer at the court of Rudolph II at Prague. That Galileo did not even mention, let alone demand, such a title is made still more striking by the fact that his chief claim to fame in 1610 lay in the astronomical discoveries he had just published in his *Sidereus Nuncius* and dedicated to his proposed employer, the grand duke of Tuscany.

Galileo's failure to seek the title of court astronomer, although curious at first glance, is not difficult to explain. In the first place, a court astronomer at that period was in fact an astrologer, or at least his primary value to his employer lay in that capacity. Any contributions he might make to theoretical or observational astronomy were the merest by-products, so far as the sovereign was concerned. As Kepler ruefully remarked, the wayward daughter astrology had to support the honest dame astronomy. Galileo was perfectly competent to cast horoscopes, but he did not enjoy doing so; on the contrary, he was openly critical of both astrology and alchemy. In the second place, he does not seem to have cared much about mathematical astronomy outside his routine public lectures, which in fact were offered by the university chiefly because of their astrological applications, deemed necessary for medical students especially.

As we have seen, the subject to which Galileo *had* devoted his principal researches during twenty years of teaching was the application of mathematics to problems of motion and mechanics. But in applying for employment by the grand duke, he could scarcely have described that specialty as physics, nor could he have asked for the title of "physicist" with any hope of being understood. Physics was no more an independent subject than was metaphysics or ethics. It was merely a branch of philosophy—and that is what throws light on Galileo's otherwise odd request for the title of "philosopher." It was, in fact, the only appropriate word, when we consider that the term "mechanic" was entirely undignified and unthinkable as a court title. The historic appropriateness of Galileo's choice of title is shown by the fact that long after his time, the term "natural philosopher" served as the official name for a physicist in England, the word "physics" itself being no more than a synonym for "nature."

I am inclined to believe that the philosophy which Galileo had in mind when he asked for the title of philosopher was that which he later described in one of his most frequently cited passages, which begins: "Philosophy is written in that grand book of nature that stands forever open to our eyes. . . ."[11] I think it is not too far-fetched to say that what Galileo was seeking, when he asked to be made mathematician and philosopher to the Tuscan court, was the world's first post as a mathematical physicist.

Support for this viewpoint is afforded by a difficulty that arose in Galileo's securing of the title he had asked for. The grand duke, doubtless in the belief that he was granting the request, sent to Galileo a document naming him chief philosopher to the court and chief mathematician at the University of Pisa. But Galileo was not satisfied with this, which is puzzling unless it was because he wanted the two titles definitely combined. Eventually he had his way and was named chief mathematician and philosopher to the grand duke and chief mathematician at the University of Pisa without obligation to reside or teach there. It may seem that he had made a major issue of a minor point, but I believe that even before Galileo moved from Padua to Florence, he had in mind the conception that completes the famous quotation of which the opening words were previously cited. To paraphrase the rest of it: ". . . that grand book of nature . . . is written in the language of mathematics, without a knowledge of which one cannot understand a word of it, but must wander about forever as in a maze."[12] What Galileo wanted, and could get only from a powerful patron, was a position in which he could openly expound the unity of mathematics and physics—and probably astronomy also, but without any astrological connotations. The grand duke could grant him this, but the departments of philosophy were too strong and the departments of mathematics too weak to accommodate such a program in the universities.

Galileo's first publication in his new position was a book on the behavior of bodies placed in water. In that book he used the principle of Archimedes and the principle of virtual velocities to refute the qualitative ideas of the Aristotelians, and he also introduced physical experiments to combat tradition and authority. His earlier use of virtual displacements had by now led him on to a true principle of virtual velocities, however primitive it may seem from a modern standpoint. Observing that the unequal arms of a steelyard in equilibrium would necessarily move their unequal weights through inversely proportional distances *in equal time,* he stated the general rule that equal weights are of equal *moment* when given inversely proportional *speeds.* As the source of this proposition, he credited the Aristotelian treatise on *Questions of Mechanics.* It enabled him to extend the principle of virtual velocities from statics to hydrostatics, as exemplified in this theorem in his book on bodies in water:

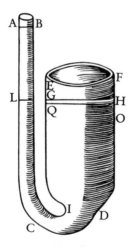

Fig. 6

Consider the above figure (which, if I am not mistaken, may serve to reveal the errors of some practical mechanicians who on false premises sometimes attempt impossible tasks) in which, to the large vessel EIDF, the narrow pipe ICAB is connected, and suppose water in them to the level LGH, which water will rest in that position. This astonishes some people, who cannot conceive how it is that the heavy weight of water GD, pressing downwards, does not lift and push away the small quantity contained in the pipe CL, which nevertheless resists and hinders it. But the wonder will cease if we suppose that the water GD goes down only to QD, and ask what the water CL has done. It, to make room for the other, descending from GH to QO, would have in the same time to ascend to the level AB. And the rise LB will be greater in porportion to the descent GD as the width of the vessel GD is to that of the pipe IC, or as the water GD is to the water CL. But since the moment of the speed of motion in one vessel compensates that of the weight in the other, what is the wonder if the swift rise of the lesser water CL shall resist the slow descent of the greater amount GD?[13]

Not only did this constitute an important addition to what Archimedes had written on hydrostatics; it also opened the door to the creation of hydrodynamics. In his earlier treatise *On Mechanics,* recognition of the fact that the force required to disturb a system in equilibrium is negligible had similarly constituted a bridge from statics to dynamics, as mentioned previously. In later years Galileo applied mathematics to the laws of falling bodies and to the analysis of strength of materials. But we have now sufficiently illustrated the effectiveness of his applications of mathematics to physics, and it is time to turn to his novel applications of physics to astronomy.

Aristotelian philosophy insisted on a complete dichotomy between terrestrial and celestial substances and motions. Astronomers were concerned not with the nature of heavenly bodies, but only with purely mathematical descriptions of the observed motions and predictions of positions. Christian theology had adopted the Aristotelian separation of base earth from noble heavens, making it dangerous as well as difficult to attack. Nevertheless, the opening sections of Galileo's *Dialogue* were devoted to a refutation of the Aristotelian assumption, as a point of departure for his pioneer attempt to unify astronomy and physics.

A complete chronological account of Galileo's efforts to bring physics and astronomy together would take us back to 1597, when he wrote to Kepler that he believed certain physical events on earth to be explicable only by its motions.[14] But his first public attempts to relate physics and astronomy are found in the *Starry Messenger* of 1610.

In announcing his first telescopic observations, Galileo declared the moon to be like another earth because of its rough, mountainous surface. Applying geometric methods familiar to land surveyors, he calculated the heights of the lunar mountains from their shadows. Denying the Peripatetic contention that all heavenly bodies were perfect spheres, he accounted in later years for the moon's roughness by assuming its material to be similar to that of the earth and similarly drawn to its common center of gravity. The darker surfaces of the moon were taken, on terrestrial analogies, to be relatively smooth as compared to the brighter parts. Conversely, he deduced from the moon's rough surface and its bright reflection of sunlight that the earth, with similar surface, must reflect sunlight to the moon; and in that way he correctly explained the secondary light on the moon, seen when it is thinly crescent. At first he suggested also that the moon had an atmosphere, but he later withdrew that further analogy between the moon and the earth. However, he postulated an atmosphere for Jupiter in order to account for changes in the appearances of its satellites in their various positions. All Galileo's physical analogies between the earth and any heavenly body, even the lowly moon, aroused strong opposition from philosophers and some protest from theologians.

When Galileo wrote the *Starry Messenger,* he was rapidly approaching his ultimate firm conviction that astronomy must be completely integrated with physics. But his interest in astronomy was then still subsidiary to his absorption in the application of mathematics to physics on which he had labored for so many years. The telescope was for a time principally a means to him for gaining fame and improving his position. Thus he first observed sunspots not later than the spring of 1611, but paid little attention to them except as a curiosity to show his friends. He did not seize immediately on them as a ready basis for expansion of his analogies between terrestrial and celestial phenomena, as one would expect him to do had he already completely formulated his program to unify mathematics, physics, and astronomy. But the sunspots were destined to be decisive in that regard when a rival astronomer proposed a theory about the spots.

Galileo's treatise on bodies placed in water was about to go to press when he received from Mark Welser three printed letters on sunspots written by a German Jesuit, Christopher Scheiner. Scheiner argued that the spots were only apparently on the sun and were in reality varying clusters of small opaque bodies rotating about it at some distance. His opinion probably had its origin in a desire to maintain, for religious and philosophical reasons, the doctrine of incorruptibility of heavenly bodies, especially the sun. Welser wrote to ask for Galileo's opinion on the whole subject, and Galileo undertook a series of careful observations, after which he replied in refutation of the Jesuit's theory.

By precise mathematical reasoning, Galileo demonstrated that the sunspots must be located either on the surface of the sun or at a negligible distance from it. He went on to say that the only proper method available for assigning the causes of distant or unfamiliar events was to apply our experience of things near at hand, and he suggested that the sunspots might better be explained as vast clouds or smokes than as stars or planets. He noted that terrestrial clouds often cover a whole province and that when a terrestrial cloud happens to be near the sun and is compared with a sunspot, it generally appears much darker than the spot. Still more significant was his explanation of the rotation of the sunspots, which he attributed to an axial rotation of the sun itself, for that in turn led him to a first attempt in the direction of celestial dynamics. Following his first published reference to an inertial principle, cited elsewhere in this volume, he wrote:

> Now if this is true, as indeed it is, what would an inert body do if continually surrounded with an ambient that moved with a motion to which it was indifferent? I do not see how one can doubt that it would move with the motion of the ambient. And the sun, a body of spherical shape suspended and balanced on its own center, cannot fail to follow the motion of its ambient, having no intrinsic repugnance or external impediment to rotation. It cannot have an internal repugnance because by such a rotation it is neither moved from its place, nor are its parts permuted among themselves. Their natural arrangement is not changed in any way, so that as far as the constitution of its parts is concerned, such movement is as if it did not exist. . . . This may be further confirmed, as it does not appear that any movable body can have

a repugnance to a movement without having a natural pro-
pensity to the opposite motion, for in indifference no repugnance exists. . . .[15]

Here Galileo's knowledge of the conservation of angular
momentum was brought to bear on a problem of celestial motion
—a real step toward the unification of physics and astronomy.
Mathematics having already been linked firmly to both the latter
sciences, Galileo's program was now essentially complete. That
program was presented successively in *The Assayer* (1623), Galileo's scientific manifesto (as it was called by Leonardo Olschki);
in the *Dialogue* (1632), dealing primarily with astronomical
arguments but heavily weighted with physics; and in the *Two New
Sciences* (1638), dealing exclusively with physics (since Galileo
was forbidden to deal with astronomy after writing the *Dialogue*)
but extending beyond mechanics to include speculations on sound,
light, and other physical topics. *The Assayer* and the *Dialogue*
offer many illustrations of Galileo's program of linking physics
with astronomy and of his simultaneous linkage of all three sciences. I shall consider a few of these here, neglecting the *Two
New Sciences,* since examples have already been given of Galileo's
methods of applying mathematics to physics.

In *The Assayer,* Galileo had occasion to discuss the so-called
third motion attributed by Copernicus to the earth in order to
maintain the earth's axis continually parallel throughout the year.
Of this he says:

> This extra rotation, opposite in direction to all other celes-
> tial motions, appeared to many people to be a most improbable
> thing. . . . I used to remove the difficulty by showing that
> such a phenomenon was far from improbable, . . . for any body
> resting freely in a thin and fluid medium will, when trans-
> ported along the circumference of a large circle, spontaneously
> acquire a rotation in the direction contrary to the larger move-
> ment. This is seen by taking in one's hand a bowl of water,
> and placing in it a floating ball. Then, turning about on one's
> toe with the hand holding the bowl extended, one sees the
> ball turn on its axis in the opposite direction, and completing
> its revolution in the same time as one's own. [Really] . . . this
> would not be a motion at all, but a kind of rest. It is certainly
> true that to the person holding the bowl, the ball appears

to move with respect to himself and to the bowl, turning on its axis. But with respect to the wall . . . the ball does not turn, and any point on its surface will continue to point at the same distant object.[16]

Galileo's appeal to familiar terrestrial observations in explanation of heavenly events was designed to pave the way to physical astronomy, which would eliminate the clumsy hypothetical apparatus of crystalline spheres which earlier astronomers had introduced as a means of accounting for the motions of heavenly bodies. The idea of relative motion, introduced in the preceding passage, became pivotal in the later *Dialogue*. Astronomers, it is true, had long been aware of the importance of optical relativity, but even Tycho Brahe had been unable to conceive of a literal physical relativity of motion. Galileo, armed with that concept and with his principles of the composition of motions, inertia, and conservation of angular momentum, was able effectively to meet many commonsense objections against motion of the earth. Thus, replying to the claim that if the earth really moves, we should see a departure from straight motion in the free fall of a body from a tower, Galileo said:

> Rather, we never *see* anything but the simple downward motion, since this other circular one, common to the earth, the tower, and ourselves, remains imperceptible and as if nonexistent. Only that motion of the stone which we do not share is perceptible, and of this, our senses show us that it is along a straight line parallel to the tower. . . . With respect to the earth, the tower, and ourselves, all of which keep moving with the diurnal motion along with the stone, the diurnal motion is as if it did not exist; it remains insensible, imperceptible and without any effect whatever. All that remains observable is the motion which we lack, and that is the grazing drop to the base of the tower. You are not the first to feel a great repugnance toward recognizing this nonoperative quality of motion among things which share it in common.[17]

A good example of Galileo's effectiveness at persuasion through the use of terrestrial and celestial analogies occurs in the First Day of the *Dialogue*. His Aristotelian opponent cannot believe that the rough, dark earth could possibly shine in the sky as brightly as the moon. Galileo points out to him that the comparison must be drawn for the moon as seen in daytime, since that is the only time we can see the earth illuminated, and then proceeds:

> Now you yourself have already admitted having seen the moon by day among little whitish clouds, and similar in appearance to one of them. This amounts to your granting that clouds, though made of elemental matter, are just as fit to receive light as the moon is. More so, if you will recall having seen some very large clouds at times, white as snow. It cannot be doubted that if such a cloud could remain equally luminous at night, it would light up the surrounding regions more than a hundred moons.
>
> If we were sure, then, that the earth is as much lighted by the sun as one of these clouds, no question would remain that it is no less brilliant than the moon. Now all doubt on this point ceases when we see those clouds, in the absence of the sun, remaining as dark as the earth all night long. And what is more, there is not one of us who has not seen such a cloud low and far off, and wondered whether it was a cloud or a mountain—a clear indication that mountains are no less luminous than clouds.[18]

Two arguments for a motion of the earth that were particularly dear to Galileo's heart, arguments which simultaneously link mathematics, astronomy, and physics, fell on deaf ears in Galileo's time. Those arguments related to the ocean tides and to cyclical changes in the paths of sunspots. Correctly understood, they were unanswerable at the time they were propounded. It may seem paradoxical, in explanation of Galileo's effectiveness, to mention two arguments of his that were (and still are) ineffective. But I think that the paradox is only apparent. The prime source of Galileo's effectiveness was his bringing together of mathematics, astronomy, and physics in an inseparable relationship. Hence even a questionable example of such a relationship given by him was still capable of revealing to others what *sort* of thing should be sought in a scientific explanation.

The tidal and sunspot arguments are the subjects of separate essays in this volume; here it suffices to outline their nature. Galileo's theory of the tides occupies the final section of the *Dialogue*. He says that, in his opinion, the ocean tides cannot be explained physically if we assume a perfectly stationary earth. So far he is quite right. He then asserts that the double motion of the earth, around its axis and around the sun, affords a purely mechanical means of explaining the tides. His argument is that the two circular motions are additive on one side of the earth and subtractive on the other, so that the extremities of any large east-west basin of water, such as an ocean, will be traveling with nonuniform velocity. Since direct experience teaches us that water in a basin is disturbed when its velocity is altered, Galileo thought that he had found a basic cause of periodic disturbances in the ocean waters.

The principal objection was that only one high tide a day would be expected from this model, whereas there are approximately two. This did not escape Galileo's attention, but neither did it bother him. So long as he had a primary mechanical cause for periodic disturbance, he was content. He pointed out that a wide variety of other factors would affect its progress, such as the length of the basin, its orientation, its depth, the shape of its coasts, the action of winds, and so on. Since Galileo had never observed tides except along the Adriatic and the Tyrrhenian seas, where they are not very impressive, it is not surprising that he thought such factors sufficient to account for the observed discrepancy of period.

On the other hand, Galileo did not neglect the fact of variations in tidal effects related to the seasons and to phases of the moon. These he accounted for in his theory by postulating cyclical changes in the earth's orbital speed, which would appear to us as related to the sun's position, and by drawing an analogy between the earth-moon system and a moving weight on a rotating rod driven by a constant force to account for monthly tidal changes.

This whole theory illustrates vividly Galileo's program of seeking mechanical explanations for all physical effects. Celestial appearances were accommodated to a tidal theory having a mechanical basis; for discrepancies with observed phenomena, he invoked further mechanical phenomena. All this was in keeping with his expressed principles; thus his admiration for Copernicus was only heightened by the latter's loyalty to heliocentrism in the face of unexplained discrepancies between the apparent and theoretical sizes of Venus at opposition and conjunction—discrepancies which were eventually reconciled by telescopic observations after the death of Copernicus.

The other argument in which Galileo combined mathematics, astronomy, and physics in support of the earth's motion concerns the annual variations in the paths of sunspots. Twice in the year, the paths are straight and tilted to the ecliptic; twice a year, they are at maximum curvature with the ends lying in the ecliptic; at all times, they change cyclically in tilt and degree of curvature. Galileo pointed out that those variations are easily explained if the earth has the two motions attributed to it by Copernicus. But for an absolutely stationary earth, they can be explained only by ascribing to the sun a highly complicated set of motions. First, the sun must have a rotation about an axis tilted to the ecliptic, having a period of about one month. Second, in its annual revolution about the earth, the sun's axis must rotate conically about another axis perpendicular to the ecliptic, in circles having a radius measured by the tilt of the first axis. The period of this conical rotation must be annual. A still further daily motion of the sun's axis would be necessary to keep the paths of the spots undisturbed on the face of the sun during each day.

The essential difference in the two cases lies in the fact that the sun presents almost exactly the same face to a terrestrial observer throughout a day. This was first known from the positions of sunspots. But the earth obviously cannot present the same face to an imaginary solar observer throughout any day. Hence the explanations required in the two systems are not simply interchangeable.

Galileo duly acknowledged that it would be theoretically possible, from a strictly geometric point of view, to endow the sun with the necessary motions to produce these appearances. But he saw that any such device led to grave difficulties from the standpoint of dynamics. Galileo was aware of the principle of conservation of angular momentum and of the inertial path of the axis of a rotating body, as mentioned earlier; thus, to him, the physical difficulties were very real. But to his contemporaries, who felt obliged only to link mathematics with astronomy and not astronomy with physics, his argument remained inconclusive.

Galileo's theory of the tides and his argument from the paths of sunspots are important in showing the manner in which he brought together simultaneously the fields of mathematics, astronomy, and physics. Whatever their defects, those two arguments for the earth's motion were founded on a fundamentally sound conception of the manner in which all physical phenomena, terrestrial and celestial, ought to be consistently explained. It was that conception which made Galileo's work more effective scientifically than the work of any one of his great contemporaries or recent predecessors. It was a conception which he himself thoroughly grasped and consciously applied to a definite program. It was a conception, moreover, which profoundly appealed to many of Galileo's contemporaries and exerted a recognizable influence upon them, suggesting a wide variety of further investigations once it had been broached. Since this particular unifying conception had been lacking in all previous science, the unsophisticated view that Galileo was the revolutionary founder of modern science is not to be rejected outright, no matter how many elements of his program may prove to have been anticipated by others before him.

Notes to Essay 5

1. The work of Simon Stevin is an example of sound mathematical physics prior to the work of Galileo. Since Galileo was born in 1564, and Stevin's first book on physics appeared in 1586, the statement above remains literally true. Stevin first published in Dutch, and his work remained relatively unnoticed until 1605, when a Latin translation appeared. Galileo was by that time far along with his own mechanical investigations. Johannes Kepler contributed to physical astronomy, but his contributions were contemporary with Galileo's. The work of René Descartes began to appear only at the close of Galileo's life.
2. Cited from R. F. Jones, *Ancients and Moderns* (Berkeley, 1965), p. 41.
3. The evidence is given in "Galileo Gleanings VII"; *Physis* I, 4 (1957), 296.
4. The *Questions of Mechanics,* unknown in the Middle Ages, played an important role in sixteenth-century physical speculations.

5. *Opere,* II, 223. "The present question [whether the earth is motion-less] is worthy of consideration, there being no lack of very great philosophers and mathematicians who, deeming the earth a star, have made it movable." Probably no passage in Galileo's writings is more widely misrepresented than that in which he explained to his students at Padua the motions that might be attributed to the earth, and the objections to its rotation, before expounding to them the geostatic theory as required by the university. In the most recent instance I have noted, the writer not only states that Galileo "taught cosmography without making the slightest allusion to an alternative way of explaining the celestial phenomena," but misquotes one of the few biographers who had correctly appraised Galileo's comments; see W. Hartner, "Galileo's Contribution to Astronomy," *Galileo Man of Science,* ed. E. McMullin (New York, 1968), p. 184, and cf. E. Wohlwill, *Galilei und sein Kampf,* vol. I (Hamburg, 1909), p. 210.

6. Slightly modified from E. A. Moody and M. Clagett, eds., *The Medieval Science of Weights* (Madison: The University of Wisconsin Press, 1952), p. 191, with permission of the copyright owners, The Regents of the University of Wisconsin.

7. For the precise argument, see *The Principal Works of Simon Stevin,* ed. E. J. Dijksterhuis, vol. I (Amsterdam, 1955), p. 177 ff.

8. I. E. Drabkin and S. Drake, *Galileo Galilei on Motion and on Mechanics* (Madison, 1960), pp. 64–65. Emphasis added.

9. Ibid., pp. 173–74. Emphasis added.

10. *Discoveries,* p. 64.

11. *Discoveries,* p. 237.

12. *Discoveries,* p. 238. This passage is often cited as an argument that Galileo believed the "real" world to be mathematical. On that argument, the "real" Hamlet must have been English.

13. *Bodies in Water,* p. 17.

14. See essay 6.

15. *Discoveries,* pp. 113–14. Preceding passages are given in essay 12.

16. *Discoveries,* pp. 264–65.

17. *Dialogue,* pp. 163, 171.

18. *Dialogue,* pp. 88–89.

6

Galileo, Kepler,
and Their Intermediaries

The relationship between Galileo and Kepler, particularly in the year 1610, has been the subject of much discussion. The question is interesting not only for its historical aspects, but also for the light it would shed, if answered in detail, on the personalities of the two men. Previous discussions of the question have usually omitted the indirect roles of several other people who stood in various relations to the two principals. Here it is intended to call particular attention to those men.

Galileo's first knowledge of Kepler's existence came with the arrival at Padua, early in August 1597, of Kepler's first book, the *Mysterium Cosmographicum* (or *Prodromus* as it is alternatively referred to). Two copies of it were brought to Italy by Kepler's friend, Paul Hamberger, and both were left with Galileo on the eve of Hamberger's return to Germany. He delivered to Kepler a note of thanks from Galileo, dated 4 August 1597, and the additional information that Galileo was sending one copy of the book to Rome and would like to have more.

Although it is commonly assumed that the books were sent by Kepler specifically to Galileo at Padua, my considered opinion is that up to this time, Kepler had no more heard of Galileo than Galileo of Kepler. Galileo had not previously written any letters to persons outside Italy; he did not show any interest in astronomical topics in any known letters written before 1597; he had published nothing on astronomy or any other subject. Moreover, Kepler's reaction to Galileo's note of thanks strongly suggests that his name had not been known before. In September 1597, writing to his former teacher, Michael Maestlin, Kepler said:

> I recently sent to Italy two copies of my (or rather, your) little work, which was received gratefully and with pleasure

by the mathematician of Padua, named Galilaeus Galilaeus, as he signs himself. He has also been of the Copernican heresy for many years. He is sending one copy to Rome, and wishes to have more. . . .[1]

The phrase "as he signs himself," suggests not only that the name was new to Kepler, but that he supposed it equally unknown to his correspondent.[2] Professor Edward Rosen suggests that Kepler employed this particular phrase only because the Latin form of Galileo's name was striking, and he wished to direct Maestlin's attention to it.[3] The view is tenable, but it seems improbable that both Kepler and Maestlin were already familiar with the Italian form of the name, as required by this hypothesis, and found the Latin surprising. For a person known to both of them, one would expect the familiar name first, and "or" in place of "named"; or, at the very least, something to indicate previous knowledge—a phrase like "the celebrated," or "of whom you have spoken."

Moreover, if the books were sent to a specific destination, person, or place, the general phrase "to Italy" sounds odd; it would be more normal to say "to Padua" or "to Galileo." Nor is it likely that two copies would be purposely sent to one man, even if he were already famous.

Kepler's remark that Galileo had been a Copernican for many years must have been intended to convey news to Maestlin, rather than a fact already known to him. His source of information was Galileo's letter, which contained almost the same words. But if it was news to Kepler that Galileo had long been a Copernican, little reason would have existed for him to have directed a copy of his book (let alone two copies) to the Italian mathematician. Furthermore, if a copy was intended for Galileo as a famous man, it would be unusual to send it without a letter requesting his opinion of the work. Hence it appears most likely that Kepler had merely asked Hamberger to carry with him to Italy two copies of the new book and to leave them with persons likely to appreciate it and make it known there.

It would be helpful to know when Hamberger left Germany, how long he was in Italy, and when he returned. The only evidence we have on these matters comes from Galileo's letter:

> Your book, most learned man, given to me by Paul Hamberger, I received not some days ago, but only a few hours;

and since this same Paul spoke to me of his return to Germany, I might indeed be thought ungrateful in spirit later unless I thanked you by this letter for the gift sent to me. . . .[4]

It is natural to read this as meaning that Hamberger was leaving at once to return to Germany, though all we can be certain of is that he was leaving Padua and would not be returning there before going back to Germany. Hamberger did not see Kepler until the first of September, so he may have remained a while in Italy, in other cities. But more probably he had already finished his journey in Italy without finding a suitable recipient for either copy, and on the eve of his return to Germany he put both copies in the hands of Galileo as professor of mathematics at Padua, perhaps requesting him to find another suitable recipient. Galileo seems to have decided to send the extra copy to Christopher Clavius, the only astronomer of his acquaintance at Rome.

Professor Rosen takes the phrase *ad me missum* addressed to Kepler to imply also "by you," and *munere* to imply "your gift." In the absence of the pronouns required to make these things specific, it is at least equally likely that Galileo's language was inspired merely by ordinary courtesy. At any rate, Kepler's reply to Galileo in October did not indicate that Galileo's fame had reached him earlier, or that the books had been sent to Galileo personally. It did urge him to make certain astronomical observations over the ensuing year, if suitable instruments were available, and asked him for a letter in payment for two additional copies of the book being transmitted at that time.

It is generally agreed that Galileo did not reply to this letter at all, and that breach of courtesy has been the basis for many deductions about Galileo's character. Certainly if there was a reply, it was no more than a perfunctory note of thanks that did not invite further correspondence.[5] Galileo was not interested in astronomy at the time. Unlike Kepler's, Galileo's correspondence is devoid of astronomical discussions until 1604, except for two letters mentioning Copernicus in 1597. The nova of 1604 attracted his attention for a few months, but it was only in 1610 that Galileo became really interested in astronomical observations, and even then they were not observations of the ordinary kind.

For about five years after the first exchange of letters between Galileo and Kepler, there were occasional indirect contacts between the two men, and actions by others affected their relationship at least potentially. On 18 July 1599 Kepler wrote to the Englishman Edmund Bruce, then at Padua.[6] He urged Bruce to solicit correspondence with him from Italians and sent greetings to Galileo, expressing surprise not to have heard further from him. The reference seems to be to Galileo's silence with regard to the astronomical observations Kepler had asked him to make from December 1597 to September 1598. Kepler now desired Galileo to make some observations regarding terrestrial magnetism. Bruce was evidently in personal contact with Galileo, for he removed the initial part of Kepler's letter (doubtless containing only personal matters) and turned over to Galileo the balance, which is still preserved among his papers. It includes many of Kepler's musical speculations relating to his attempt to reduce planetary distances and speeds to a pattern based on rules of harmony, a topic later expanded by Kepler in his *Harmonice Mundi.*

During this period, Kepler had entered also into correspondence with Tycho Brahe. Shortly after Tycho's death, Kepler wrote for the first time to Giovanni Antonio Magini, giving an account of himself and of his relation with Tycho, and requesting Magini to collaborate in his work. Magini, a noted astronomer, had won the chair of mathematics at Bologna in competition with Galileo, and subsequently lost to him the chair at Padua, Magini's own city. He was the author of no less than nine published works by 1597, when Kepler sent his first book to Italy. Magini's *Novae coelestium orbium theoricae congruenties cum observatione N. Copernici* had been published at Venice in 1589.[7] As the title implies, Magini was no Copernican; he adopted only the observations of Copernicus, and not his theory.

In writing to Magini for the first time in 1601, Kepler said: "Since 1594 I have avidly pursued the mathematical discipline, assisted by a stipend from the Styrian province. In 1595 I wrote a book entitled *Mysterium Cosmographicum.* If a copy was sent to you at Padua, this was done as I wished."[8] The wording is strange; it implies that a copy had been sent to Padua for Magini four years earlier, that Kepler did not know whether it had reached him, but that if it had not, the fault was not Kepler's. This is only an implication, though; a flat statement was avoided. Kepler was vague about the date of the possible transmission, saying that he composed the book in 1595, which is true enough, though the title page was dated 1596 and the book did not issue from the press until 1597. He was equally vague about the identity of the person who should have transmitted a copy to Magini, giving the latter no clue to the manner in which the book might still be retrieved if not yet delivered.

Possibly one of the copies sent to Italy with Hamberger was intended by Kepler for Magini, though that seems unlikely. If Hamberger had known that a book was meant for Magini, nothing would have been easier than for him to tell Galileo so and to ask him to forward one copy to Bologna in return for the gift of the other. But Galileo volunteered to send the spare copy to Rome, and neither Hamberger nor Kepler objected. Nor did Kepler, in sending two additional copies to Galileo in October 1597, ask him to send one on to Magini. That he did not send a copy to Bruce at Padua for Magini will be evident shortly. On the whole, it appears that Kepler's carefully worded conditional sentence in his introductory letter to Magini was mere diplomacy: "If you did get a copy of my book at Padua, you have me to thank for it." But this innocent compliment to Magini's fame (if such it was) miscarried badly. Magini received the impression that Galileo, with whom he was anything but friendly, had received a book intended for him and had kept it.

Magini did not reply to Kepler's letter in 1601, for a reason that will be explained later. But in 1602 he visited Padua, his native city, and it appears that he there asked Galileo whether Kepler had sent one of his books for delivery to him and received a negative reply. In Padua he also conversed with Bruce, who was going to Florence, so they journeyed together as far as Bologna, where Bruce stayed overnight with Magini. At Florence, on 15 August 1602, he wrote to Kepler: "I showed him [Magini] your *Prodromus,* and told him you are greatly astonished that he had never replied to your letter; he then swore to me that he never saw your *Prodromus,* but daily expected its arrival; and he faithfully promised to send you a letter shortly. He admitted that he not only likes you, but admires you for your discoveries. Galileo moreover told me that he wrote to you, and received your book, which however he denied to Magini, of whom he spoke ill while praising you gently. For this I know certainly, that he offers your discoveries as his own to his students and others. But I did, and do [contrive] that all this redounds to your honor and not to his."[9]

Interpretation of this letter varies according to what one thinks of the several personalities involved. I believe that it was the beginning of a serious misunderstanding. My interpretation is that Galileo had told Bruce long before (probably in 1599) that he had received Kepler's book and had written to him, apropos of the letter to Bruce from Kepler at that time in which Kepler had expressed his surprise not to have heard further from Galileo. In the summer of 1602, Magini visited Padua and there asked Galileo if he had a book for him that had been sent by Kepler. Galileo replied that he did not. On the journey to Bologna, or at Magini's house there, Bruce showed him Kepler's book. Magini told Bruce that Galileo denied having received a copy sent to Padua for him. Bruce, remembering his earlier conversation with Galileo, interpreted this as a denial on Galileo's part that he had received Kepler's book at all, and was naturally indignant at this supposed duplicity. Hence he notified Kepler, adding that Galileo was passing off as his own certain of Kepler's discoveries.

But what were these discoveries of Kepler's that so fascinated Galileo as to induce him to try to steal them? They could hardly have been the doctrine of inscribed and circumscribed Platonic solids for planetary orbits that dominated the *Mysterium Cosmographicum,* nor was there anything else in that book that Galileo was likely to adopt. Since Kepler had not published anything further of importance by 1602, the only source for the discoveries said to have been appropriated by Galileo is the letter turned over to him by Bruce in 1599. Now, the theory of planetary relations to musical harmony set forth in that letter was as unlikely to have excited Galileo as Kepler's published ideas on the Platonic solids. Not only is there no trace of admiration on Galileo's part for those doctrines in any letter or published work during his entire life, but on the contrary there are adverse comments on Kepler's flights of fancy and his method of theorizing. Only one thing remains, then, and this (I believe) is the key to Bruce's charge. It occurs at the end of Kepler's 1599 letter: "Third, I ardently wish from Galileo, after determining exactly the meridian line, that he observe the magnetic declination [i.e., dip] from that meridian, by putting a magnetic needle in a square frame perpendicularly erect and applied to the meridian. For a wonder of the magnet is promised, if there be diligent observers consulting different magnets, none disagreeing. I was long ago of the opinion that the point to which the magnet turns is the original place of the pole of the world, and its motion has a magnetic cause. . . . Mercator puts the magnetic pole 16½ degrees from that of the world. From Dutch observations, I perceive it to be not more than 6½ degrees, which suits this purpose better. . . ."[10]

And in fact, Galileo did interest himself in magnetic phenomena about the time of Bruce's charge that he had appropriated Kepler's ideas. Later in the *Dialogue* he mentioned that a Paduan professor of philosophy gave him a copy of Gilbert's book on the magnet, published in 1600. He particularly interested himself in the variation of magnetic dip with latitude, discussed by Gilbert and here noted by Kepler as a possible cosmological clue. Whether Galileo's interest in the magnet came from Kepler or Gilbert, and whether he expounded only his own conclusions (which were quite different from Kepler's), or Kepler's as his own, or both, it is impossible now to tell. The first hint of Galileo's magnetic researches in surviving letters came on 2 September 1602, in a letter to Galileo from Paolo Sarpi concerning Gilbert's book.

A year elapsed without a reply from Kepler to Bruce, who then wrote again (21 August 1603) to say that there was no news, but that from recent letters from Germany he knew that Kepler was still alive, though he had thought him dead, having received no answer and in fact having his letters returned to him. He added that he had been thinking of seeing Kepler again before returning to England, as there was no one in the world he would rather talk to, and if Kepler knew how many learned men in Italy spoke of him, he would know that Bruce was not his only admirer. He had spoken to them of Kepler's marvelous musical discoveries and of his observations of Mars, and had shown his book to many who had praised it and awaited his further books. "Magini was here more than a week, and recently received your *Prodromus* as a gift from some noble Venetian. Galileo has your book and propounds your discoveries as his own to his students; I should write much more if time permitted."[11]

This makes it sound as if it were the contents of Kepler's book that Galileo taught as his own discoveries, but it does not actually say that. Bruce, knowing that his previous letter had not reached Kepler, merely repeated hurriedly what he had written before and had been returned to him undelivered.

The noble Venetian who gave Kepler's book to Magini early in 1603 was Giovanni Francesco Sagredo. The copy may have been sent to him for delivery to Magini before Kepler wrote directly to Magini in mid-1601, or it may have been given to Sagredo by Galileo, for they were close friends by 1603. Kepler probably first heard of Sagredo earlier, when the Venetian transmitted to Magini at least one letter from Tycho early in 1600. At that time Tycho sought to have a laudatory biography of himself written and published in Italy, a complex story which will be outlined here for its relevance to our main theme.

Francis Tengnagel, a young pupil of Tycho's, was sent by him to Rome in 1599 with the confidential mission of finding some astronomer who would write a glowing account of Tycho's life and work. The purpose was to impress his imperial employer. Tycho wished the biography to be written in Italy so that it would appear to have originated quite independently of his influence. To that end, Tengnagel visited Magini late in 1599, giving him a number of letters and documents to be used in the work. Tycho himself wrote to Magini on the matter, and Magini replied in February 1600, mentioning that Sagredo had forwarded Tycho's letter. Magini did not want the job of praising a rival astronomer, but neither did he wish to offend Tycho. He tried to get out of his uncomfortable position by recommending Bernardino Baldi, who was known to have compiled some two hundred biographies of mathematicians of all epochs. The biography desired by Tycho was never written, and Magini's embarrassing position was terminated by Tycho's death in 1601, shortly before Magini first heard from Kepler. Magini's failure to reply to Kepler, mentioned previously, was largely the result of his fear of getting entangled again in the same project, in which he (incorrectly) assumed Kepler to be concerned.

Tengnagel had met Galileo in Padua at the home of his friend and patron, Giovanni Vincenzio Pinelli. Early in 1600 Tycho wrote to Pinelli, hinting that he would like to hear from Galileo, doubtless in another attempt to secure an authorship for the laudatory biography. Receiving no response, Tycho wrote directly to Galileo on 4 May 1600, inviting direct correspondence. That the biography was the real objective can hardly be doubted. The recent return of Tengnagel was mentioned in Tycho's letter, and Tengnagel's whole job in Italy had been to negotiate the biography. But Galileo doubtless knew from Tengnagel or through Sagredo of Magini's connection with the matter, and decided to stay out of the affair at all costs. At any rate, he never answered Tycho. Tengnagel was later hostile toward both Sagredo and Galileo. In 1603 he wrote indignantly to Magini about the envious detractors of Tycho, mentioning particularly two little men who, raging furiously in the Paduan lecture halls and in private among crude people, took from Tycho's name the splendors that belonged to it in the republic of letters. One, God save the mark, was a professor of mathematics, who had never published anything by reason of his ineptitude; the other, his brother in ignorance, was a Venetian.[12] The two men were, of course, Galileo and Sagredo. It might be mentioned that by the time he wrote this letter, Tengnagel had also become suspicious of Kepler.

As to Magini's acquisition of Kepler's *Mysterium Cosmographicum,* Bruce can hardly have been mistaken in saying that Sagredo gave him a copy early in 1603. Yet in 1610 Magini wrote to Kepler that he had first obtained a copy from a young German who had arrived only a short time before. The person meant was Martin Horky, who is remembered for the violence of his published attack on Galileo in 1610 and for his attempt at that time to alienate Kepler from Galileo. But the prime mover behind this, as behind most other sharp attacks on Galileo around this time, was Magini—despite his numerous denials of the fact.

To Bruce's letter of 21 August 1603, Kepler replied at once. He asked Bruce not to praise him too extravagantly in Italy, and added: "Do not worry about Galileo, or vindicate me. My witnesses are time and light, and those who hear those witnesses, as will the erudite and upright. . . . Farewell, and continue to love me. Greet Magini and Galileo. . . ."[13]

Bruce replied on 5 November, this being the last letter of his to have survived. In it he spoke of the plurality of worlds, of the source of solar and planetary lights, of the oval figure of the earth, and other similar speculations. He did not mention Galileo. Many years later, on 5 April 1610, Kepler reread this letter and wrote on it some comments of admiration concerning the anticipation by Bruce of many of his own ideas, even saying: "This letter seems almost a compendium of my *Celestial Physics*."[14] Only three days after Kepler wrote these words, a copy of Galileo's *Starry Messenger* was put into his hands by Thomas Seggeth at the request of Giuliano de' Medici, the Tuscan ambassador at Prague.

When Galileo's book issued from the press on 12 March 1610, he had been out of touch with Kepler for more than twelve years. Even his indirect contact through Bruce had ended no later than 1603, and perhaps earlier. Galileo had not received (and appears not even to have heard of) Kepler's *Astronomia pars optica* of 1604 until after the *Starry Messenger* was published. There is no mention in his correspondence of Kepler's book on the nova of 1604, published in 1605, though Galileo took an interest in that phenomenon. Thus he appears to have lost touch not only with Kepler personally, but even with his publications. It is therefore risky to assume that Kepler's name, or the possibility of his support, entered Galileo's mind during the feverish period from January to March 1610, when he was making his first telescopic astronomical observations and writing the *Starry Messenger*.

Nevertheless, it is commonly assumed now that Galileo made haste to obtain Kepler's support against a host of enemies who assailed the validity of his claim to new discoveries in the heavens. In so doing, he is represented as having sought by devious means to reopen the correspondence that he himself had impolitely broken off long before. The entire fabric of that representation needs examination.

It is true that a number of men attacked Galileo's *Starry Messenger*, but only after the lapse of some time. The earliest references to the book show that at first it aroused only admiration and bewilderment; it caused a sensation and was in demand everywhere. Even Martin Horky, who was soon to become Galileo's bitterest opponent in the matter of Jupiter's satellites, wrote to Kepler from Bologna on the last day of March to say of the claimed discovery: "It is a marvelous thing, a stupendous thing; whether true or false, I know not."[15] Thus it was not before April

that doubt and controversy arose, even in the anti-Galileo circle
of Magini at Bologna.

Kepler's opinion was solicited in Galileo's letter to Giuliano
de' Medici, the Tuscan ambassador at Prague. This letter and a
copy of the book arrived at Prague on 7 April. It must therefore
have been sent from Venice about 25 March, judging by the fact
that the return courier took twelve days for the trip (from 19 April
to 1 May). But up to 25 March, or even a week after that, there
is no evidence that Galileo had reason to feel need for any external support. It may be that he foresaw trouble and moved to
be ready to counter it, but that assumption seems to me far-
fetched in view of his generally sanguine nature. There is a much
more plausible explanation (than fear of attack) for Galileo's
letter to Giuliano de' Medici and his request for Kepler's written
opinion, to which I shall return presently. First we may reconstruct
the events from Kepler's narrative and the letters of Galileo's
friend, Martin Hasdale.

Accounts of the new discoveries first reached Prague by word
of mouth about 15 March, according to Kepler. His own acquaintance with them came more than a week later, through a visit
from Wackher von Wackhenfels. This visit occurred after 22
March, for on that date Kepler wrote to Magini without mentioning or inquiring about the surprising news from Italy. There was
then a lapse of one or two weeks between Kepler's first excited
conversation with Wackher and his sight of the actual book. The
latter event may be dated almost certainly as occurring on 6 April.
A few days earlier, Kepler appears to have written to the imperial
ambassador at Venice, George Fugger, to ask whether a copy of
the *Starry Messenger* had been forwarded to the emperor. This
letter, now lost, was probably written about the first of April,
shortly after Wackher's first visit. Fugger replied in the negative
in mid-April.[16]

Hasdale, writing to Galileo of 15 April, recounted that on
3 April he was dining with the Spanish ambassador, where Mark
Welser had brought a copy of Galileo's new book. This copy
belonged to the Elector of Cologne, to whom it had been sent
by the grand duke of Tuscany, and I believe that it was the first
copy to reach Prague. The ambassador told Hasdale that he wished

to have Kepler's opinion of its contents. Hasdale met Kepler at breakfast with the Saxon ambassador on 15 April; Kepler had brought along a copy of his *Prodromus* of 1597 and attempted to show that in his book he had anticipated some of the new discoveries. Kepler had praised Galileo highly in talking with Hasdale, ranking him even above Tycho. Both men were invited to breakfast with the Tuscan ambassador on the following day. Hasdale told Galileo that news of the book had swept the imperial court with admiration and stupor, and that every ambassador and nobleman was calling on the mathematicians to refute it.[17]

It is generally said that the first copy of the *Starry Messenger* seen by Kepler belonged to the emperor, but I think this is an error. As previously mentioned, no copy had been sent to him by his ambassador at Venice, and the only copy sent by Galileo to Prague was a personal gift to the Tuscan ambassador, accompanied by a request to share it with Kepler. A copy might have been sent to the emperor by the grand duke of Tuscany, to whom it was dedicated, but this seems unlikely; first, because if a copy had come to him, his imperial astronomer would not have had to write to Fugger at Venice, and second, because the emperor did not give Kepler a copy to study when requesting his opinion. Kepler says that he first saw a copy "by permission of the emperor," and had a chance only to leaf through it. This took place after 5 April and before 8 April. From Hasdale's account, we know that the Spanish ambassador requested Kepler's opinion after seeing the copy in Welser's possession on 3 April. The most probable reconstruction is that Kepler applied to the emperor and obtained permission to inspect Welser's copy. This idea is borne out by the fact that in Kepler's narrative, the direct request from the emperor for his opinion came a few days later, after he had seen the book briefly (6 April) and had been reproached by Wackher (7 April) for having read it himself without showing it to his friend.

These dates are further confirmed by the fact that the notations made by Kepler on Bruce's last letter, which are dated 5 April 1610, contained no reference to the surprising news of Galileo's new discoveries in the heavens. It will be recalled that ten days later, Kepler wanted to show how his *Prodromus* had already anticipated such discoveries. If he had actually read the *Starry Messenger* before making his notations of 5 April on a letter speculating about the plurality of worlds (as against his merely having heard unconfirmed rumors about Galileo's discoveries), it is overwhelmingly probable that he would have included a further note about this, and about his having anticipated it.

In any case, the copy sent by Galileo to Giuliano de' Medici was put into Kepler's hands by Thomas Seggeth on 8 April, and he proceeded to write out his opinions at length in a letter to Galileo dated 19 April. The contents, with very few important changes, were published in May with a dedication to Giuliano de' Medici, under the title *A Conversation with the Starry Messenger*. In this way the requests for Kepler's opinion, not only from Galileo, but from the Saxon and Spanish ambassadors, the emperor, and others, were satisfied.

Giorgio Tabaroni has recently suggested that Galileo did not in fact ask for Kepler's opinion at all and that the supposed request was really fabricated by Giuliano de' Medici. "The able diplomat," Tabaroni wrote, "in fact obtained the speedy reply by pretending that it had been requested by Galileo, and by feigning that the copy of the *Starry Messenger,* which really had been sent to him personally (for otherwise one cannot explain his warm thanks for it) was intended for Kepler."[18] Tabaroni believes that the initiative was either the ambassador's own, or was carried out by him on instructions from Florence, where many remained unconvinced of the truth of Galileo's claimed discoveries. This hypothesis is interesting, and supporting arguments can be found for it. But against it is the fact that Kepler clearly related that the ambassador had read to him, from Galileo's letter, many kind words of praise and a request for his opinion. Had the ambassador merely told Kepler of such a letter, that is what Kepler would have recounted. It is likely enough that he would be shown the letter, which was in Italian, and that even if he did not request it, the ambassador would translate it for him. Kepler's account of the matter is very circumstantial; in his dedication of the *Conversation* to Giuliano, he wrote: "You made an appointment for me to meet you on 13 April. Then, when I appeared, you read me Galileo's request in his communication to you, and added your own exhortation."[19] In the text of the book, which preserves the form of the letter addressed to Galileo, Kepler said: "While I was thinking the matter over, your letter to the ambassador . . . of Tuscany arrived, full of affection for me. You did me the honor of thinking that so great a man [the ambassador] should particularly encourage me to write; and you sent along a copy of the book and added your own admonition. With the utmost graciousness, the ambassador fulfilled this function as a courtesy to you, and he most generously placed me under his patronage."[20]

It is evident that the "request" made by Galileo was that the ambassador himself ask Kepler to send him a written opinion on the contents of the book. This request was carried out by the ambassador with the addition of his own "exhortation." This leaves us the question of what additional "admonition" from Galileo was to be delivered to Kepler. The word is hardly appropriate to describe a further request on Galileo's part, addressed directly to Kepler.

I think that the "admonition" is likely to have been of this kind: "and if you do make the request, please tell him that he is to say precisely what he thinks, without regard to courtesies and formalities, for a mere flattering assent would be of little use to me." Similar terms had been used by Kepler to Galileo in October 1597, in requesting an opinion on the *Mysterium Cosmographicum*.[21] The words were conventional, were in keeping with Galileo's character and his probable purpose, and would also throw light on Kepler's oft-quoted remark in the preface to the *Conversation:* "I do not think that the Italian, Galileo, has treated me, a German, so well that I must in return flatter him, with injury to the truth or my deepest conviction."[22] These words, usually interpreted as a reproach for Galileo's long silence, were more probably intended to disabuse the reader of any idea that Kepler's approval was insincere, or that he owed the foreigner any special favor.

A question that has been widely discussed in connection with this whole affair is why Galileo did not approach Kepler directly, rather than through the Tuscan ambassador. Many think that he was hesitant to do so because of bad conscience about his long neglect to respond to Kepler's earlier requests for observations. Tabaroni suggested that Galileo, whatever his reasons, did not approach Kepler even indirectly; that the ambassador fabricated the whole story. Now it is true that if Galileo had had reason to believe that Kepler might feel any rancor toward him, he could best approach Kepler through a third party of high rank. But there is no evidence of bad conscience on Galileo's part, or of rancor on Kepler's. These are gratuitous hypotheses of historians and biographers. Against them is the fact that despite Bruce's accounts of duplicity and plagiarism on Galileo's part (if we read his letters in that way), Kepler continued to send his greetings to Galileo through Bruce, gently rebuked Bruce for excessive praise, and never wrote a word to anyone showing resentment toward Galileo. Modern writers treat Galileo's dropping of the correspondence in 1597 as if it were deliberate discourtesy. But during the same period, Kepler's own former teacher, Maestlin, let a letter from him go unanswered for five years. Magini did not answer Kepler's request for collaboration in 1601 at all. When Bruce notified Galileo in 1599 that Kepler was expecting a further letter, he replied that he had written to Kepler and had received his book. Galileo appears to have felt that his own obligations were discharged; otherwise he would have at least made some further promise or apology to be relayed to Kepler by Bruce.

In place of the prevailing interpretation of Galileo's indirect approach to Kepler, I suggest an alternative view that has at least some circumstantial support outside of character evaluations. It has already been remarked above that Kepler cannot have been on Galileo's mind early in 1610, when he was writing the *Starry Messenger*. At the time of constructing his first telescope, in mid-1609, Galileo had already been negotiating quietly for a post at the Florentine court. When his improved telescope opened up new fame to him, he speedily determined to press those negotiations. On the very day that Kepler completed and signed his lengthy opinion in the form of a letter to Galileo, Galileo was in Pisa en route to Florence for a brief visit, returning early in May. Two months later, his appointment by Cosimo II was a reality, and soon afterward Galileo left Padua forever.

It was this negotiation, I believe, that was uppermost in Galileo's mind when he wrote to Giuliano de' Medici in March of 1610, and not any possible opposition that might develop toward his book. It is likely that Galileo's choice of the Tuscan ambassador as intermediary was simply a part of his wish to renew acquaintances swiftly in Tuscan court circles. The diplomatic pouch, moreover, was the speediest and safest channel; indeed, contemporary practices may have made it the only proper channel for important correspondence of Tuscan subjects residing abroad. In any event, for Galileo's purposes, the endorsement of the mathematician to the Holy Roman Emperor, obtained through the Tuscan Embassy, had an importance much greater than the support of the leading German astronomer as such. It is noteworthy that when Galileo wrote to the Tuscan secretary of state announcing his receipt of the opinion in letter form, he used Kepler's title to identify the author rather than his name, which would have meant little to Florentine officialdom.

Perhaps the most impressive fact that emerges under nearly any reconstruction of events from the surviving documents is the undisturbed good faith that Kepler reposed in Galileo despite the efforts of intermediaries such as Bruce, Tengnagel, Horky, and Magini to diminish or destroy it. Considering the information that was in Kepler's hands at any time during the period discussed here, only his perceptive recognition of the characters of the various persons concerned can have enabled him to keep that faith. That he did keep it is a fact that must be taken into account when we attempt to judge the actions and motives of Galileo, to say nothing of those of other men concerning whom we know little, whereas Galileo and Kepler knew a great deal.

Notes to Essay 6

1. *Opere*, X, 69: *Nuper in Italiam misi 2 exemplaria mei opuscoli (sive tui potius), quae gratissimo et lubentissimo animo accepit Paduanus Mathematicus, nomine Galilaeus Galilaeus, uti se subscripsit. Est enim in Copernicana haeresi inde a multis annis. Unum exemplar misit Romam, et plura habere desideravit. . . .*
2. I have not found any letters in which Maestlin mentions Galileo, though I have read that he spoke slightingly of him.
3. E. Rosen, "Galileo and Kepler: Their First Two Contacts," *Isis*, 57 (1966), 262.
4. *Opere*, X, 67: *Librum tuum, doctissime vir, a Paulo Amberger ad me missum, accepi non quidem diebus, sed paucis abhinc horis; cumque idem Paulus de suo reditu in Germaniam mecum verba faceret, ingrati profecto animi futurum esse existimavi, nisi hisce literis tibi de munere accepto gratias agerem.*

5. Rosen, in the article cited above, states positively that Galileo did not reply; yet in a subsequent publication he has Kepler say, referring to the period immediately before the appearance of the *Starry Messenger* in 1610: "For a long time I had stayed home to rest, thinking of nothing but you, most distinguished Galileo, and your letters." This implies that he had received more than one letter from Galileo before 1610. See Rosen, *Kepler's Conversation with Galileo's Starry Messenger* (New York, 1965), p. 9.

6. J. Kepler, *Gesammelte Werke,* ed. M. Caspar, vol. XIV (Munich, 1949), pp. 7–16.

7. The title page described Magini as a Paduan, but also gave his title as professor at Bologna.

8. Kepler, *Werke,* XIV, 173.

9. *Opere,* X, 90; Kepler, *Werke,* XIV, 256. Bruce consistently misspelled Galileo's name, suggesting that his acquaintance with him was very slight.

10. *Opere,* X, 75–76; Kepler, *Werke,* XIV, 15–16.

11. *Opere,* X, 104; Kepler, *Werke,* XIV, 441.

12. *Opere,* X, 104–5.

13. Kepler, *Werke,* XIV, 445.

14. Kepler, *Werke,* XIV, 451. The work meant is Kepler's *Astronomia Nova* of 1609.

15. *Opere,* X, 308.

16. *Opere,* X, 316.

17. *Opere,* X, 314–15.

18. G. Tabaroni, review of E. Rosen (see note 3 above), *Physis,* 9 (1967), 253.

19. *Opere,* III, pt. 1, p. 101; Rosen, *Kepler's Conversation,* p. 3.

20. *Opere,* III, pt. 1, pp. 106–7; Rosen, *Kepler's Conversation,* p. 12.

21. Cf. *Opere,* X, 69: *Existimo namque te ab eo tempore, si ocium tibi fuit, libellum meum penitus cognovisse; inde cupido me vehemens incessit censurae efflagitare; et mihi credas velim, malo unius cordati censuram, quamvis acrem, quam totius vulgi inconsideratos applausus.*

22. *Opere,* III, pt. 1, p. 104; Rosen, *Kepler's Conversation,* p. 7.

7

Galileo and the Telescope

Wide differences of opinion have been—and are—expressed about
Galileo's role in the invention, development, and astronomical use
of the telescope. Some of the issues perennially raised are illusory,
as when he is reproached for having claimed the original invention
of the instrument, a claim he never made. Others are genuine
problems, capable of more precise solutions than they are generally
given; for example, the chronology of Galileo's first involvement
with the instrument. Still other issues must remain in the area of
probability and conjecture; among these is the question of the
extent of Galileo's knowledge of the optical principles involved
in the construction of his telescopes. The present essay is concerned principally with the order of events in Galileo's early work
with the telescope, though some light may be shed on other issues
in the course of that discussion.

Galileo's first published account of his own connection with
the telescope, given in March 1610, ran as follows:

> About ten months ago a report reached my ears that a
> certain Fleming had constructed a spyglass by means of which
> visible objects, though very distant from the eye of the observer,
> were distinctly seen as if nearby. Of this truly remarkable effect
> several experiences were related, to which some persons gave
> credence while others denied them. A few days later the report
> was confirmed to me in a letter from a noble Frenchman at
> Paris, Jacques Badovere, which caused me to apply myself
> wholeheartedly to inquire into the means by which I might
> arrive at the invention of a similar instrument. This I did
> shortly afterwards, my basis being the theory of refraction.
> First I prepared a tube of lead, at the ends of which I fitted
> two glass lenses, both plane on one side while on the other

side one was spherically concave and the other convex. Then, placing my eye near the concave lens, I perceived objects satisfactorily large and near, for they appeared three times closer and nine times larger than when seen with the naked eye alone. Next I constructed another one, more accurate, which represented objects as enlarged more than sixty times [that is, of about eight power, equivalent in magnification to the usual field glass of today].[1]

It was this instrument that he presented to the Venetian government late in August 1609.

Galileo made no claim to the original discovery, but only to its independent duplication and subsequent improvement, in this first printed narrative. In his letter of presentation to the Venetian government, however, he spoke of his instrument as having been developed by reflection on the principles of perspective, without mentioning the work of others. That statement is often portrayed as a false representation and deserves comment in passing.

It was impossible for Galileo to pretend successfully to the Venetian government, late in August 1609, that the telescope as such was his own invention. This is so evident from existing documents that it would scarcely be worth mentioning, were that preposterous idea not frequently put forth as a part of the evidence against Galileo's integrity and honesty. Numerous letters of the period show not only that word of the Dutch invention had reached Italy by the first of August 1609, but that an unidentified person visited Padua in July with a telescope in his possession, and then traveled on to Venice in the hope of selling it.[2] The Venetian government referred the matter to Fra Paolo Sarpi for his opinion, and on his recommendation the offer was refused. All this was known to Galileo, whose instrument was accepted by the same government a short time afterward. In addressing them, he claimed only that *his own* instrument had been devised on optical principles, and this was quite consistent with what he wrote and published elsewhere, though his terminology varied.

The change from the word "perspective" in the letter of presentation to the word "refraction" in the *Starry Messenger* to identify the optical basis of his telescope has given rise to doubts about Galileo's own knowledge of the theoretical principles involved. Such doubts are in part created by misunderstanding of the sense of the word "perspective" at the time. The name "perspective glasses" had been applied in England for at least thirty years to single lenses or concave mirrors capable of enlarging the images of distant objects. The word "perspective" was the standard Latin synonym for the Greek "optics" in the nomenclature of mathematical sciences during the Middle Ages and throughout the sixteenth century. Tartaglia, in his preface to Euclid, included under "Perspective Science" the works of both Witelo and Albrecht Dürer, whereas we should be inclined to speak of Witelo's optics and Dürer's perspective. Hence there exists no suitable basis in the words alone for concluding that Galileo was either ignorant or was bluffing. His knowledge of perspective was at least equal to that of the ordinary professor of mathematics in any Italian university of the time, and his knowledge of refraction equaled that of any other professor of astronomy. In order to move from a three-power to an eight-power instrument in a very short time—a move that Dutch and French makers had not made in several months—Galileo probably did apply his knowledge of optics. If he did not, he certainly had extraordinary luck in improving the instrument to eight power, to say nothing of incredible luck about the end of the year in moving on to a thirty-power telescope, which he applied to the heavens. Others were still unable to produce an equivalent instrument for a very long time afterward.

Jacques Badovere had been a pupil of Galileo's at Padua, residing in his house in 1598. He was a frequent visitor from France. In 1607 he provided an affidavit, for use in legal proceedings, concerning the manufacture of the proportional compass by Galileo. But no correspondence between Galileo and Badovere is known to exist. Badovere (more properly Badoer) was the son of a rich Venetian merchant who had been converted to Protestantism and migrated to France. Jacques returned to the Catholic faith and became closely associated with the French Jesuits, for whom he undertook various risky enterprises. For a time he held a diplomatic post with the French government, abruptly terminated by vigorous opposition from Sully and other important ministers. Scandalous rumors were circulated against him, but he remains a shadowy figure. If he ever wrote to Galileo about the telescope, or anything else, the letter is lost. Yet one would expect Galileo to have kept such a letter if he had received it, particularly in view of his having referred to it in print.

The Fleming referred to by Galileo was Hans Lipperhey (originally the family name was La Prey), who had obtained a patent from Count Maurice of Nassau for his invention. Fra Paolo Sarpi, who was appointed to report on the foreigner's instrument to the Venetian government and was the pivotal figure in its rejection, had been the first man in Italy to learn of the Flemish invention. His information came from Francesco Castrino in November of 1608, only a month after Lipperhey applied for the patent. In a letter to Castrino dated 9 December 1608, Sarpi acknowledged receiving "a month ago" a report of the embassy of the king of Siara to Count Maurice and news of the new "spectacles."[3] Writing to Jerome Groslot de L'Isle on 6 January 1609, Sarpi said:

> I have had word of the new spectacles more than a month, and believe it sufficiently not to seek further, Socrates forbidding us to philosophize about experiences not seen by ourselves. When I was young I thought of such a thing, and it occurred to me that a glass parabolically shaped could produce such an effect. I had a demonstration, but since these are abstract matters and do not take into account the fractiousness of matter, I sensed some difficulty. Hence I was not much inclined to the labor, which would have been very tiresome, so I did not confirm or refute my idea by experiment. I do not know whether perhaps that [Flemish] artisan has hit upon my idea—if indeed that matter has not been swelled by report, as usual, in the course of its journeys.[4]

Probably a similar account of Sarpi's own speculations had been sent to Badovere, with whom Sarpi (unlike Galileo) was definitely in correspondence at this time. Sarpi maintained an extensive correspondence with foreigners, Protestant and Catholic alike, concerning every kind of political and religious development in Europe and every important item of news. On 30 March 1609 he wrote to Badovere:

> . . . I have given you my opinion of the Holland spectacles. There may be something further; if you know more about them, I should like to learn what is thought there. I have

practically abandoned thinking about physical and mathematical matters, and to tell the truth my mind has become, either through age or habit, a bit dense for such contemplations. You would hardly be able to believe how much I have lost, both in health and in composure, through attention to politics.[5]

There is little doubt that Badovere replied to this letter, confirming the effectiveness of the instrument. Perhaps he also described the two lenses employed in it, particularly if Sarpi had sent to him the same conjecture about a parabolic glass that he sent to Groslot de L'Isle. Since there is no known correspondence between Galileo and Badovere about any subject, and there was a correspondence between Sarpi and Badovere about this particular matter, the chances are that what Galileo saw (and reported in his *Starry Messenger*) was Badovere's letter to their common friend Sarpi. Galileo's account does not exclude this course of events, for he says that the truth of the reports was "confirmed to me from Paris in a letter from the noble Frenchman Jacques Badovere," not "confirmed in a letter to me . . . from Jacques Badovere."[6] Nor is it said that he was at Padua when he received that confirmation. In all probability he was at Venice, for in a later account he wrote:

> . . . At Venice, where I happened to be at the time, news arrived that a Fleming had presented to Count Maurice a glass by means of which distant objects might be seen as distinctly as if they were nearby. That was all. Upon hearing this news I returned to Padua, where I then resided, and set myself to thinking about the problem. The first night after my return I solved it, and on the following day I constructed the instrument and sent word of this to those same friends at Venice with whom I had discussed the matter the previous day. Immediately afterward I applied myself to the construction of another and better one, which six days later I took to Venice, where it was seen with great admiration by nearly all the principal gentlemen of that Republic for more than a month on end, to my considerable fatigue.[7]

Thanks to the labors of Professor Antonio Favaro, who edited and published the definitive edition of Galileo's works between the years 1890 and 1910, there are easily accessible not only Galileo's published works but virtually every scrap of writing in his hand that has been preserved. Among these are accounts of grocery bills, payments to servants, and records of his dealings with instrument makers, copyists, boarders, and private students. These seemingly trivial documents are not devoid of interest to the historian, since it is safe to say that the 700-odd entries made in Galileo's journals between 1599 and 1610 supply us with dates on which he was physically present in Padua. A careful comparison of entry dates with surviving correspondence and other sources of information discloses but two entries in conflict with this assumption. One is the implied absurd date of 30 February 1610, which can clearly be shown to mean 30 March, the error arising from the mistaken use of the word *detto*. The other appears to be a slip in which *7mbre* was written for *9mbre*. In any case, two errors in seven hundred entries might occur in dates put down by a bookkeeper, let alone a professor keeping his own accounts.

Assuming, then, that Galileo's journal entries and the dates on his letters provide us with accurate information about his presence in Padua, it is possible to establish with considerable confidence the chronology of production of his first telescopes and of the exhibition at Venice of one of these.

During that summer one of Galileo's university students, Count Montalban, remained to complete his work for a doctorate. He resided at Galileo's house and paid for room and board monthly. Normally these payments were entered toward the end of the month, as in April and June of 1609, but collections were made early in August and in September, suggesting that Galileo was absent from Padua at the end of July and again at the end of August. Montalban had studied with Galileo since 1604 but had never previously remained in the summer. A student's presence would have made it difficult for Galileo to be away for extended periods. Journal entries show that he was in Padua on the twenty-third, twenty-eighth, and twenty-ninth of June. On the third of July he wrote from Padua mentioning an illness; on the eleventh and eighteenth of July he again made account entries, as he did also on the twentieth of August and on the first and third days of September.

Toward the end of June, Galileo had spoken with Pietro Duodo at Padua concerning the possibility of improving his salary. Duodo was discouraging about the prospects. It is evident that

Galileo was not yet on the track of a new and wonderful discovery late in June 1609, but that he was anxious to increase his income. We know that he was in Venice twice during the next two months, hearing of the new instrument on the first visit and exhibiting his own on the second, having returned to Padua between the two visits.

The first of these visits may have begun at any time after 18 July. It was probably at Venice during his first visit that the rumors of the new instrument were discussed in Galileo's presence, some believing them and some rejecting them. It would be quite natural for Galileo to visit Paolo Sarpi when in Venice, where he was accustomed to discuss scientific problems with him. It has already been shown that Sarpi was in correspondence with Badovere on the topic, and it was probably in response to Galileo's inquiry for his opinion on the rumors that Sarpi showed him a letter from Badovere, amply confirming the truth of the rumors. Galileo was then seeking an increase in salary, and it would be in keeping with all that is known about him if he saw at once the possibility of utilizing the new device for the purpose.

It was precisely at this time, toward the end of July, that a foreigner visited Padua with one of the instruments in hand.[8] He showed it to Lorenzo Pignoria, a friend of Galileo's, who wrote on the first of August to another friend of Galileo's, Paolo Gualdo, about it. Gualdo was then at Rome. The rumors had spread all over Italy in that month; for example, Federico Cesi at Rome wrote to Giovanni Battista Porta at Naples for his opinion, probably in July. Porta replied on the first of August with a sketch of the device and his contemptuous dismissal of it as a mere toy. I believe that word of the presence of the foreigner at Padua with an actual instrument could not fail to reach nearby Venice swiftly. Galileo says that he left Venice immediately after discussions of the device with friends there. Very likely he had also heard of the visit of the stranger, and his motive was to find him and to examine the instrument for himself.

But here he was disappointed; when Galileo arrived back in Padua on the third of August, the stranger had already left for Venice to sell the "secret" to the government. Galileo's situation was now one in which he had to act with great speed or lose all hope of benefit from the opportunity. And he did act with speed.

It appears that he promptly verified his first conjecture about the construction of the instrument. He recounted this later as follows:

> My reasoning was this. The device needs either a single glass or more than one. It cannot consist of one glass alone, because its shape would have to be convex . . . concave . . . or bounded by parallel surfaces. But the last-named does not alter visible objects in any way, either by enlarging or reducing them; the concave diminishes them; and the convex, though it does enlarge them, shows them indistinct and confused. . . . Knowing that a glass with parallel faces alters nothing . . . I was confined to considering what would be done by a combination of the convex and the concave. You see how this gave me what I sought.[9]

Galileo's account, written much later, may or may not be historical. It certainly has no logical force, and in fact the combination of two convex lenses can produce much better telescopes than the combination he chose. No "principles of perspective" or "doctrines of refraction" are involved in any way in Galileo's own account of his actual (and feverish) procedure in hitting on the nature of the device. Very likely they were only minimally considered in its immediate improvement.[10] This now occupied him for several days, during which he obtained a tube and ground, or had his instrument maker grind, spherical lenses of different radii of curvature. It was not difficult to divine some connection between the ratio of those radii and the degree of magnification. At any rate, within two weeks Galileo was ready for his return to Venice on a trip that brought him undying fame, and incidentally secured him an increase in salary far beyond anything he had aspired to in June.

Meanwhile, however, the foreigner had arrived in Venice with his instrument. There can be little question that the person to whom Galileo immediately sent word of his initial success in divining the "secret" was Paolo Sarpi. Sarpi was very close to the Venetian government as its theological adviser, having recently refuted Cardinal Bellarmine over the rights of Rome and counseled defiance of the interdict placed on Venice by Paul V. Before this appointment, Sarpi was already noted as a scientific expert. It was therefore natural that he was put in a position to referee the foreigner's demands. The foreigner would not allow Sarpi to do more than look through the instrument, refusing anyone the right to take it apart. His price was a thousand florins. Sarpi, confident that Galileo could make at least as good an instrument and probably better, advised the government to reject the offer, and the foreigner departed. It is highly improbable that Galileo ever met him or saw his instrument.

The events, according to this reconstruction, took place as follows:

About 19 July 1609	Galileo leaves Padua to visit friends at Venice.
20–27 July	He hears rumors of the Dutch instrument and discussions of their veracity. Visitor arrives at Padua with a telescope.
About 27 July	Galileo visits Sarpi, asks his opinion of the rumors, and is shown Badovere's confirming letter.
1 August	Pignoria writes to Gualdo concerning the visitor. Galileo hears at Venice of the same event.
3 August	Galileo arrives in Padua, learns that the foreigner has gone to Venice to sell his "secret," and forms his own conjecture as to its nature.
4 August	Verifies his conjecture by trial and sends word to Sarpi that he has the "secret."
5–20 August	Sarpi advises Venetian government to reject the foreign instrument. Galileo succeeds in constructing an eight-power telescope.
21 August	Galileo returns to Venice and exhibits his telescope to officials from the campanile of St. Mark.
24–25 August	Exhibits telescope to the Signoria and presents it to the Senate, receiving life tenure and increased salary.

Galileo's later statement that he had exhibited the telescope to the principal dignitaries of Venice for more than a month on end is surely mistaken. There was no period in the summer of 1609 during which Galileo could have been in Venice for an entire month. By the first of September he had returned to Padua and was making preparations for a speedy trip to Florence before the beginning of the new academic year. In the account written more than ten years later, Galileo recollected that he had demonstrated his new instrument to distinguished people for more than a month on end, to his considerable fatigue. But not all these dignitaries were at Venice; some were at Florence.

There is a third account of the events, written by Galileo right at the time. Addressed to his brother-in-law at Florence, and extant only in a contemporary copy, the letter embodying this account has been questioned as to authenticity on various grounds. Edward Rosen has argued very strongly for acceptance of the letter, and I agree entirely with his conclusions, though not with his interpretation of the circumstances.[11] It reads as follows:

Dear and Honored Brother-in-Law:

I did not write after receiving the wine you sent me, for lack of anything to say. Now I write to you because I have something to tell you which makes me question whether the news will give you more pleasure or displeasure, since all my hope of my returning home is taken away, but by a useful and honorable event.

You must know, then, that it is nearly two months since news was spread here that in Flanders there had been presented to Count Maurice a spy-glass, made in such a way that very distant things are made by it to look quite close, so that a man two miles away can be distinctly seen. This seemed to me so marvellous an effect that it gave me occasion for thought; and as it appeared to me that it must be founded on the science of perspective, I undertook to think about its fabrication; which I finally found, and so perfectly that one which I made far surpassed the reputation of the Flemish one. And word having reached Venice that I had made one, it is six days since I was called by the Signoria, to which I had to show it together with the entire Senate, to the infinite amazement of all; and there have been numerous gentlemen and senators who, though old, have more than once scaled the stairs of the highest campaniles in Venice to observe at sea sails and vessels so far away that, coming under full sail to port, two hours or more were required before they could be seen without my spy-glass. For in fact the effect of this instrument is to represent an object that is, for example, fifty miles away, as large and near as if it were only five.

Now having known how useful this would be for maritime as well as land affairs, and seeing it desired by the Venetian government, I resolved on the 25th of this month to appear in the College and make a free gift of it to His Lordship. And having been ordered in the name of the College to wait in the room of the Pregadi, there appeared presently the Procurator Priuli, who is one of the governors of the University. Coming out of the College, he took my hand and told me how that body, knowing the manner in which I had served for seventeen years in Padua, and moreover recognizing my courtesy in making such an acceptable gift, had immediately ordered the Honorable Governors [of the University] that, if I were content, they should renew my appointment for life and with a salary of one thousand florins per year; and that since a year remained before the expiration of my term, they desired that the salary should begin to run immediately in the current year, making me a gift of the increase for one year, which is 480 florins at 6 lire 4 soldi per florin. I, knowing that hope has feeble wings and fortune swift ones, said I would be content with whatever pleased His Lordship. Then Signor Priuli, embracing me said: "Since I am chairman this week, and can command as I please, I wish after dinner to convene the Pregadi, that is the Senate, and your reappointment shall be read to you and voted on." And so it was, winning with all the votes.[12] Thus I find myself here, held for life, and I shall have to be satisfied to enjoy my native land sometimes during the vacation months.

Well, that is all I have for now to tell you. Do not fail to send me news of you and your work, and greet all my friends for me, remembering me to Virginia and the family. God prosper you.

From Venice, 29 August 1609.
Your affectionate brother-in-law
GALILEO GALILEI[13]

Antonio Favaro neglected to state the reasons for which he felt the style of this letter to be not Galilean at certain points, but that objection seems pointed at the opening and closing paragraphs. These are quite extraordinarily awkward, so much so that at first sight they seem to exclude Galileo as the writer. But they may be readily reconciled with his authorship if those two paragraphs are considered as having been hurriedly tacked on to the body of the letter, which itself had been very carefully drafted, simply to supply Galileo with a pretext for sending it to Landucci and having its contents conveyed to friends. Galileo was never on good terms with Landucci, even though he had exerted himself to obtain a minor government post for him a short time before. Certainly Landucci did not care whether Galileo ever returned to Florence, and (as Favaro observed) Galileo had other correspondents at Florence who would normally have been more suitable recipients of this stirring news.

The main body of the letter makes it very plausible to suppose that it was written for other eyes than those of Galileo's brother-in-law. To Landucci's eyes, the parade of dignitaries and the high salary offered would have been an intolerable display of boasting. As Galileo well knew, Landucci's own job carried no salary and brought him fees amounting to no more than sixty florins a year. There could be no sense in Galileo's telling him that when offered a salary of one thousand florins a year for life, he had accepted it only because "hope has feeble wings and fortune swift ones." What more, Landucci might exclaim, could a man possibly want? But this phrase would have a very real significance to the grand duke, who had delayed too long in acting on Galileo's appeals for employment, and for whose eyes I believe the letter was really intended.

If my reconstruction of the events is correct, Galileo was embarrassed to admit to Cosimo de' Medici that he had suddenly committed himself to remain in the service of the Venetian Republic for life while negotiating for a post at the Court of Tuscany. Nevertheless, he felt a need to have this news reach the Florentine court from himself before word got there from others. Accordingly he sent his message as a family letter to his brother-in-law, who held a minor government post, with specific instructions to greet all his friends for him. Landucci did convey the news promptly, and the interest that was immediately shown at the court in the topic doubtless accounts for the survival of this letter in a contemporary manuscript copy, whereas any other letters Galileo may have written to Landucci are lost.

Galileo's phrase "if I were content," coupled with his insistence on the impossibility of his ever returning permanently to Florence, implies that he had accepted as a condition of the increase in salary the stipulation that he remain for life. If we accept the letter as genuine, and consider how soon after the events it was written, we are obliged to believe that such a promise was exacted. In that way a great deal of light is thrown upon some subsequent events, especially upon the bitterness that was created at Venice by Galileo's later departure. The letter implies also that Galileo had been given to understand by Priuli that the increase in salary would take place immediately, and that he was not told of any restriction against future increases. In the official award, the increase was made effective in the following year, not the academic year about to begin, and it was stipulated that no further increase could ever be made. It is possible that Priuli misunderstood these stipulations when he conveyed the offer to Galileo, or that Galileo misunderstood Priuli concerning them. In any event, differences between the terms of the subsequent contract and their description in the letter do not condemn the letter as unauthentic. On the other hand, once we accept the letter as genuine, it becomes easier to understand Galileo's subsequent behavior, his mounting irritation at the university, and his final departure from Venice within the year.

The occasion for Galileo's having written this letter becomes clear when the presence of the foreigner at Padua and Venice is taken into account. Had there been no immediate pressure to act swiftly, Galileo might have taken his new instrument to Florence rather than to Venice. Negotiations for his employment by the grand duke of Tuscany, a former pupil, had been in progress for some time but showed no signs of coming to a head. The presentation of a telescope, useful for military purposes, would have been a good inducement to conclude them. But as things stood, Galileo could not delay. He knew that others already had similar instruments, and if none were yet as good as his, he had no reason to think that others would not soon equal or better his achievement. At best, by the time he could reach Florence, it would be known there that a similar instrument was being shown at Venice, and any claim of superiority for his telescope would be difficult to establish. Hence his best procedure was to devote all his efforts to forestalling action at Venice on the rival instrument, produce a better one himself, and hurry back with it to Venice, a mere twenty-five miles from Padua. Thus, from the moment he learned that the stranger had left Padua for Venice, Galileo may be presumed to have worked only at beating him at his own game.

When he succeeded in doing so, however, the next thing he had to do was to communicate the news to the grand duke, his natural prince and former pupil. This was embarrassing. To the duke, he had to present the circumstances in a light that would explain his failure to return to Florence and would justify his gift of the new and important device to a foreign government. The recital of events he prepared was plausible, if not precise in all regards. He said it was nearly two months since the rumors spread, but he did not say that he himself had heard the rumors at that time. He said that word had reached Venice of his having penetrated the secret, but not that it was he himself who had promptly sent news of his success to friends there. The manner in which he recounted events for the ears of Florentines was designed to make it appear that he was the victim of circumstances, and had acted from that time under orders of the government which employed him. "It is six days since I was called by the Signoria," he wrote, making the context imply that this elite body had called him to Venice from Padua; in fact, on the twenty-third of August he was already in Venice and had shown the instrument to others before he was officially called to show it to the Signoria. On the two succeeding days it was shown first to them and then to the whole Senate. The offer made to him was generous; had he refused it, he could not have been sure of doing so well at Florence. Such was the story as written for the eyes of Cosimo. It may, in the light of later events, have been an oblique reopening of Galileo's application for a court position.

If Galileo tried by this letter to be first to get the news to Florence, however, he did not succeed. On the same day that his letter was posted at Venice, Eneas Piccolomini wrote from Florence at the request of the grand duke to inquire about the instrument and solicit the gift of one or instructions for making one. Galileo did more than comply with this request; he personally made a hurried trip to Florence. There he repaired any damage that had been done, and paved the way for negotiations the following spring that culminated in his long-desired appointment by Cosimo.

Why did Galileo, after his spectacular success in wresting from the Venetian government a lifetime appointment at a large increase in pay, continue to improve the telescope? It seems to be widely assumed that he expected a still stronger telescope to reveal discoveries in the heavens. I cannot see the slightest reason for him to expect such a thing, even if he had been interested in astronomy at the time. The idea of using a telescope at night would not have occurred to any sensible person on rational grounds. A point of light, magnified many times, is still a point of light. Nevertheless, Galileo did apply himself to the improvement of his telescope and even brought it to the practicable limit of power, for the lens-system he employed, by the beginning of 1610. It is possible that he had previously observed the moon with a weaker instrument and wished to enlarge that body still more, but there is no mention of any lunar (or other astronomical) observations before 1610 in his notes or correspondence.

It is my opinion that there was no specific scientific purpose in Galileo's mind when he resumed the improvement of the tele-scope late in 1609. He was still pressing for a post at Florence, and he may have wished to present to the grand duke a better telescope than anyone else then had. Galileo undoubtedly liked to tinker, and he had a well-equipped workshop. The clue to higher power was implicit in the eight-power and three-power telescopes he had already built. His later lenses bear the radii of curvature scratched in the glass, and the "secret" of their ratio to the power was not a hard one to find. It is indeed surprising that other makers had not hit on it. The widespread production of three-power toys suggests that they used spectacle lenses. The real reason that Galileo's were for a long time the only telescopes adequate for celestial observations was probably that he concentrated on the grinding of short-focus concave eyepieces. The production of such lenses entailed considerable technical difficulties.

In any case, Galileo's first celestial observations appear to have been made early in January 1610. Probably they were ac-cidental in their origin. A glimpse of the moon, low in the heavens, during terrestrial observations made about dusk, would have been sufficient to start him on them. Two months later they were the talk of Europe.

Those who argue that Galileo knew nothing of optics and was unable himself to explain properly the construction and theory of the telescope may be assuming absence of knowledge where there was only unwillingness to give away advantages. His critics also point out that Galileo never built a Keplerian telescope, with its superior field of view and higher limit of power. They overlook the fact that Galileo had a good deal of trouble convincing others that what the telescope disclosed in the heavens was really there, and was not just an illusion created by the lenses. In arguing the contrary, Galileo was much assisted by the fact that his telescopes gave an erect image, so that objects observed close at hand were in no way altered (except as to size) by the instrument. An inverting lens system would only have made his task harder in this regard. Nor was higher power any advantage in making the initial discoveries; high-power telescopes need rather elaborate supports.

There are many debated points concerning the invention and improvement of the telescope. Credit for the original invention was early in dispute and has been widely debated ever since. The safest attribution is to Hans Lipperhey, who first applied for a patent on the device in October 1608. Descartes, however, credited the invention to Jacob Metius. In 1634 Isaac Beeckman entered in his journal the claim of Zacharias Janson, as put forth by his son, under whom Beeckman was then learning the technique of lens-grinding. His journal entry was discovered early in the present century, and reads as follows:

> Johannes, son of Zacharias, says that his father made the first telescope here in the year 1604, after an Italian one on which was written "anno 190 [i.e., 1590?]."[14]

The credence due to Beeckman, a highly intelligent and upright man, has been unreasonably transferred to the story he heard from Johannes. Beeckman accurately reported what he had been told, but his informant was unreliable, not only as an interested party, but as a man who later submitted a palpably false sworn affidavit on the same matter. The story is itself improbable to the highest degree. Johannes was born in 1611, seven years after the claimed events, and was accordingly obliged to rely on a family story for his information. His father, the claimant, was born in 1588, and was thus but sixteen years of age in 1604. Later a convicted counterfeiter, the father is hardly a credible witness on his own behalf. His son's later affidavit, in 1655, claimed the invention by his father for the year 1590, when in fact his father was an infant of two years, and Johannes deliberately falsified his father's age.

Yet it is by no means impossible that a telescope was built in Italy in 1590, or even earlier. Either Giambattista Porta or Marcantonio de Dominis would have been quite capable of constructing one. Porta, however, later regretted that he had never done more than to describe it as a toy, so it is unlikely that he had ever built an instrument worthy of having the date engraved on it. The relevant work of de Dominis, supposed to have been composed in 1590, was not published until 1611. Moreover, if a worthy instrument was made in Italy, dated, transported as far as Holland, and copied there, it seems to have escaped mention in any letter or book. The case was quite different in 1608–9. Then the instrument, from its very first public mention, became the subject of widespread correspondence and printed reports in journals. None of this correspondence appears to have called forth memories of a predecessor instrument (or report of one) four years earlier, or of a more remote one in 1590.

Reports of optical experiments by Leonard Digges and John Dee in England as early as the 1570s have occasioned speculations that telescopes were made and used there long before 1590. Those speculations are not idle with respect to the history of the reflecting telescope, introduced astronomically much later by Sir Isaac Newton. But the idea of a combination of lenses enclosed in a tube appears not to have been involved in the English experiments. William Bourne left a manuscript account of them that is probably reasonably complete.[15] It is clear from this document that the concave mirror alone, or its combination with plane or with other concave mirrors, was the basis of the magnifying effects obtained by Digges and Dee. An effective portable magnifying device such as the Galilean or Keplerian lens system would not be likely to have gone unremarked or neglected, particularly in a seafaring nation. Bourne suggested that a series of concave mirrors might be arranged for greater magnification. He also suggested, in his *Inventions or Devices* of 1578, the use of a single large convex lens (burning glass) in combination with a plane mirror. The passage is of considerable interest, and since the book is rare, it deserves citation:

For to see any small thing a great distance of[f] from you, it requireth the aid of two glasses, and one glasse must be made of purpose, and it may be such sort, that you may see a small thing a great distance of[f], as this, to reade a letter that is set open neare a quarter of a myle from you, and also to see a man foure or five myles from you. . . . [It must be] like the small burning glasses of that kind of glasse, and must be round, and set in a frame as those bee, but that it must bee made very large, of a foote, or 14 or 16 inches broade. . . . But now to use this glasse, to see a small thing a great distance, then doo this, the thing or place that you would view and discerne, set that glasse fast, and the middle of the glasse to stand [at] right [angles] with the place assigned, and be sure that it doo not stand oblique or awry by no means, and that done, then take a very fayre large looking glasse that is well polished, and set that glasse directly right with the side against i.e., towards ye first glasse, to the intent to receive the beame or shadow that cometh thorow the first placed glasse, and set it at such a distance off, that the thing shall marke the beame or shadowe so large, that it may serve your turne, and so by that meanes you shall see in the looking glass a small thing a great distance. . . .[16]

This description, I believe, precludes the possibility that Bourne, who was very well informed about the state of the arts at his time, had ever heard of any kind of portable telescope.

Notes to Essay 7

1. Galileo, *Starry Messenger;* cf. *Discoveries,* pp. 28–29.
2. These letters will be found in *Opere,* X, 250–55.
3. *Atti del R. Ist. Veneto di Scienze, Lettere ed Arti,* 87 (1927), pt. 2, p. 1069. The embassy is usually said to have been from Siam. Siara (Ceará) was a province in northern Brazil that submitted to the Dutch in 1637.
4. *Sarpi, Lettere ai Protestanti,* ed. M. L. Busnelli (Bari, 1931), I, 58.
5. *Atti del R. Ist. Veneto . . . ,* 87 (1927), pt. 2, p. 1160.
6. *Mihi per literas a nobili Gallo Iacobo Badovere ex Lutetia confirmatus est* (*Opere,* III, pt. 1, p. 60).
7. Galileo, *The Assayer;* cf. *Discoveries,* p. 244.

8. The visitor was probably the same one whose telescope was seen in Milan by Geronimo Sirturi in May 1609, as reported in his *Telescopium* (Frankfort, 1618). Sarpi had heard of a telescope brought to Italy by 21 July 1609, when he mentioned the news in a letter to a friend.

9. Galileo, *The Assayer;* cf. *Discoveries,* pp. 245–46.

10. In his *Starry Messenger,* Galileo mentions refraction in relation to the angle subtended by the visual image, which determines the apparent size. He does not discuss the lenses separately, but only their joint effect. The omission is more likely due to his desire to diminish competition than to ignorance on his part.

11. E. Rosen, "The Authenticity of Galileo's Letter to Landucci," *Modern Language Quarterly,* 12 (1951), 473–86; "When Did Galileo Make His First Telescope?" *Centaurus,* 2 (1951), 44–51.

12. The vote was not unanimous, which has contributed to doubts about the authenticity of this letter. But Galileo does not say "winning all the votes." "Winning with all the votes" may simply mean after all votes had been counted.

13. *Opere,* X, 252.

14. *Journal tenu par Isaac Beeckman,* ed. De Waard, vol. 3 (The Hague, 1945), p. 376.

15. Published by J. O. Halliwell-Phillips in *Rara Mathematica* (London, 1839), pp. 32–47, reprinted 1967.

16. William Bourne, *Inuentions or Deuices very necessary for all Generalles . . . as well by Sea as by Land* (London, 1578), pp. 96–97.

8

The Dispute over Bodies
in Water

In June of 1611 Galileo returned from a visit to Rome, aptly described by a contemporary as a "tour of triumph," during which he exhibited his telescopic discoveries, was made a member of the Lincean Academy, and opened with Cardinal Bellarmine a discussion of the merits of the Copernican system. Accompanying him on the return to Florence were G. B. Strozzi and his young protégé Giovanni Ciampoli.

The journey was very tiring, and Galileo was ill for some weeks after his return. In the latter part of July he was present at a meeting of literati which probably took place at the house of Filippo Salviati in Florence. Here a dispute over floating bodies originated, but the matter of hydrostatic principles did not come up directly. The point argued was philosophical—that cold produced condensation—and ice was introduced as an example by Vincenzio di Grazia, professor of philosophy at Pisa.[1] Galileo countered with the paradoxical position that ice must be rarefied water, being lighter than water, as shown by its floating. Di Grazia attempted to explain the floating of ice by its shape. Galileo successfully answered di Grazia's arguments, but did not really convince him. It is probable that at this first philosophical argument there was present also Giorgio Coresio, professor of Greek at Pisa and a staunch Aristotelian.[2]

Three days later di Grazia told Galileo that in discussing the arguments with other friends, he had encountered one who had volunteered to demonstrate the falsity of Galileo's denial that shape played a role in the floating of bodies, and would do so by means of actual experiments. This new opponent was Ludovico delle Colombe, who first entered the dispute only in connection with this Aristotelian point. Galileo agreed to meet Colombe at the house of Canon Francesco Nori. The meeting took place in the early part of August, and at that time an agreement was signed fixing the conditions of the contest.[3] A date was set for the exhibition of the experiments, probably about the middle of August, at Nori's house, with Filippo Arrighetti as co-referee.

Colombe promptly began to exhibit to various people and in public places the materials he intended to use for his experiments, boasting that Galileo was already vanquished. His apparatus consisted of pieces of ebony, some in the form of thin chips or lamina and some in spherical or cylindrical shapes. Since the former could be floated while the latter would invariably sink, Colombe advanced this as experimental proof that shape affected the floating or sinking of bodies in water. Considering the wording of the written agreement, it may be that he had the best of it on literal grounds, but so far as the essential issue was concerned, his proposed experiment was the merest quibble.

It is a curious fact that Colombe failed to appear at Nori's house for the final contest, as we know not only from Galileo's statement but from that of a friend, Lodovico (Cardi di) Cigoli, then at Rome, where word of the dispute had already reached.[4] From what is known of Colombe, his failure to pursue the quibble can be accounted for in only one way. News of his activities had quickly reached Galileo's ears, and Galileo did not wish to engage in quarrels over wording.[5] Accordingly, it may be presumed that he spoke directly to Nori and Arrighetti, both of them former pupils and friends of his, complaining that Colombe's proposed experiment was not germane to the issue and should be rejected. Assuming further that they agreed, Colombe was left with no alternative but to remain away or face defeat at the hands of the judges themselves.

Galileo, however, extended to his adversaries an opportunity to continue the debate if they were willing to put aside quibbles. This he did by sending to them a new form of the proposition to be put to test, under which all materials used would be entirely wetted—that is, actually placed in water and not merely on it. Colombe appears to have made a new appointment to pursue the matter, this time at Salviati's house, and there he appeared with a number of followers, including Giovanni de' Medici.[6] By then, however, the controversy had become notorious, and Galileo's foes had been using it to discredit him at court with his august employer, Cosimo II. Perhaps Giovanni de' Medici was instrumental in accomplishing this. At any rate it seems that Cosimo had already diplomatically rebuked his mathematician for engaging in public disputes and cautioned him to abstain from further oral controversies and commit his arguments to writing. Galileo accordingly refused to be drawn into argument with Colombe, or to submit to his experiments without limitations on the size of the objects used; rather, he said, he would write out his arguments. From the apologetic tone of the essay which he proceeded to compose during the month of September, it is clear that Galileo was on the defensive at court during this period.[7]

In the summer of 1611, about the time the dispute began, Flaminio Papazzoni of Bologna had been appointed to the chair of philosophy at Pisa vacated by the death of Galileo's stubborn opponent Giulio Libri at the end of 1610. Galileo had secured the post for Papazzoni, who came strongly recommended by Galileo's friend and ally, G. A. Roffeni, giving him preference over Camillo Belloni of Padua, whose nomination was vigorously pressed by old friends of Galileo's there. Toward the middle of September Papazzoni arrived at Florence, whence he had been called for some specific purpose which he seems to have been rather reluctant to carry out.[8]

Now Galileo, in applying for his own position at the Tuscan court, had insisted upon the title of philosopher as well as that of mathematician to the grand duke, and refused to accept the post until that was granted. In support of his demand he had asserted that he would prove his right to the title as soon as he was given opportunity to debate against the most eminent philosophers in the presence of Their Highnesses. The arrival of Papazzoni at Florence at this moment, when Galileo had lost some ground at court, provided an excellent occasion to make good his previous boast. Indeed, the coincidence and its aftermath suggest that Galileo himself may have requested Papazzoni to come to Florence at this time and defend the Peripatetic position on floating bodies against him at court. In any event, several such debates ensued at the ducal table between Papazzoni and his erstwhile sponsor.[9] Colombe was not present at these debates, which constituted the third phase of the dispute over floating bodies in 1611.

Toward the end of September, Maffeo Barberini left his episcopal residence at Spoleto to take up residence as cardinal legate in Bologna, where he arrived on 4 October. On 30 September he visited two nieces at a convent in Florence and remained as guest of the grand duke for a few days. During this visit, Cardinal Gonzaga happened also to be present in Florence, and Cosimo invited Galileo and Papazzoni to repeat their arguments before the two distinguished visitors. Immediately afterward, Galileo fell ill again and was unable to pay his respects to Barberini when he departed for Bologna, probably on 3 October.[10]

Galileo's new illness was a long and serious one which continued into January of the following year. But on the first of October he was not yet ill, for on that day he wrote to Cigoli at Rome: "I am obliged to answer two very welcome letters of yours, but as I am very busy finishing an essay of fifteen pages, regarding a certain contest during these past days between certain of these Peripatetic philosophers and myself, which I am doing for the grand duke and which perhaps will be published, I am forced to be quite brief with you."[11] Those familiar with Galileo's correspondence will recognize the extreme improbability of his being ill when he wrote this, or having recently been ill, without mentioning the fact or using it as an excuse for having failed to reply earlier. Still more important to us is the implication that the famed debate before the two cardinals had not yet taken place; a triumph of such magnitude could scarcely have escaped mention. That famous event, therefore, probably occurred on the second of October, just before Barberini's departure.

The "essay of fifteen pages" was neither the *Discourse* nor a draft of it, as has hitherto been supposed. It was a finished work with a literary peroration, written mainly, if not entirely, before the grand duke had heard Galileo's arguments and bearing little resemblance to the later *Discourse*. Colombe, replying to the latter, recalled how, on the occasion of the last meeting at Salviati's house, Galileo had declined to argue and had undertaken to write instead.[12] The essay remained unpublished, but has survived nearly intact in manuscript. Addressed to the grand duke in the form of a letter, it began as follows:

> Many are the reasons, Most Serene Lord, for which I have set myself to the writing out at length of the controversy which

in past days has led to so much debate by others. Of these, the first and most cogent has been your hint, and your praise of the pen as the unique remedy for purging and separating clear and sequential reasoning from confused and intermittent altercations in which they especially who defend the side of error deny noisily on one occasion that which they had previously affirmed, and on another, pressed by the force of reason, they attempt, with inappropriate distinctions and classifications, cavils, and strained interpretations of words, to slip through one's fingers and escape by their subtleties and twistings about, not hesitating to produce a thousand chimeras and fantastic caprices little understood by themselves and not at all by their listeners. By these the mind is bewildered and confusedly bandied from one phantasm to another, just as, in a dream, one passes from a palace to a ship and thence to a grotto or a beach, and finally, when one awakes and the dream vanishes (and for the most part all memory of it also), one finds that one has been idly sleeping and has passed the hours without profit of any sort.

The second reason is that I desire that your Highness should become fully and frankly informed of what has taken place in this affair; for the nature of contests being what it is, those who through carelessness are induced to support error will shout loudest and make themselves more heard in public places than those through whom speaks truth, which unmasks itself tranquilly and quietly, though slowly. Hence I can well believe that just as in the squares and temples and other public places, the voices of those who dissent from what I assert have been far more often heard than those of others who agree with me, so likewise at court have they tried to advance their opinion by forestalling me there with their sophisms and cavils; these I hope to disperse and send up in smoke, even though they may have gained the ear and assent of some men prior to a careful reading of this essay of mine.

In the third place, I have deemed it good not to leave this matter unresolved, for just as at the outset the erroneous side had for nearly everyone the face and appearance of truth, so it might continue to deceive many persons with that same appearance, causing them on some momentous occasions to fall into serious error by taking false axioms for true principles.

Finally, having been chosen by your Highness as your personal mathematician and philosopher, I cannot permit the malignity, envy, or ignorance (and perhaps all three) of anyone to bear stupidly against your prudence; for this would be to abuse your incomparable benignity. On the contrary, I shall always put down (and with very little trouble) their every impudence, and this I do with the invincible shield of truth, demonstrating that what I have asserted in the past was and is absolutely true, and that to the extent that I have departed from the commonly accepted Peripatetic opinions, this has not come about from my not having read Aristotle, or not having understood as well as they his reasoning, but because I possess stronger demonstrations and more evident experiments than theirs. And in the present dispute, in addition to showing the approach I take to the study of Aristotle, I shall reveal whether I have well understood his meaning in two or three readings only, compared with them, to some of whom the reading of Aristotle fifty times may seem a small matter; and then I shall show whether I have perhaps better investigated the causes of the matters which constitute the subject of the present contest than did Aristotle. . . .

[I have thought it good in this essay of mine not to name any of my adversaries—not because I do not esteem and appreciate them, but because it has reached my ears that they, for whatever reason, do not want their affairs published to the world, and hence I, being unable to hide the things, shall hide the persons, which comes to the same thing. Besides, if (as I expect) it shall happen that I resolve their every argument and irrefutably conclude in favor of my own position, then I think it will not displease them that I have thus kept silent. But if the contrary should happen, it will be up to them to identify themselves in refuting and reprimanding my paralogisms, for which I shall be much indebted, as I glory not in triumphing over my adversaries, but only that truth shall triumph over falsehood.

[I know that your Highness well recalls how, four years ago, I happened in your presence to contradict some engineers, otherwise excellent in their profession, who were devising a method of weaving together a very broad esplanade of timbers. By virtue of the lightness of wood and by a great quantity of wooden tubs made concave and filled with air, on which the esplanade should rest when placed in the water, these men made a great point of the increase in support from the broadness of surface spread over a large body of water, expecting that this would necessarily be capable of sustaining without sinking two or three times as much weight as that which could be precisely and accurately computed for the said planks and beams. Concerning that belief, I said that no great faith should be put in that framework, however spacious, as supporting any more than its separate and disunited parts, or those parts joined in any other framework; and I concluded in general that shape could be neither help nor hindrance to solid bodies with respect to their floating or sinking in water.][13]

It was necessary for me some days ago to repeat the same conclusion, and the occasion was a discussion in a circle of gentlemen concerning the four basic qualities.[14] A professor of philosophy said something that is commonplace in the Peripatetic schools, which is that the action of cold was to condense, and he adduced by way of experience the case of ice, affirming that this was nothing but condensed water. Now I, questioning this, remarked that ice should rather be said to be rarefied water; for if it is true that condensation brings about greater heaviness and rarefaction lightness, then since we see that ice is lighter than water, we must also believe that it is less dense. I went on to add that I doubted whether he had not equivocated from "dense" to "hard," and that he meant to say that ice is harder than water, not denser—just as steel is harder, but not denser, than gold. The philosopher immediately denied that ice was less heavy than water and asserted the contrary, to which I replied that this was most evident, since ice floats on water. Thereupon I heard it promptly rejoined that not the lesser heavinesss of ice was the cause of its floating on water, being really heavier than water, but rather the cause was its broad and flat shape, which, being unable to cleave the resistance of the water, keeps it on top. Now to this I had two answers: first, I said that not only broad and thin plates of ice remain afloat on water, but pieces of any shape; and I then added that if it were true that ice is really heavier than water, but that a broad and thin plate of it would not submerge, being sustained by the unsuitability of its shape for penetrating the continuous body of the water, one might test this by driving the ice forcibly under the water and then releasing it; and doubtless one would see it return to float, penetrating and dividing the resistance of the water while going upwards even though that resistance were assisted by the heaviness of the plate which was unable to divide it by descending. At this point, having nothing else to reply [and the gravity of disputation making it necessary for him to stand fixed and

immovable upon anything once pronounced], an attempt was
made to oppose my demonstration by another experiment. He
said that he had observed a thousand times that when the surface of water was struck with the flat of a sword, great resistance
to its penetration was felt; whereas a blow with the edge, on
the other hand, divided and penetrated it without hindrance.
I pointed out his second equivocation by telling him that he
now had gone off to another question—that it was one thing
to investigate whether different shapes made a difference in the
absolute motion or rest of a thing, and quite another to inquire
whether it made a difference in its moving more or less swiftly.
I added that it is indeed true that broad shapes move slowly
while thin ones move swiftly through the same medium; hence
the flat of the sword, moved swiftly, meets with greater resistance
on striking the water than it would if it were moving with like
speed edgewise; nevertheless, a flat shape cannot prevent the
sinking of those solid bodies which would go to the bottom
in other shapes. And summing up, I concluded my argument
with him by this proposition: That a solid body which falls to
the bottom in water when reduced to a spherical shape, will
also fall there in any other shape, so that in brief, the difference
of shape in bodies of the same material does not alter its sinking or not sinking, rising or not rising, in a given medium.

The philosopher departed, and having thought the matter
over and conferred about it with other students of philosophy,
he came to find me three days later and said to me that having
reasoned on this point with some friends, he had found one
who did not fear to contend with me over the question, and who
would by reasons and experiments make evident to me the
falsity of my proposition. I, ever ready to learn from anyone,
replied that I should take it as a favor to converse with this
friend of his and reason about the subject.[15]

The game being agreed to by both sides, the place and
time were set; but these were not observed by the other party,
who not only failed to appear on the appointed day but for
many days thereafter. Now this would have mattered little were
it not that this second philosopher, instead of conversing with
me and showing me his reasons and experiments, set himself
in many public places in the city to show a great multitude
of people some little balls and chips of his, first of walnut
wood and later of ebony, chanting his triumph and saying that
he had me beaten—though he had not so much as spoken with

me. Advised of these artifices of his, I comprehended his entire strategy before we ever met; but, the philosophic dispute having thus degenerated into a contentious rivalry, making it impossible to treat the dispute with propriety, I decided that in order to escape from odious contests it would be best to propose in writing a single general argument as the basis and foundation of that which I had asserted, and if this were overthrown, I should admit myself vanquished. And since the experiment produced against me by the adversary was a thin chip of ebony, which, placed on water so that its upper surface is not wetted, does not sink, and a ball of the same material the size of a nut, which goes to the bottom, I, having considered that the cause of this difference proceeds not from shape but from the chip being not wholly wetted, proposed and sent to the adversaries this argument: Every kind of shape, of any size, when wetted, goes to the bottom in water, but if any part of the same shape is not wetted, it will rest without sinking; therefore, not the shape and not the size is the cause of sinking or not sinking, but complete or incomplete wetting.[16]

The next event was described by Colombe as follows:

> On the prescribed day, I appeared at the house of Signor Filippo Salviati, a principal gentleman of our city and as rich in endowments of the mind as in those of fortune, there being present the illustrious and most excellent Signor Don Giovanni Medici, with a host of noble literati, to hear us dispute together. But Signor Galileo could neither be brought to dispute, nor did he wish to perform the experiment with materials of a suitable size, shape, and quantity of material. Rather, he was resolved (and let everyone judge the reason for himself) to publish a treatise of his on this subject, hoping to make others believe by reasoning that which he could not show to the senses; for by altering and adding, and deviating from the agreement and the truth, one may easily draw the true conclusion from false premises and assumptions.[17]

The treatise to which Galileo had thus alluded in conversation with Colombe was, of course, the essay of which the opening pages have been set forth above. It concluded, after a number of arguments and demonstrations which it is unnecessary to repeat here, as follows:

Here I expect a terrible rebuke from one of my adversaries, and I can almost hear him shouting in my ears that it is one thing to deal with matters physically, and quite another to do so mathematically, and that geometers should stick to their fantasies and not get entangled in philosophical matters—as if truth could ever be more than one; as if geometry up to our time had prejudiced the acquisition of true philosophy; as if it were impossible to be a geometer as well as a philosopher— and we must infer as a necessary consequence that anyone who knows geometry cannot know physics, and cannot reason about and deal with physical matters physically! Consequences no less foolish than that of a certain physician who, moved by a fit of spleen, said that the great doctor Acquapendente,[18] being a famous anatomist and surgeon, should content himself to remain among his scalpels and ointments, without trying to effect cures by medicine—as if knowledge of surgery destroyed and opposed a knowledge of medicine. I replied to him that having many times recovered my health through the supreme excellence of Signor Acquapendente, I could depose and certify that he had never given me to drink any compound of cerates, caustics, threads, bandages, probes, and razors, nor had he ever, instead of feeling my pulse, cauterized me or pulled a tooth from my mouth. Rather, as an excellent physician, he purged me with manna, cassia, or rhubarb, and used other remedies suitable to my ailments. Let my adversaries see whether I treat the material in the same terms as Aristotle, and whether he himself does not, where necessary, introduce geometric demonstrations. And then let them have the kindness to desist from their bitter enmity toward geometry—to my astonishment indeed, since I had not thought anyone could be enemy to a total stranger.

Finally, Aristotle says at the end of his text that one must compare the heaviness of the body with the resistance to division of the medium, because if the power of the heaviness exceeds the resistance of the medium, the body will descend, and if not, it will float. I need not trouble to reply beyond that which has already been said: that it is not resistance to division (which does not exist in air or in water), but rather it is the heaviness of the medium which must be compared with the heaviness of the body, and if the heaviness be greater in the medium, the body will not descend therein, nor can it be entirely submerged, but a part only, since in the space which it occupies in the water there cannot exist a body which weighs less than an equal quantity of water. But if the body be heavier than the water, it will descend to the bottom, where it is more natural for it to rest than a less heavy body. And this is the true, unique, proper, and absolute cause of floating or sinking.

As for your chip, gentle adversaries, it will float when it is coupled with so much air as to form with it a composite body less heavy than as much water as would fill the space which the said composite occupies in the water; but if you put simple ebony in the water, in accordance with our agreements, it will go to the bottom though you make it thinner than paper.

Most Serene Lord, I have taken the trouble (as your Highness has seen) to keep alive my true proposition, and along with it many others that follow therefrom, preserving it from the voracity of the falsehood overthrown and slain by me. I know not whether the adversaries will give me credit for the work thus accomplished, or whether they, finding themselves under a strict oath obliged to sustain religiously every decree of Aristotle (perhaps fearing that, if disdained, he might invoke to their destruction a great company of his most invincible heroes), have resolved to choke me off and exterminate me as a profaner of his sacred laws. In this they would imitate the inhabitants of the Isle of Pianto when, angered against Orlando, in recompense for his having liberated so many innocent virgins from the horrible holocaust of the monster, they moved against him, lamenting their strange religion and vainly fearing the wrath of Proteus, terrified of submersion in the vast ocean.[19] And indeed they would have succeeded had not he, impenetrable though naked to their arrows, behaved as does the bear toward small dogs that deafen him with vain and noisy barking. Now I, who am no Orlando, possess nothing impenetrable but the shield of truth; for the rest, naked and unarmed, I take refuge in the protection of your Highness, at whose mere glance must fall any madman who imperiously attempts to mount unreasonable assaults.[20]

Immediately after the debates before the grand duke about the beginning of October, Galileo fell seriously ill. During his recuperation in the winter of 1611, he composed the *Discourse* as published in 1612 and discarded the previously completed essay. The difference in tone of the two documents is very marked. Having thoroughly vindicated himself in the eyes of his prince and employer, he did not hesitate to turn his book into a bold and uncompromising blow against the very foundations of Aristotelian physics. Its effectiveness was much enhanced by the colloquial Italian in which it was written.[21] Perhaps of equal importance in this regard was the simplicity and inherent interest of the experiments described, the relevance of which to the decision of the controversy was indisputable. This could not fail to weaken the long-standing tradition under which such disputes were customarily settled by appeal to authority, a tradition that remained the chief obstacle to the development of modern scientific notions.

Colombe took the *Discourse* to be directed against himself, even though it dealt with disputes at which he had not even been present. But it was the earlier essay that really had been aimed at Colombe, and this was discarded in favor of a general attack upon Peripatetic physics after the triumph at the ducal table. Hence, when Galileo replied to Colombe through the agency of Castelli, he scorned the idea that the *Discourse* had been directed against him. Nevertheless, Colombe has ever since been credited with a disproportionate share in the entire controversy.

Di Grazia and Coresio also published replies to the *Discourse,* feeling obliged to uphold their positions. One other booklet in reply to Galileo appeared anonymously, and it remains to comment upon the authorship of that work, which has not generally been properly linked with the disputes that led to Galileo's first book on physics.

The *Discourse* emerged from the press late in May 1612. By the middle of July a reply by an "Unknown Academician" was given to the printers at Pisa.[22] The work is dignified in tone, and it was unquestionably written by a philosopher intimately familiar with the literature of his subject. The author does not associate himself with the adversaries of Galileo, but attempts to find a middle ground, describing himself in his concluding sentence as "one who loves peace." Other writers, in the same year, also dissociated this author and Papazzoni from the "league" which had been formed against Galileo by his opponents.

The identity of the Academician, though well known at the time, was not specified in surviving letters. From the fact that some references to him under the appellation of *pippione* were found, an early historian concluded that he was Thomas Palmerini, a literary man of little merit who was often called by that contemptuous term. But whoever the Academician was, he was certainly dead before 1615, as Castelli withheld any answer to his book for that reason. Palmerini was still living several years later, eliminating his candidacy. Favaro believed the author to have been Arturo Pannochieschi de' Conti d'Elci, overseer of the University of Pisa, who evinced his hostility to Galileo's ideas in 1613 and who died in the following year. D'Elci had signed the dedication of the book, representing himself as its translator only; but this assertion Favaro dismissed as a more or less customary disclaimer of responsibility. Several years later Favaro discovered a letter from d'Elci to Cardinal Borromeo, transmitting some considerations on Galileo's book. This seemed to him to establish beyond doubt his previous conjecture, and so it has appeared to all subsequent writers.

There are, however, powerful objections to Favaro's reasoning, as well as some cogent arguments against d'Elci from internal evidence. If d'Elci had valid reasons to conceal his identity, it would seem foolish for him to put his name in the book at all, and still more so to reveal his authorship to Borromeo, when the latter was friendly with both Galileo and Ciampoli. And it is not apparent in any case why he should wish to conceal his identity. He had nothing to fear from Galileo, and the book was not a vigorous attack such as would lead to reprisals. On the contrary, it was a rather creditable performance of which the author might be proud, certainly more so than any of the other answers. Nor is there any evidence of d'Elci's competence as a philosopher in his own right. To compose and publish such a work within six or eight weeks after reading the *Discourse* would have required intimate familiarity with the subject.

The evidence against d'Elci as the Unknown Academician is automatically evidence in favor of Papazzoni. In his case both the philosophical competence and the previous familiarity with the material existed. But common courtesy would have required him to conceal his identity, at least formally, as he owed his recent appointment to Galileo and could not decently oppose him so soon in print. At the same time his honor was at stake, as he was known to have upheld the rival position before the grand duke. The ordinary rules of conduct in such disputes would require him to reply, and indeed to be first to reply, as I believe he was.[23] Moreover, the neutral tone in which the Academician speaks of Galileo's adversaries, among which he does not count himself, accords well with the actual role of Papazzoni when he had to defend at court the Peripatetic views on a subject which had previously been disputed between Galileo and his avowed adversaries.

Papazzoni, like d'Elci, died in 1614, so that the previously mentioned action of Castelli would apply equally well in either case. There is some indirect evidence that Papazzoni may have replied to Galileo's book in the summer of 1612, as at that time he told Ciampoli that he blushed to write against Galileo on this subject.[24] Perhaps even more significant is the fact that when the booklet arrived at Rome, G. B. Agucchi quickly identified it as the production of Papazzoni, even though he seems not to have known about his previous participation in the debates.[25]

The physical arrangement of the book bears out the idea that d'Elci was not solely responsible for it. It begins with a dedication to the archduchess, signed by d'Elci and dated 15 July. This is followed by a greeting from the Academician to Severo Giocondi, dated 1 July, which in turn is followed by a jeu d'esprit in the form of a salutation to his book by its author, and only then do we come to the text. The semidedication of 1 July seems quite pointless, both as to date and content, unless it constituted a letter of transmittal by the true author which the translator did not wish to omit. D'Elci says in the dedication that he has translated most of the work from Latin; presumably the parts already in Italian were the two prefatory salutations, to which d'Elci then added his own dedication. In his subsequent letter to Cardinal Borromeo, discovered by Favaro, d'Elci said: "Having been detained this year at Pisa almost all of August, I undertook to make certain brief Considerations on the Discourse of Signor Galileo Galilei, merely because of my detention and as an exercise in style, and to test whether for once I might be able to write on something weighty. . . ."[26] Thus the claim of authorship of what was sent is unequivocal; but it may be asked why, if the work was completed and dedicated at Pisa in the middle of July, the month of August should be mentioned as the period of its composition. It seems quite possible that what accompanied d'Elci's letter was not the printed *Considerations of the Unknown Academician,* but rather an essay of d'Elci's own which he had composed after he had translated Papazzoni's work and sent it to the printers. The co-incidence of title would not be remarkable, as the word "considerations" was very widely used for such polemic works.

Notes to Essay 8

1. It is my opinion that di Grazia first raised the point. Galileo says only that it was "a professor of philosophy," but he mentions di Grazia in a contemporary note about the controversy; *Opere,* IV, 32, line 20. Di Grazia wrote one of the four replies to Galileo's book on the subject.

2. Coresio was the first author to reply openly to Galileo's book on the subject. His ostensible reason is that of turning an accidental contention into something useful for philosophy, which seems to recall the circumstances of its origin; see *Opere,* IV, 204.

3. Colombe gives the text as follows, saying it was written in Galileo's own hand: "Signor Lodovico delle Colombe being of the opinion that shape affects solid bodies with regard to their descending (or) not descending (and) ascending or not ascending in a given medium, such as water, and in such a manner that for example a solid of spherical figure which would go to the bottom would not do so if altered to some other figure; and I, Galileo Galilei, on the contrary deeming this not to be true, but rather affirming that a solid body which sinks to the bottom in spherical or any other shape will also sink no matter what its shape is, being opposed to Signor Colombe in this particular, am content that we proceed to make experiments of it. And since these experiments might be made in various ways, I am content that the Very Reverend Signor Canon Nori, as our common friend, shall choose among the experiments that we shall submit, selecting those that may seem to him best suited to reveal the truth, as I also defer to his judgement the decision and the settling of controversies that may arise between the parties in making the said experiments." Colombe then added in his handwriting, "That the body is to be of the same material and the same weight, but the different shapes are at the choice of Lodovico; and the choice of bodies, which shall be chosen as nearly equal as possible in density [to water?] at the election of Lodovico; and the test shall be made several times, with the same material, but with as many pieces of that material as the number of times the experiment shall be made." Filippo Arrighetti was then made co-judge with Nori; see *Opere,* IV, 318–19. It should

be noted that nothing said by either man concerns floating as such, but only the rising or sinking of bodies.

4. *Opere,* IV, 34; XI, 176.

5. *Opere,* IV, 20 ff., 34 ff.

6. *Opere,* IV, 319. The names of Nori and Arrighetti are not mentioned; hence Colombe's claim that he appeared "at the appointed time" must refer to a subsequent and not the original engagement. The presence of Giovanni de' Medici, to whom Colombe later dedicated his book, was of particular significance if it is true that Galileo had offended this dignitary in 1592 by rejecting a contrivance designed by him to dredge the Bay of Leghorn, especially if hydrostatic principles were involved. See *Opere,* XIX, 606, but compare p. 638 of the same volume.

7. *Opere,* IV, 30–51. Rumors of Galileo's discontent reached Padua, where it was said he might return; see *Opere,* XI, 230. The essay is partly translated below.

8. *Opere,* XI, 207. Upon his return to Bologna, Papazzoni seems to have felt that he had been badly used by Galileo, and was reluctant to go through with his move to Pisa. Roffeni also felt that Galileo should make amends; *Opere,* VI, 217.

9. *Opere,* XI, 453; IV, 517, 537–38.

10. *Opere,* XI, 216. The fact that Galileo did not mention his triumph in the presence of the cardinals to any of his correspondents at the time would be remarkable were it not for the fact that he fell ill immediately afterward, and as a result wrote scarcely any letters from the beginning of October to the middle of December.

11. *Opere,* XI, 213–14. Favaro's dating of late September for the debate before the cardinals depended on his belief that the fifteen-page essay mentioned in this letter was either the *Discourse* itself or a first draft of it.

12. *Opere,* IV, 319. Galileo's behavior at this meeting indicated that in all probability he had already (late August) been cautioned by Cosimo not to indulge in further oral arguments. A similar warning came from his friend Cigoli at Rome (*Opere,* XI, 176).

13. Passages in square brackets were later canceled in the manuscript by Galileo.

14. That is, the qualities of heat, cold, moisture, and dryness, which were made to account for all other properties in the Peripatetic philosophy. At this period, "circles" for philosophical discussions were formed in many parts of Italy and were very popular at Pisa and at Florence.

15. Galileo did not supply here the actual wording of the question agreed to be debated, or the conditions of the contest. These are preserved, however, in Colombe's later published account of the affair; see note 3 above.

16. *Opere,* IV, 30–35.

17. *Opere,* IV, 319.
18. Hieronymus Fabricius of Acquapendente, discoverer of the valves in the veins and teacher of William Harvey, who was physician to Galileo and his close friend.
19. See Ariosto, *Orlando Furioso,* canto vi, 45 ff.
20. *Opere,* IV, 49–51.
21. Galileo gave his reasons for composing this book in Italian, rather than in the scholarly Latin usually used for such treatises, in a celebrated letter to Paolo Gualdo: "I am induced to do this by seeing how young men are sent through the universities at random to be made physicians, philosophers, and so on; thus many of them are committed to professions for which they are unsuited, while other men who would be fitted for these are taken up by family cares and other occupations remote from literature. . . . Now I want them to see that just as nature has given to them, as well as to philosophers, eyes to see her works, so she has also given them brains capable of penetrating and understanding them." (*Opere,* XI, 326; *Discoveries,* p. 84).
22. *Considerazioni sopra il Discorso del Galileo Galilei . . . da Accademico Incognito* (Pisa, 1612); *Opere,* IV, 145–82.
23. Galileo expected him to reply, or perhaps suspected that he had already replied under the veil of anonymity, and wrote to him sending sheets of the second edition of the *Discourse,* in which it is worth noting that Galileo had made one insertion specifically replying to the Academician (a defense of the use of the colloquial term *moment*). Papazzoni's answer was somewhat evasive, asserting that he would not have time to reply to the book because of duties at the university which were about to resume; but he did not deny having already replied, or refer in any way to the anonymous book which he certainly must have seen and about which some comment must have been made in Galileo's letter, now lost. See *Opere,* XI, 405–6. In 1613 Galileo sent to Papazzoni a copy of his *Letters on Sunspots,* and seems to have challenged him to reply to that, for Papazzoni's answering letter says, with simple dignity, that he will always defer to Galileo "save where my honor and the truth in defending Aristotle" are concerned (ibid., 496).
24. *Opere,* XI, 454, lines 32–33. The syntax makes it impossible to say whether Papazzoni said that he was ashamed to have written against Galileo, or that he was ashamed to write against him. The letter is undated, but was certainly written about the time the *Considerations* of the Academician were going to the printer at Pisa. Probably it was addressed to Strozzi, and the copy came into Galileo's hands in the summer of 1612, when he was preparing the second edition of the *Discourse;* if so, it would have furnished the pretext for sending Papazzoni sheets of that work and inquiring whether he intended to reply; see preceding note.

25. *Opere,* XI, 390. Agucchi's identification of author by style and content is not to be lightly passed over; an excellent judge, he did not hesitate to select Papazzoni from a large field of possible candidates.

26. *Opere,* XI, 384. The letter is dated from Florence, 27 August 1612. On the back of it one of Borromeo's secretaries has written, *Il Conte Arturo d'Elci manda alc.ᵉ Conside.: fatte sopra'l discorso del Galilei.* The word *alcune* raises grave doubt that a printed book was meant.

9

Sunspots, Sizzi, and Scheiner

Francesco Sizzi has a tiny niche in history as one of the many victims of savage court intrigue at Paris during the reign of Louis XIII. In the history of science he has thus far had a slightly larger but still less distinguished place as the author of an attempted refutation of Galileo's first telescopic discoveries.[1] Both Kepler and Porta promptly dismissed this work (quite correctly) as trifling, the latter writing to Federico Cesi: "I have received the book against Signor Galileo, than which I have never seen anything more absurd on earth."[2] Only Galileo seems to have had a kind word for Sizzi at that time. Transmitting to Filippo Salviati a copy of Kepler's remarks about the *Dianoia,* he wrote in part: "As I have often told you and others, I had much rather gain the friendship of Sig. Sizzi by forgiving him all insults than have him as an enemy through conquest. And for that reason I have managed also to apologize for him among the Jesuit fathers, who read his puerilities with vast amusement."[3]

Galileo's judgment of the man turned out to be correct, for despite the silly and mystical arguments Sizzi had presented in his book, he soon afterwards made a real contribution to science. Such, at any rate, is the thesis to be offered here. Long after his death he was destined to figure anonymously in a dramatic struggle between two more famous men, a struggle which was not without grave consequences to the history of astronomy in Italy. Nor is that all. Galileo has never been entirely exonerated from grave charges that have been made against his character, almost uninterruptedly, from his day to our own. If the reconstruction of events presented below is correct, the keystone of that arch of calumny will have been removed, or at least loosened.

Of Sizzi himself, little is positively known. By birth a

Florentine patrician, he appears to have left his native city for Paris shortly after the publication of his book in 1611. There he entered the service of Leonora Galigai (or of her brother, the archbishop of Tours). Wife of the Florentine adventurer Concino Concini, Marechal d'Ancre, this remarkable woman for a time exercised virtually the power of a queen of France through her ascendancy over the regent-mother, Marie de' Medici. Concini, for several years the most influential man at the French court, was murdered in the summer of 1617 at the instance, or at least with the consent, of the young Louis XIII. Not long afterward Mme la Marechale was arrested and sentenced to death on flimsy charges of treason, heresy, and the practice of magic. It is possible that Sizzi had cast some of the horoscopes seized among her papers, which were used to bolster the absurd charges laid against her. But whether or not Sizzi was implicated directly in 1617, he was barbarously executed a year later. The circumstances may be partly reconstructed from the following accounts.

G. B. Nelli, citing an anonymous manuscript in his possession, said of Sizzi that, "This unfortunate author, seven years after trying to contend against Galileo, had the imprudence to write at Paris a book against the King of France and his government, for which he was stretched on the wheel and garotted on the 19th July, 1618. Thus he learned how much difference there is between criticizing a philosopher and censuring the actions of a monarch."[4]

Cardinal Richelieu described in more detail the events leading up to Sizzi's death. Writing of M. de Luynes, he said:

> While strengthening his own position on the one hand, he undertook on the other to ruin so far as he was able the opposing party, to repress Barbin, and to blame him for the entire conduct of the Queen. This business made a good deal of noise at court. . . . Some persons became involved in this affair who imprudently produced ill-advised writings on the subject of Luynes and the affairs of the times. Durand was imprisoned for this, as well as a man named Sity, a Florentine, who had been secretary to the Archbishop of Tours, brother of the Marechale d'Ancre. A single book was imputed to both men, and for this they were ordered to be broken and burned, together with their writings . . . while a brother of the said Sity, who had merely transcribed a copy of it, was hanged.[5]

If Richelieu is correct in saying that but one book was in question, it must have been the *Ripozographie* mentioned in a note to the memoirs of the marquis de Fontenay-Mareuil: "Put to death at this time were Durand, who made all the king's ballets, and two Italians who had been of the household of the Marechal d'Ancre, for some writings in praise of the Queen-mother and against the existing government."[6] To this statement by the marquis, the editors have appended the identifying note: "Marie Durand, accused of being the author of a pamphlet against Luynes entitled *Ripozographie*." On the whole it would appear that Sizzi's was at worst a case of imprudence and perhaps no more than one of guilt by association.

During Sizzi's residence in Paris, however, he did not spend all his time casting horoscopes or meddling in politics. Not long after his arrival he fell in with a group of competent mathematicians—among them Jacques Aleaume, a pupil of Vieta's. This association soon removed his previous hostility to the new sciences, vindicating the judgment of him that Galileo had already expressed privately to his friends. For in July 1613, Father Horatio Morandi at Rome wrote to Galileo a letter that commenced as follows:

> I am sending you the letter of Signor Francesco Sizzi, so that you and others may be confirmed by this new event in the conviction that truth is one, and that all men who are born with the ability to accommodate their minds to it must sooner or later fall under the victorious banner of those who philosophize by contemplating the ample and beautiful book of nature, and do not league themselves with the sophistries of men who have attempted not only to imprison this unhappy science, but even to fetter it with unworthy chains of Aristotelian opinions and the crippling manacles of capricious philosophasters who swear by the words of unsound masters. I assure you of my pleasure at hearing that Signor Sizzi has emerged from the obstinate confusion into which he was once led by the mad throng; he seems to me to have been reborn, and by losing all he had to have regained it. But truly his fine mind could not long remain submerged in the murky sea of so many errors.[7]

The letter which Morandi enclosed had been sent to him by

Sizzi from Paris on 10 April 1613. Among the things dealt with was the dispute over floating bodies which had led to several publications by Galileo and certain Peripatetics. This dispute had begun about the time Sizzi left Florence; though it was waged by his former philosophical allies there, he now acknowledged the entire justice of Galileo's position as against theirs. The historically significant passages of Sizzi's letter, however, dealt with quite another matter. To appreciate their importance, we must run ahead to some events which did not take place until nearly two decades later, long after Sizzi's voice had been stilled by death.

In discussions with Pope Urban VIII which paved the way for the publication of Galileo's long-promised treatise on the Ptolemaic and Copernican systems, Galileo was expressly forbidden to attempt any physical proofs of the motion of the earth. So long as he confined himself to philosophical arguments and considerations of mathematical simplicity, he would be safe—or so he was told. Nevertheless, in writing his *Dialogue* he did employ two arguments which he himself regarded as physical proofs. One of these was based on the apparent paths of sunspots, and the other on the existence of the ocean tides. The latter argument, in substantially the form in which it occupies the last "day" of the *Dialogue,* had been composed as early as 1616. The argument from sunspots, however, made its first appearance in the *Dialogue,* where it occupied some ten pages. This argument depends entirely upon the inclination with respect to the ecliptic of the sun's axis of rotation, and neither in Galileo's published writings nor in his surviving letters is there any mention of this tilt prior to 1632. On the contrary, he had previously described the paths of sunspots as parallel to the ecliptic, notably in his *Letters on Sunspots* of 1613.[8]

Now, about two years before the *Dialogue* was published, and not long after its manuscript had been submitted to the censors, the Jesuit Father Christopher Scheiner had published his *Rosa Ursina,*[9] in which the annual variations in the apparent paths of sunspots were correctly described. Inasmuch as Scheiner had long been a rival claimant for priority in the discovery of sunspots, and in view of certain other circumstances which will be mentioned presently, Galileo's late appearance in print concerning this matter has been regarded as highly suspicious. In this connection the suggestions of

Emil Strauss have been very generally accepted. Strauss wrote, in part, as follows:

> The account of the discovery of sunspots which Galileo puts into the mouth of Salviati[10] has the purpose of establishing his priority over Scheiner. Scheiner's claims had been based upon his observations of March, 1611, mentioned in the letters which he wrote under the pseudonym of Apelles. Prior to 1630 there had been no open conflict between Scheiner and Galileo; yet a conflict must have taken place in private circles, as otherwise there would be no point to Galileo's attack in *Il Saggiatore*. Scheiner had merely written in the *Mathematical Disquisitions* of 1614[11] that the spots "had been portrayed by Apelles in two pictures, whence also by Galileo . . . ," and thereby in apparent good faith he had already made the attempt to establish his priority, which had previously been contested only by an incidental remark of Galileo's in his first letter to Welser. Antagonism to Galileo was in fact so far from Scheiner's thoughts at this time that in the book mentioned he refers to him frequently with the highest respect, and he sent Galileo a copy of the book with a very courtly letter of transmittal.
>
> The literary feud in a hostile sense was begun by Galileo— perhaps, as remarked above, upon provocation from Scheiner by word of mouth. Without naming any names, Galileo quite unmistakably suggested in *Il Saggiatore* that Scheiner had tried to wrest from him the glory of the discovery of sunspots. Against this assault Scheiner bitterly took up arms in the *Rosa Ursina*, which was completed and published at Bracciano in 1630.
>
> Galileo's *Dialogue* was first published in 1632, but it had been ready for the press in the middle of May, 1630; hence it had no relation to the *Rosa Ursina*, though the contrary has often been asserted. During the writing of the *Dialogue*, Galileo knew of the impending publication of the *Rosa*, and probably of its polemic tone; perhaps even of its scientific content. Accordingly . . . he inaugurated a new battle against his opponent. . . .[12]

More striking than Galileo's assertion that he had already seen sunspots at Padua in 1610 is his remark that the yearly period of the spots had been known to him in Salviati's lifetime. Salviati died in March, 1614. Hence during the more than sixteen years which had elapsed before the completion of the *Dialogue,* Galileo would have been aware of a fact to which he assigned the highest importance, and one (if we are to put any faith in this passage) whose significance he recognized at the moment of the discovery. Now would Galileo, who already had so many priority battles on his hands, have let this go by for all of sixteen years without making any communication of it? That would have been quite contrary to his practice, especially at first. Would he not have recorded his discovery, if necessary under the protection of an anagram? Instead, and precisely at the time when his rival Scheiner communicated the same fact to the scientific world in his *Rosa Ursina,* Galileo decides at last to reveal the secret which he has so long hidden for no apparent reason.

One can hardly repress the suspicion that Galileo either was actually acquainted with the *Rosa Ursina* when he composed the passage in question, and that he utilized the long interval which elapsed between completion of the *Dialogue* in 1630 and its publication [in 1632] to insert this passage; or that just as he knew of the pending appearance of the *Rosa,* so he knew also something of its content, and in order to anticipate his rival he finally turned to further observations of the sunspots and made the discovery for himself.

. . . If Galileo wanted his story to be credible, he ought at the very least to have given a reason for his enigmatical silence. Yet even later, in his letter to Fulgenzio Micanzio of 9th February 1636, he merely says that "I discovered it [the tilt of the sun's axis to the ecliptic] before him, of that I am convinced; but I had no occasion to speak of it outside of the *Dialogue.*"[13]

The suspicion thus cast on Galileo is indeed serious, and the evidence in its favor may at first seem overwhelming. To steal a scientific discovery is bad enough in any case; but to plagiarize from the very rival whom one has previously accused of plagiarism on the same general topic is entirely beyond the pale of decency. Hence so long as such a suspicion has rested on Galileo, many other charges of bad conduct on his part have managed to retain some spark of life—even some that have been adequately answered, refuted, and discredited in the minds of fair men. Yet this, the gravest charge of all, is unique in having gone entirely unanswered.

Before we proceed to examine it, let us recall that when

Strauss wrote his notes to the *Dialogue* (which have been exten-
sively utilized in subsequent English, Polish, and Russian translations and have not yet been surpassed in general excellence), no
relevant document had been published which could throw light on
the difficult questions that he raised. Such a document was published shortly after his death, but its relevance to this point appears
to have escaped even the vigilance of the great scholar who
brought it to light in his monumental edition of Galileo's works.
It is to that document that we now turn our attention.

The letter which Sizzi wrote to Morandi in 1613 is extant
in the original, as well as in a contemporary copy corrected in
several places by Galileo's own hand. Thus there can be no doubt
either as to the authenticity of the letter or the fact that Galileo had
read it attentively and preserved it all his life. Both the original
and the copy are clearly legible; hence no question exists about
Sizzi's words, though his meaning in certain places is vexingly
ambiguous or obscure. Here is a translation of the crucial passages:

> . . . concerning the opinion of Galileo and those other
> literati about the sunspots, I should take it as a great favor if
> you would speak more at length. And to give you a reason, I
> shall tell you what is known to us by continued observations
> of almost a year. This makes us believe (with due respect to
> the authority of Galileo and those others, whose pupils we
> recognize ourselves to be) that the said spots are not always
> being newly generated and dissolved about the body of the
> sun. . . .
>
> Our arguments against this opinion are: the equable
> motion they maintain in passing across the solar surface; the
> distance preserved between them (except as this varies through
> the plane representation of a globular figure); the size of the
> angles between the spots, together with the regular motion
> of both one and the other; the definite and uniform change
> of place that occurs between the rising and setting of the sun
> (except that this partly opposes that of midday); all which have
> been minutely observed by us. To this I can add the specific
> appearances according to the variation in tilt of the ecliptic in
> the solar surface; for the angles made by the spots at the
> equinoxes with the imaginary perpendicular line in the sun and
> parallel to our view differ from those made at the solstices—
> which in turn differ between themselves, since the angle which

at one solstice will be considered as in one of the four quadrants of the solar surface will [at the other solstice] be in the opposite quadrant. . . .[14]

Sizzi goes on to tell Morandi that he has deliberately withheld his further conclusions in order to stimulate in others the same curiosity which he and his friends have experienced concerning these matters. Perhaps some of the expressions in the passages just quoted were deliberately made cryptic for a similar reason, or perhaps these merely exhibit Sizzi's characteristic style, which had drawn exasperated comments from Kepler and Galileo concerning the *Dianoia*. Alternative translations might be given of the passages quoted. But in any translation, the hints supplied by Sizzi's letter were more than adequate to direct the attention of an interested astronomer to the existence of variations in angle between the sunspot paths and the ecliptic at various seasons of the year.

Sizzi's letter came into Galileo's hands about six months after he had published his *Letters on Sunspots*. Recognizing it as a possible source of Galileo's first acquaintance with those appearances which implied a tilt of the sun's axis of rotation, let us consider the probable course of events which followed.

It has already been remarked that the tidal argument for the earth's motion had been written early in 1616, when Galileo was at Rome to battle against prohibition of the Copernican system. On that occasion he certainly employed every argument he could muster, unhampered as yet by official restrictions against "physical" proofs; yet he made no mention of an argument based on sunspots. It seems safe to conclude that at that time this line of reasoning had not yet occurred to him. But this in no way contradicts his having read Sizzi's letter. It is one thing to know of an annual variation in the sunspot paths, and quite another to link this with the motion of the earth. The connection is so far from obvious that Strauss, centuries later, rejected Galileo's reasoning as entirely fallacious, though it is far from being so. The sunspot argument would in fact have afforded Galileo a much more powerful means of convincing his mathematical opponents that *some* terrestrial motion must exist than the erroneous tidal argument which he invoked during his desperate effort to save Copernicus from prohibition by the Church.

After the Church's condemnation of the heliocentric theory in 1616, Galileo was for several years in no position to utilize any new arguments for the earth's motion, if any occurred to him. Probably none did, as he was not in the habit of dwelling upon matters that could be of no use to him. He was ill a good deal of the time, and much of the rest he spent upon such safe projects as that of determining longitudes at sea. For seven years he published nothing. In *The Assayer* of 1623 he was still careful to abstain from pressing the Copernican view; in fact he tried to appear as having forever rejected it. It was not until the following year that this situation had altered sufficiently for him to feel free once more to turn his mind to these arguments.

When Galileo wrote to Micanzio that he had discovered the tilt of the sun's axis long before Scheiner, but had had no occasion to mention it until the *Dialogue,* the latter statement was literally true. Quite possibly the former one was too. But he certainly did not deduce anything about the earth's motion from this until late in 1629. On 21 April of that year, writing to Cesare Marsili apropos of recent news that Scheiner would soon publish a thick folio volume on sunspots, he remarked that any such book would surely be filled with irrelevancies, as there was no more to be said on the subject than he had already published in his *Letters on Sunspots* sixteen years before. It is most improbable that he was here dissembling any additional knowledge; that was never his habit, at least when writing to personal friends.

At the time he wrote to Marsili, Galileo had laid aside the *Dialogue* for more than two years. But on the twenty-ninth of October in the same year, he wrote to Elia Diodati at Paris to say that about a month previously he had resumed work on it and would soon publish it; that it would be filled with novelties and contain ample confirmation of the views of Copernicus. Within two or three months the book was completed. In February 1630 he was writing the marginal notes and additions necessary to round it out, and in May he arrived at Rome to submit the manuscript to the censors.

For various reasons, printing did not begin until June 1631—more than a year later—but even then Galileo had not actually seen a copy of the *Rosa Ursina,* and his knowledge that it contained a bitter attack on himself seems not to have moved him to try very hard to get one. It was only in September 1631, when the printing of the *Dialogue* was about one-half completed, that the *Rosa Ursina* came into his hands. Having seen it, he at once wrote letters of indignant protest to friends and to the powerful nobleman to whom it was dedicated—something he clearly would have done before if he had seen the book.

It was the opinion of Strauss, who did not know of Sizzi's letter, that Galileo got his clue to the tilt of the sun's axis either directly from the *Rosa Ursina* or by means of further observations, conducted in the knowledge that Scheiner was attacking him on the subject of sunspots. There are fatal objections to these suggestions, both from internal and external evidence. The internal evidence depends on the fact that although Galileo in his own ten-page discussion uses the most acute mathematical reasoning, he displays entire ignorance or complete neglect of the observational data. His argument is, in the main, that if the sun's axis had some (undefined) tilt with respect to the ecliptic, then the paths of the sunspots would appear sometimes curved and sometimes straight as the earth made its annual trip around it, and that the same appearances could be accounted for only by the most complicated and implausible motions of the sun if the earth remained stationary. At the conclusion of this hypothetical reasoning he asserts that protracted observations have confirmed its premises. He does not state the times of year when the paths would appear straight, nor the degree of the observed tilt, as Strauss duly noted.[15] However, it would be natural enough for him to omit these data from a popular book, so long as he did not know that his ancient rival had discovered, published, and crowed over them. But if he knew that, he would in this way be deliberately taking second place; and that was not his custom.

Even that is not all. To the extent that Galileo's argument did imply a degree of axis tilt and a timing for the path shapes, these were utterly wrong. Surely Galileo would not have invented and published a theory irreconcilable with observed data as set forth by an antagonist if he had seen those—and Scheiner's description of the phenomena is very detailed and accurate. He states quite clearly in the *Rosa Ursina* that the times of rectilinear motion of the spots occur in summer and winter, while their "equilibrations" with the ecliptic take place at the beginning of

March and September.[16] Galileo, on the other hand, implies almost the exact opposite, if he does not ignore these questions completely.[17] Hence he can hardly have stolen his data from Scheiner. Likewise, observations of any duration made for himself would have prevented his implicit reversal of the facts. And if he had any hint that his rival had discovered something new on this subject, that ought to have deterred him from publishing a mere guess. Thus, the most plausible explanation of Galileo's argument is that it resulted from a "thought-experiment" during the winter of 1629–30, when he was pressing to find every possible argument for Copernicus. His interest, for this purpose, was merely in the general consequences of a tilted axis. If his only data were Sizzi's ambiguous and general remarks about seasonal changes in the apparent sunspot paths, it would be easy for Galileo to have fallen into precisely the error imputed to him.[18]

It remains to give the external evidences that the sunspot argument was not inserted in the *Dialogue* after Galileo had seen the *Rosa Ursina*. At that time the book was half-printed. It is perfectly possible that Galileo then added a clause supporting his original sunspot priority by invoking the testimony of certain Venetians who were still living, as Favaro suggested. But it is not possible that he added ten pages of text which contained a brand new argument for Copernicus. One need only recall that the *Dialogue* was already a notoriously controversial book, that it had been subjected to unusual and unreasonable delays and revisions to satisfy the censor at Rome, and that it had then been subjected to a complete review by the authorities at Florence. It is most unlikely that the printer of such a book would accept this quantity and kind of new material from the author without specific approval of the censor, or that the Florentine censor would neglect in turn to consult Rome about it.

Even apart from this, there is adequate evidence that no such addition took place. The sunspot argument is one of the three powerful points in favor of Copernicus that is singled out for special mention in the closing pages of the *Dialogue*. These closing pages, like the famous preface, had been the subject of almost endless scrutiny, revision, and criticism at Rome for over a year. Separate copies of them had been made and sent back to Rome after Galileo had taken the manuscript to Florence. Hence, if the ten pages in question had been added to the middle of the book during printing without consultation of, or without objection by, the Florentine censor and without having been referred to Rome for approval, the fact of their insertion could not have been concealed later. The corresponding change in the final pages would surely have been detected by the special commission appointed at Rome after publication of the *Dialogue* to search it for any pretext on which Galileo could be prosecuted. Such a violation of the imprimatur would have been evident and would have provided ample grounds for prosecution in place of the flimsy charges actually brought by the commission against the book.

The existence of Sizzi's letter thus undermines any ground for suspicion that Galileo plagiarized from Scheiner any information in the *Dialogue*. Nevertheless, Scheiner was convinced that he had been ill-treated, and he exerted all his influence at Rome to have the *Dialogue* condemned and its author punished.

Because the controversy between Galileo and Scheiner has figured so prominently in this study, it seems appropriate to review in conclusion the widely held theory that Galileo brought all his troubles on himself by vigorously attacking Scheiner in *The Assayer.* That book opened with a long (and eminently justified) complaint against the many persons who had stolen or belittled its author's ideas and discoveries. Coming to the matter of sunspots, Galileo wrote:

> How many men attacked my *Letters on Sunspots,* and under what disguises! The material contained therein ought to have opened to the mind's eye much room for admirable speculation; instead, it met with scorn and derision. Many disbelieved it or failed to appreciate it. Others, not wanting to agree with my ideas, advanced ridiculous and impossible opinions against me; and some, overwhelmed and convinced by my arguments, attempted to rob me of that glory which was mine, pretending not to have seen my writings and trying to represent themselves as the original discoverers of these impressive marvels.[19]

It was natural enough for Scheiner to take this accusation as directed at himself, and equally natural for him to feel outraged. If it had been directed solely against him, the utter injustice of the final passages would have afforded an adequate excuse for almost any steps he might have taken in reply. We may forgive Scheiner for his misinterpretation, as he was not acquainted personally with Galileo and did not know that injustice of any kind was foreign to his nature. But that it was a misinterpretation is abundantly clear. The final words cannot by any stretch of the imagination apply to Scheiner. He had been disposed of in the opening passage with the words "under what disguises."[20] At most he may have been included again as one who "advanced ridiculous and impossible opinions." But he could not possibly be described as "overwhelmed and convinced" by Galileo's arguments; still less could Galileo have meant to reproach Scheiner for "pretending not to have seen my writings." As a matter of fact, Scheiner's letters on this subject preceded and were the publicly acknowledged reason for Galileo's own first writings about sunspots. And to Galileo's first letter, before it was published, Scheiner wrote a published reply.

Scheiner says in the opening page of the *Rosa Ursina* that when he came to Rome in 1624 and was shown this passage, he at first thought that his "Italian critic" must have meant somebody else; but that when he searched, he could not find that anyone but Apelles (i.e., himself) had written, spoken, or done anything whatever on sunspots. Here he was seriously in error. There had been another writer, of whom we shall speak presently, shortly before *The Assayer* was published, and Scheiner had as much reason to resent him as Galileo did. Others also had publicly debated and discussed Galileo's sunspot views in Italy ten years before Scheiner arrived there, and they were still in Galileo's mind. The Jesuit fathers at the Roman College, where Scheiner made observations mentioned in the *Rosa Ursina,* could have informed him of at least one of these debates, for many years earlier they had defended Scheiner's views against a Dominican who supported Galileo's.[21] Moreover, there was at least one other man whom Galileo resented as a claimant for priority, possibly one who "pretended not to have seen my writings." This was Domenico Passignani at Rome, to whom Galileo is said to have intended to give honorable mention in his published *Letters on Sunspots.*[22] Hence there were indeed other men referred to in the passage that offended Scheiner; and Galileo's repeated plurals in that passage, his "many," his "others," and his "some" could hardly all be taken as exaggerations by any reasonable person, as if they alluded over and over again to the lone Apelles. Nevertheless, so far as I know, all writers on this topic have agreed with Strauss in believing that open hostilities were commenced by Galileo in *The Assayer*.

Scheiner was not even right in saying that no others had written (that is, published) on the topic. In November 1614 Galileo received a visit at Florence from Jean Tarde, to whom he showed his sunspot data and with whom he discussed at length the dispute with Scheiner and his own conclusions. Tarde recorded the entire interview in his diary and later acknowledged by letter the receipt of Galileo's *Letters on Sunspots*. But five years afterward, he scratched out his diary entries of conversations with Galileo about sunspots and proceeded to publish a book of his own on the subject. It appeared at Paris under the title *Borbonia sydera, id est planetae qui Solis lumina circumvolitant motu proprio ac regulari, falso hactenus ab helioscopis maculae Solis nuncupati,* etc. In 1623 Tarde published a French version of the book; this time the title was still more specific: *Les Astres de Borbon et apologie pour le Soleil. Monstrant et verifiant que les apparences qui se voient dans la face du Soleil sont des planetes et non des taches, comme quelques italiens et allemands observateurs d'icelles luy ont impose.* The irony of this is that Tarde's planetary explanation of sunspots was a plagiarism of Scheiner's original theory, not Galileo's. The *allemand observateur,* inventor of the helioscope, had indeed called the spots *maculae* in the title of his first book, but in the text he had contended that they were stars. In overlooking Tarde, Scheiner had ignored a worse foe than Galileo, at least so far as the original dispute was concerned.

A complete account of the tragic enmity between Galileo and Scheiner would be out of place here. It suffices to have indicated that there was no unreasonably violent attack directed openly and intentionally by either man against the other before 1630. Despite the assumptions made by Scheiner himself in the *Rosa Ursina* and adopted by many historians, Galileo had in mind many other men than Scheiner when he published his complaint in *The Assayer*. But the *Rosa Ursina* fueled a long-smoldering fire into a blaze of destruction. The well-informed Gabriel Naudé was convinced that Galileo's final trial and condemnation was the work of Scheiner.[23] Despite the fact that he was the only Jesuit responsibly named by contemporary writers, the Jesuits in general have ever since received the brunt of the blame.

It is interesting that the innocent cause of the final debacle may have been the long-dead Francesco Sizzi, whom Galileo had once defended against the derision of the Jesuits at the Roman College.

The strength of Galileo's argument drawn from the sunspots in favor of a motion of the earth has been challenged by a long train of writers, from Scheiner's posthumous *Prodromus pro sole mobile* of 1651 down to Arthur Koestler's *Sleepwalkers* of 1959. Among the modern writers who have perceived its strength, the best exposition is that of the late Filippo Soccorsi, S.J. His account deserves wider attention than it has received. Soccorsi wrote:

> Galileo considers the circular paths described by sunspots and notes not only that the sun revolves on itself, but also that its axis of rotation is, over the course of a year, differently inclined with respect to the earth. In fact, the paths of the spots, over a yearly period, appear sometimes straight and sometimes curved upward or downward, as well as tilted to the right or to the left.
>
> Here we are concerned with a phenomenon of relative motion that is explained in the heliocentric system by assuming the axis of the sun to be tilted with respect to the terrestrial orbit; and it is also explained in the geocentric system if we suppose that the sun in its annual motion with respect to the stars carries its axis parallel to itself. Thus the argument is not peremptory, and Galileo himself does not treat it as such.
>
> Nevertheless, Galileo rejects the geocentric interpretation as "very hard and almost impossible," because of the complicated motions that it must assume, whereas the heliocentric explanation is very simple. It must be admitted that Galileo interpreted in a complicated way—not to say "obscure," as he admits— something that would definitely be resolved by a simple carrying of the sun's axis parallel to itself. However, it cannot be allowed to pass unnoted that the simplicity of explanation is confined to the *annual* motion of the sun; it would not have remained simple if Galileo had brought into his argument on sunspots, and insisted on considering simultaneously, both the sun's annual motion with respect to the stars and its diurnal motion with respect to the earth.

In fact, in the brief daily period, the sunspots do not show any detectable movement to the right or left, or up or down. For this fact, an explanation may be given, either in the heliocentric or the geocentric interpretation; in the former it is a simple explanation from a kinematic point of view; but for the latter it is indeed complex, and goes against the laws of dynamics.

Given that in a day's turn, the sunspots undergo no noticeable change, two necessary conclusions follow: first, that in the period from sunrise to sunset, the sun always turns virtually the same face toward the earth; otherwise the spots would be carried across the sun's disc along some of their respective parallels. In the second place (and to this we must turn our attention) in this same brief space of a day, the solar axis cannot sensibly *change* its tilt with respect to the earth, or else the observer would see the sunspots move upward or downward.

Now this second condition is obviously verified in the heliocentric interpretation, since the apparent motion of the sun in that case is due to the rotation of the earth on its axis, and the terrestrial rotation cannot in any way change the tilt of the sun's axis. But under the geocentric hypothesis one must suppose that the sun, in revolving about the earth, keeps its axis directed as if rigidly connected with the earth's axis. Without such a connection, the respective orientations of those two axes would visibly change, and the spots would rise or fall [on the sun's face, as seen] even in the short space of a day.

Therefore, to save the geocentric interpretation of the phenomena, one must attribute to the sun a complex movement, the resultant of two heterogeneous rotations around the earth —one of annual period, in which the sun's axis, carried parallel to itself, describes about the earth a cylindrical surface; and another of daily period, in which the sun's axis is not carried parallel to itself but is carried around in rigid connection with the earth, describing about it a surface called a hyperboloid. This is a surface generated by the rotation, about one axis, of a skew line with respect to that axis. It is a surface rather like a cone, but in which the generating line no longer intersects the axis of rotation and thus does not turn about a fixed point (vertex of the cone), but remains skew to the axis and runs along a circle of radius equal to the minimum distance between the two axes. From the combination of the two movements there results a unique variable complex motion, the sun's axis describing around the earth a surface that passes continuously from the form of a cone (when the solar axis cuts the terrestrial axis) to that of the hyperboloid of which the guide-circle increases progressively to a maximum value, only to draw in again and disappear at the vertex of the cone.

There results a complicated cosmic picture which, though irreproachable as an abstract geometric and kinematic interpretation of the celestial motions, appears quite implausible as a physical reality. One may add that this hypothetical turning of the axis about the earth without remaining parallel to itself is contrary to the laws of dynamics applied to planetary motions. At the time of the Copernican controversy, those laws were still not definite; but Galileo had already perspicuously observed certain phenomena that he did not hesitate to ascribe to a general inertial principle, according to which bodies rotating "and balancing in a fluid and yielding medium" conserved "naturally the axis of rotation parallel to itself."

Put in this way, the argument would have been strengthened by dynamic facts and would have brought into serious consideration the idea that at least the *diurnal* rotation should be given to the earth, and not the sun. This would not have resolved the controversy over the annual motion and the geocentric or heliocentric structure of the system; but the diurnal rotation of the earth in itself would have been sufficient to bring to light the true sense of the Bible, destroying the motives for opposing the Copernican thesis.

Father [Adolf] Müller has already emphasized that if consideration were given to the diurnal motion of the sun, the examination of the sunspot paths would effectively have excluded the geocentric interpretation of the phenomenon. Müller puts the argument in different terms, but they are equivalent to those given here. . . .[24]

I believe that the reverend fathers are mistaken only in supposing that Galileo did not carry out the same reasoning and try to explain it to his readers. The fact that the argument appears in the Third Day of the *Dialogue,* which is devoted especially to the annual motion of the earth, is not conclusive regarding Galileo's intention in offering it. The daily motion had already been discussed in the Second Day, where the seasonal variation of sunspot paths would have been out of place. But that does not mean that all problems involving the diurnal motion had to be excluded from the Third Day; on the contrary, that was the only logical place to introduce an argument involving *both* motions. The case of the sunspot argument is like that of the tidal argument that occupies the Fourth Day; both motions are involved, and to attempt to refute either argument by a consideration of only one motion is to miss (or conceal) its force. That Galileo did intend the daily as well as the annual motion to be taken into account is evident in his summing up of the difficulties in a geostatic explanation of the appearances:

> Hence finally it will be necessary, in order to keep the earth fixed in the center, to attribute to the sun two movements about its own center, one of which would complete its rotation in a year [the annual cycle of shapes of sunspot paths] and the other in less than a month [the rotation of a particular spot] . . . and two other movements around the earth *on different axes,* tracing out the ecliptic in a year with one of these, and with the other, forming spirals or circles parallel to the equinoctial plane, *one a day.* . . . As to that which must convey the axis and poles of this monthly one [i.e., the first motion named above], no reason whatever is to be seen why it should complete its motion in a year . . . rather than *in twenty-four hours* as dependent on the diurnal motion [i.e., the last named above] about the poles of the equinoctial.[25]

This last remark calls attention to the fact that in the geostatic explanation, the sun is carried around the earth daily, and hence that the presence of an annual cyclic change in sunspot paths is hard to reconcile with the absence of a daily cyclic change of the same character. Galileo remarks that if this is obscure to his readers, it will become clear when the so-called "third motion" attributed to the earth by Copernicus is discussed. The Copernican "third motion" is precisely analogous to the geostatic requirement that the sun's axis of rotation be transported daily as if in rigid connection with the earth's center, in order to prevent observable daily displacements of the sunspot paths. Galileo goes on to say:

> Now if these four motions, so incongruous with each other and yet necessarily all attributable [geostatically] to the single

body of the sun, could be reduced to a single and very simple one [in the sun], the sun being assigned one unchanging axis; and if with no innovations in the movements assigned by so many other observations to the terrestrial globe [day and night, the seasons, retrogressions of planets, etc.], one could still easily preserve the many peculiar appearances of sunspots—then really it seems to me that the latter decision could not be rejected.[26]

Thus Galileo makes two objections to the geostatic position: complexity and incongruity of motions. The objection of complexity rests on the need for two solar rotations, that of its body about an axis, and that of the axis in annual conical rotation. A single solar rotation on a fixed axis suffices in the heliocentric system. The other movements are two in number under either system—for the geostatic, those described above; and for the heliostatic, the earth's diurnal rotation and annual revolution.

The objection of "incongruity" is not further explained by Galileo. He cannot have been referring to a mathematical incongruity, for he made no claim that the necessary motions could not be described geometrically. It is hard to see how he can have referred to anything but a physical incongruity, particularly after having promised his readers that the puzzle of annual rather than daily cycles of sunspot paths will be clarified by the disposition of the Copernican "third motion." That motion he showed to be unnecessary, pointing out that the transport of the earth's axis parallel to itself was in reality not still another motion, but a kind of rest; that is, a kind of inertial behavior. This he exemplified by the behavior of a ball in a basin of water held by a person who turns completely around; with respect to the rim of the basin there is rotation, but with respect to the fixed objects in the room there is rest. The literal motion demanded of the sun's axis to keep the same face of that body toward the earth all day was, for Galileo, a physical incongruity in a theory that demanded also a slow rotation of that same axis about the center of the sun during the year. The conservation of a double rotation, of different periods, in the same axis of a freely floating sphere, was likewise incongruous with the behavior of observed terrestrial spheres.

The thoughtlessness of Galileo's modern critics is shown by this diagram, given as self-explanatory by one of them:

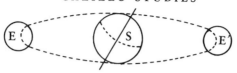

a. Copernican

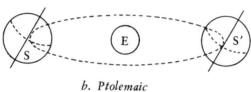

b. Ptolemaic

Fig. 7

If the second figure is taken literally for a perfectly stationary earth, the condition demanded by Galileo's own opponents, then it means that from any given point on the earth, the sun is invisible for half the year. The modern adversary knows, but his diagram fails to show, that the earth revolves on its own axis daily; if he tries to stop that rotation and send the sun instead hurtling around the earth daily, the diagram will no longer prove what he wants to prove. The sunspot paths in the second figure will then not vary gradually throughout the year, though they will twist about through the same set of paths every day. But that is not what is observed.

Notes to Essay 9

1. *ΔΙΑΝΟΙΑ astronomica, optica, physica, qua Syderei Nuncii rumor de quatuor planetis a Galilaeo Galilaeo mathematico celeberrimo recens perspicilli cuiusdam ope conspectis, vanus redditur.* Auctore Francisco Sitio florentino. Venetiis, MDCXI.
2. *Opere*, XI, 157.
3. *Opere*, XI, 91.
4. Nelli, *Vita e Commercio Letterario di Galileo Galilei* (Lausanne, 1793), I, 236. Nelli was the owner of virtually all Galileo's manuscripts. The place and date of publication are false; the book was printed at Florence, probably about 1818.

5. Michaud and Pouloulat, *Nouvelle Collection des memoires pour servir a l'histoire de France* . . . (Paris, 1837), VII, 183–84.
6. Ibid., V, 131.
7. *Opere*, XI, 530.
8. *Opere*, V, 189; *Discoveries*, p. 125.
9. *Rosa Ursina sive Sol ex admirando facularum et macularum suarum phoenomenon varius* . . . a Christophoro Scheiner germano suevo e societate Jesu . . . Bracciani . . . Impressio coepta anno 1626, finita vero 1630, Id. Junii.
10. *Dialogue*, pp. 345–56.
11. *Disquisitiones mathematicae de controversiis et novitatibus astronomicis. Quas sub praesidio Christophori Scheiner . . . publice disputandas posuit, propugnavit . . . Joannes Georgius Locher . . .* Ingolstadii . . . MDCXIV. Although the work is nominally by Locher, Scheiner had sent a copy of it to Galileo and was widely considered its real author. Galileo identified Scheiner as its author in indexing the postils to the *Dialogue*, but not in the postil itself. This last-minute addition by Galileo is evidence that he had not intended to attack Scheiner personally, and hence that he had not seen the *Rosa Ursina*, when the printing of the *Dialogue* began; see further below.
12. *Dialog über die beiden hauptsächlichen Weltsysteme*, trans. E. Strauss (Leipzig, 1891), pp. 553–54.
13. Ibid., p. 555. In this argument Strauss exaggerated the importance of Salviati's having died in 1614. So far as that goes, Galileo never saw Sagredo after 1609. Many of the conclusions he reached in later years were nevertheless placed in the mouths of these two men when he wrote the *Dialogue*, which after all was no less a literary than a scientific work. And as a matter of fact the passage Strauss refers to states specifically that some years had elapsed between the publication of the *Letters on Sunspots* and the discovery of the tilted axis (*Opere*, VII, 374; *Dialogue*, p. 346). Hence Galileo made no pretense of having formulated the argument in Salviati's lifetime; the use of his friend's voice was merely a necessary literary device.
14. *Opere*, XI, 491–92.
15. Strauss, *Dialog*, p. 556. Strauss raised some interesting problems regarding Galileo's use of the word "meridian" in his sunspot argument. In an earlier passage (*Dialogue*, p. 263) Galileo put the sun's axis parallel to the earth's. He may have read Sizzi's remark as suggesting that our equinoxes and solstices correspond exactly to maximum and minimum tilt of sunspot paths. Cf. note 17 below.
16. *Rosa Ursina*, pp. 161–62, 225.
17. If Galileo meant "meridian" literally when he first introduced it in his sunspot argument, then this implied that the straight paths

would occur at the equinoxes. When the argument first occurred to him, he seems to have assumed this, and also that the tilt of the sun's axis was the same as the earth's; cf. note 15 above. In developing the detailed ten-page argument he abandoned the latter assumption and left the tilt of the sun's axis completely undetermined. Perhaps he wished also not to commit himself on the times of maximum tilt (minimum curvature) of sunspot paths, overlooking that to leave the word "meridian" at the beginning defeated that purpose. Galileo's argument does bear the mark of haste, but not at all in the sense implied by Strauss. The haste was in completing the manuscript, not in composing a new argument after the book had gone to press. The sunspot section seems to have been altered more than once, with signs that specific statements were replaced by general ones. But it does not show evidence of having been dashed off in a hurry. The complexity of the argument alone virtually precludes the latter possibility.

18. Whether Galileo held the incorrect view, or failed to note the implication, the conclusion would still follow.

19. *Discoveries*, p. 232.

20. Scheiner's original letters on sunspots, written to Mark Welser, had been published by the latter over the pseudonym "Apelles," as Scheiner's superior is said to have forbidden him to jeopardize the reputation of his order by publishing observations that might be mistaken and were contrary to Aristotle. Galileo forbore in *The Assayer* from referring directly to this nom de plume, but a contemptuous reference to it had been made in 1619 in a book which Galileo was known to have written, though it was published over the name of a pupil. Scheiner was exasperated at the time, saying that he would pay Galileo back in his own coin. See *Opere*, VI, 47–48; XII, 489.

21. *Opere*, XI, 395, 418.

22. As a matter of fact, Passignani very likely did discover sunspots independently shortly before the date of Scheiner's first published observations. He asked Galileo's friend Ludovico Cigoli to transmit his findings to the Florentine astronomer, and Cigoli's letter includes the first mention of sunspots in the surviving correspondence. From Galileo's reply, however, it is apparent that sunspots were nothing new to him; and it may be that Passignani observed them only because Galileo had aroused interest in the subject while at Rome a few months before. At any rate, when Passignani later insisted loudly that it was his discovery, Galileo reversed his attention to mention him. See *Opere*, XI, 208–9, 212–14, 253, 268, 276–77, 348.

23. *Opere*, XV, 88, 164.

24. Filippo Soccorsi, S.J., *Il Processo di Galileo* (Rome, 1947), pp. 75–78. Adolf Müller had earlier perceived the dynamic cogency of

Galileo's argument, but believed that Galileo himself could not have done so. See "Die Sonnenflecke im Zusammenhang mit dem Copernicanischen Weltsysteme," *Stimmen aus Maria Laach,* 52 (1897).

25. *Dialogue,* p. 355.
26. *Dialogue,* p. 355.

10

Galileo's Theory
of the Tides

In a letter to Kepler dated 4 August 1597, Galileo declared that he had been an adherent of the Copernican theory for several years, and stated further that by means of this theory he had been able to discover the causes of several physical effects which could perhaps not be satisfactorily explained under the geostatic theory.[1] Had he written again to comment on Kepler's first book, as Kepler requested him to do, he might also have disclosed precisely what effects he thus referred to.[2] Scholars who have pondered over this question have generally concluded that Galileo must have had in mind the tidal theory he developed at length in the *Dialogue* nearly half a century later. As Emil Strauss pointed out, no terrestrial phenomenon except that of the tides was ever maintained by Galileo to be incapable of explanation (without recourse to the miraculous) under either cosmological theory.[3] Nevertheless, the earliest surviving mention by Galileo of his tidal theory came in 1616, when it was embodied in a discourse addressed to Cardinal Orsini.

Until quite recently no concrete evidence had been published, so far as I know, that anyone had formulated such a tidal theory as early as 1597. This theory, which was highly esteemed by Galileo and was vigorously claimed by him as his own invention, remains virtually the only thing he ever published for which no rival claim of priority was ever entered, either in his own time or by recent historians, on behalf of someone else. Probably it has gone unchallenged because in his day it was dangerous to champion the assumption of the earth's motions on which the theory rested, and since his death the theory itself has generally been considered worthless. A review of these matters is the purpose of the present study.

Kepler himself, as early as 1598, conjectured that the physical effects hinted at in Galileo's first letter were the tidal phenomena.[4] Kepler, however, assumed that Galileo had in mind no more than the mistaken idea, broached by Kepler's friend Herwart, that any motion of the earth would cause a commotion in the waters and in the air, producing tides and winds.[5] Accordingly he gave no serious thought to the matter, remarking only that the evident relation of the moon's motion to the tidal periods made it necessary to base any rational explanation of the tides on the action of the moon. Now Galileo's theory depended not on a single motion of the earth, but on a composition of the diurnal and annual motions, and Galileo thought he could account for an apparent influence of the moon on mechanical grounds, without any need to invoke a special dominion of the moon over the waters as such. It was for Kepler's apparent support of the latter idea that he was respectfully reproached by Galileo later in the *Dialogue,* for to Galileo, such occult qualities were the bane of natural philosophy.[6]

That the tidal theory later put forth by Galileo had already been formulated as early as 1597 can now be verified by certain entries in the notebooks of Paolo Sarpi concerning philosophical, physical, and mathematical problems. Sarpi's original notebooks have perished, but a reliable copy is extant which preserves even the occasional marginal notations of dates that serve to establish a rough chronology of the entries. The notebooks contain 655 numbered paragraphs written during a period of about thirty-five years, but chiefly from 1578 to 1597. Among these there are four consecutive paragraphs dealing with the tides, written in 1595. The content of these paragraphs is as follows:

> 568. —The diameter of the earth subtends six minutes, and a bit less, in the orbit of annual motion; so that, the center [of the earth] moving less than 60 [minutes, or one degree, per day], in the upper part the daily motion advances one-fifth in thirty minutes [of arc; that is, in half a day], and in the other thirty [minutes, or half-day] it is retarded by that amount. The upper [part] is the night, and the lower, the day. Whence every point on the surface is now fast, now average, and now slow, as in [i.e., with respect to] the [stellar] sphere.

> 569. —Any water carried in a basin, at the beginning of its

transport, remains behind and rises at the rear, because the motion has not been thoroughly received; and when stopped, the water continues to be moved by the received motion and rises at the front. The seas are waters in basins and by the annual motion of the earth make that effect, being now swift, now slow, and again average through the diurnal [motion], which is seen in the moving of the basin diversely. And if the seas are so large that they have a [quarter-sphere(?)] so that part is in the swift and part in the average [motion], there will be a greater diversity, and still greater if they have a half-sphere, so that part is in the swift and part in the slow [motion].

570. —Hence it is manifest that lakes and small seas do not produce this effect, being insensible basins. It is also manifest how the variation of the eccentricity [i.e., differences in latitude] varying the ratios of the annual and diurnal motion equalizes [sic] the augmentations and decrements. Also it is manifest how the various positions of the shores may cause variation, if their length be along or across the motion. Finally it is manifest how the motion of the seasons, carrying the shores now to one site and now to another, makes an annual variation of the augmentations and decrements.

571. —The motion of the sea will therefore be a motion composed of two things: first, of the resting behind and rising of the water when the motion passes from slow to swift; and, from its natural [tendency] to return to equilibrium, the second, of following the motion when it passes from slow to swift [sic], and therefore to rise with its natural [tendency] to return to equilibrium.[7]

The notebooks contain little else to suggest that Sarpi was a Copernican. There are two other references to a motion of the earth; one of these is in a Cusanian rather than a Copernican sense, while the other is dubitative. There is only a single mention of the name of Copernicus, and that occurs in connection not with the motion of the earth but with a theorem of Apollonius and its relation to a dictum of Aristotle's.[8] The absence of previous or subsequent notes relating to the tides or to arguments for or against Copernicus suggests that the above paragraphs merely record an interesting theory heard from Galileo, with whom Sarpi often talked at Venice or at Padua in these years, rather than one which Sarpi himself had thought out. The compactness and relative completeness of the summary tend to support such a view. Nowhere in the notebooks is the name of any of Sarpi's contemporaries mentioned, and though in general the thoughts recorded may be presumed to have been his own, there is nothing to exclude the possibility that on occasion he noted down the ideas of others.

An examination of the text of the last three paragraphs cited lends support to this conjecture. In particular, the confusions or contradictions marked by the word *sic* occur at places where it would seem that the author of the ideas could scarcely fail to be precise. In the first of these, whatever may have been intended by the word "eccentricity," the context seems to demand the phrase "renders unequal" rather than the word "equalizes." In the second, it is apparent that the motion of the container and not of the water is the subject of the verb "passes," and hence that the order of the words "slow" and "swift" should be reversed. The examples of the quarter-sphere and half-sphere seas are trademarks of Galileo's two later expositions, one of which was widely circulated during Sarpi's lifetime, without protest on his part. And the reference to the seasonal motion (Copernicus's "third motion") is suggestive. If the originator of this tidal theory was a literal adherent of Copernicus, he ought to have expected a special tidal effect from that motion. Galileo, however, recognized it as an inertial phenomenon and not a true motion, so he limited its effect to a gradual annual alteration of the components in his primary cause of the tides, precisely as the writer of the summary has done. It is highly improbable that Sarpi should have won through to this conception in a single stroke, without having made any critique of or other note on the "third motion" of Copernicus.

Yet if Sarpi made these entries to record a theory heard in conversation, it is undeniably odd that four separate paragraphs rather than a single one should be devoted to it. Perhaps the last two entries represent additions made after Sarpi had raised further questions which were clarified in subsequent conversations. In support of this idea, attention is called particularly to the last paragraph, for what it says is not quite what it appears to be at first glance. This paragraph is not an attempt to summarize the general cause of tides, which was said in the second paragraph to be the unequal motions of parts of the earth. In the final paragraph the word "sea" (*mare*) is used in the singular, and refers not to seas in general (as does the plural in the first paragraph), but probably to the Adriatic (or perhaps the Mediterranean) in particular. The period of the tides there was known to Sarpi, and it would be quite natural for him to object that this did not conform to the implications of the proposed primary causes, after he had had time to consider them. And in fact the principal explanation Galileo offered for this was the reciprocal coursing of water seeking equilibrium, which varied with the length of the basin. A person recording the answer to a specific query would be far more likely to abbreviate this explanation, as Sarpi has done here, than would the originator of the theory when working it out.

Indirect evidence that Sarpi was not the author of this tidal theory is afforded by writings of his intimate friend and first biographer, Fulgenzio Micanzio, who was also a fast friend of Galileo's. Micanzio had seen a treatise of Sarpi's on the tides (now lost), addressed to one Marioti.[9] He was also thoroughly familiar with Galileo's theory as set forth in the *Dialogue* and with his uncompromising claim to its authorship in the preface to that book. Micanzio not only praised the *Dialogue* for its clarity and originality, but undertook at Galileo's request to carry out for him further observations of the tides at Venice. Yet nowhere in his biography of Sarpi, published after Galileo's death, or in his correspondence with Galileo, is there any suggestion by Micanzio that Galileo owed to Sarpi any part of his tidal theory. In contrast, Micanzio makes it clear in the biography that Sarpi had more than a little to do with Galileo's success in constructing his first telescope.[10] Furthermore, he is very severe with Fabricius of Acquapendente for not giving Sarpi proper credit for his discovery and explanation of the valves in the veins.[11]

The fate of Galileo's tidal theory is a curious one and deserves even more attention than can be given to it here. It was warmly accepted by friends of Galileo's like Sagredo, who had the critical ability and honesty to challenge certain other ideas of his esteemed teacher. It continued to find some support from other able men up to the promulgation of the theory of universal gravitation by Newton in 1687. Foremost among these was John Wallis, who admired the device by which Galileo attempted to account mechanically for the well-known relation of the motion of the moon to the tides, and Wallis attempted to improve on this.[12] After

Newton, of course, Galileo's theory fell into oblivion except for occasional comments by biographers and historians.

The opinion of most of these writers has resembled that of Drinkwater, who recognized the ingenuity of Galileo's theory but assured his readers that despite its plausibility, it did not in the least account for the tides for reasons too technical to set forth.[13] Emil Strauss, however, opined that the causes alleged by Galileo might have some tidal influence that was too small to be detected under the much greater effects of gravitation, and even of winds and currents.[14] Most subsequent historians have preferred the view of Ernst Mach, who maintained that the "Galileo effect" was entirely illusory, and attempted to illustrate this by means of a thought-experiment utilizing the Galilean principle of relativity of translatory motion.[15] Emil Wohlwill, writing in 1909, remarked on Strauss's credulity but stated that he himself had encountered technically trained persons who leaned toward a similar view.[16] Later writers have agreed that no such effect is possible, and have suggested that Galileo either blundered into an absurd contradiction of his own principles of mechanics out of fondness for his tidal theory, or saw the contradiction and deliberately played upon the ignorance of his readers.[17] Some say that Galileo's refusal to accept the theory of Kepler, with its remarkable anticipation of the theory of gravitation, is a sad commentary on Galileo's attitude toward his great contemporary. It does not appear to me that these commentaries hit the nail on the head, while some of them merely illustrate the perils that assail the historian of science when he fails to assess the views of earlier periods in terms of the knowledge available to the men who first expressed them, or attempts to construe too literally some of the generalizations of modern mathematical physics.

Let us consider first the notion that Galileo's theory was absurd or is demonstrably irreconcilable with the principles of modern physics. This may be so, though I am inclined to doubt it. But whether true or not, it is certainly not settled by Mach's thought-experiment. Mach imparts to an isolated rotating globe of water a translatory motion and correctly asserts that this will have no further effect. One may feel that Mach's argument, utilizing one rotation and one translation, is justified by the fact that the motion of the earth around the sun for a single day is pretty much a straight line. But this empirical fact is irrelevant to any evaluation of Galileo's theory, which did not attempt to discuss quantitative effects, partly because Galileo believed them to be the product of the widest diversity of causes independent of his primary thesis.[18] Galileo's theory depends specifically on the compounding of two circular motions, not of a rotation and a translation. Hence, in order to attack his theory, one is obliged to consider both the annual and the diurnal motions as circular. Mach did not do this. With that in mind, let us attempt our own thought-experiment, confining ourselves to a framework which Galileo himself might have used.[19]

Imagine a grindstone pierced by two fairly large holes placed near its rim and about thirty degrees apart, connected by two cylindrical passages, one near the rim and the other near the base of each hole. These are half-filled with colored water, and then covered with glass to permit observation. Let the grindstone be rotated horizontally on an axle held in a U-shaped fork to which a long cable is attached, provided with a handle at one end and a saddle near the fork. As we crank the stone to a moderate speed, we shall see the water recede into the hole which is further back in the direction of rotation, but once we have got it to considerable speed and let it rotate freely, the water will distribute itself along the passage and between the two cavities in such a way as to get as close to the rim as possible. Next we mount the saddle, and

Acceleration   *Uniform Rotation*

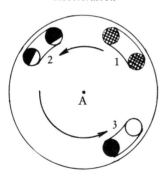
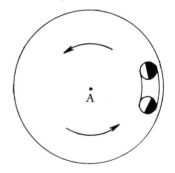

Fig. 8. At rest, (1) water lies evenly across bottom of both chambers and connecting tubes. As rotation begins, (2) water moves toward rim and toward rear chamber (3).

Fig. 9. At constant speed of rotation sufficient to overcome gravity, water half-fills each chamber and presses toward rim of grindstone.

at our command an Olympic hammer-slinger begins to revolve the whole framework, while we watch the grindstone from our seat in the saddle. With each rotation of the stone on its axle, the distribution of the water between the two holes and their connecting passage will be altered cyclically. The tidal effect thus produced would vary considerably for different relative radii and speeds, but reciprocating flows could undoubtedly be produced.

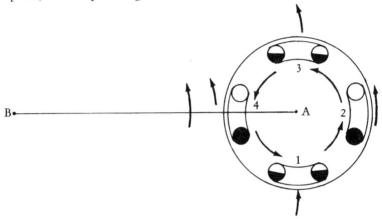

Fig. 10. Interior arrows show direction of rotation of grindstone around its center A. Exterior arrows show direction of rotation of cable AB and of virtual motions imparted to points on rim by this rotation around B. At point 1, rotation around B increases pressure of water toward rim of grindstone, created by rotation around A. Approaching point 2, rotation around B causes water to accumulate in rear chamber. Approaching point 3, rotation around B presses water toward center of grindstone. Approaching point 4, rotation around B causes water to accumulate in forward chamber.

It is true that this thought-experiment appeals to a physical intuition of tangential velocities (or centrifugal forces), whereas Galileo appealed to differential velocities at the ends of the cavities. Also, it does not produce its effect on external seas, though it may easily be modified to do this.[20] And the reciprocal inertial motions of the waters, which play a large part in Galileo's theory, will scarcely be perceptible in this model at most speeds. These and similar objections, however, seem to me inconsequential for the present purpose, which is to induce some spirit of skepticism in historians of science with regard to the application of physical principles of great generality when attempting to criticize the thought of early physicists. Whether the "Galileo effect" could be observed in some hypothetical universe in which multiple attracting bodies were given such masses, distances, and periodic positions as virtually to cancel out their tidal effects, I do not know; but I should not wonder if mathematical physicists could produce such a universe to order. It is less to the discredit of Galileo that he happened not to live in such a universe, than it is to the discredit of his modern critics that they believe such a universe to be impossible, or submit his ideas to critiques inconsistent with his stated postulates.

A typical criticism of Galileo's tidal theory, for instance, asserts that it would imply only one high tide, precisely at noon, every day. One critic has gone so far as to say that Galileo postulated such a condition.[21] As a matter of fact, Galileo postulated only that the tides must be accounted for either supernaturally or by motions of the earth; as to periodicity, he asserted that there was no general period for tides, but that each basin had its characteristic period. In any case, a contemporary of his had pointed out to Galileo himself this supposed implication of his theory of the tides, before he published it.[22] Thus it is evident that he considered that he had freed his theory from any such implication. Galileo believed that virtually no rising or falling of water was to be found except at the extremities of large seas; in the central parts, he thought, the water would merely course more rapidly in one direction or the other. Hence it would make a good deal of difference in the time of high tide whether the observer happened to be at the end of a large sea-basin, or on a small island in an ocean. It would also make a difference whether he was at the eastern or western end of a basin; for it is not at all obvious that just because the maximum daily tide would occur at noon (or shortly after noon, to allow for Galileo's remark that water continues in motion for some time) at the eastern shore, while the western shore was still retarding its motion as it approached noon, the maximum daily tide would also occur at noon for the western shore, by which time the eastern end of the basin would be accelerating away from that shore.

Suppose, for example, that the Straits of Gibraltar are closed, and you are stationed on the Rock a little before noon. Your position is approaching its slowest daily net motion, on Galileo's hypothesis, so the waters of the Atlantic are piling up against the Rock. But what about the waters of the Mediterranean? Like the waters of the Atlantic, they are engaged in the general eastward movement, and hence should be moving away from the Rock at approximately the speed with which the Atlantic waters are piling up against it, unless they are being pressed back by waters receding from the earlier high tide at the eastern end of the same basin. Thus on Galileo's theory, during the last few minutes before noon, the tide might be rising on the western side of Gibraltar and falling on the eastern side. Again, it might be rising on both sides, or falling on both sides, depending on the period of reciprocation for each basin. Hence the common objection that Galileo's theory must result in a high tide at noon each day is based on a gross misunderstanding of his opinion. At any rate, the objection did not worry him in the least, because he quite definitely and specifically attributed the observed tidal periods on any coast to the length and depth of the adjacent sea-basin.

Thus, with regard to the Mediterranean tides, he wrote: "Six hours, then, is not a more proper or natural period for these reciprocations than any other interval of time, though perhaps it has been the one most generally observed because it is that of our Mediterranean, which has been the only place practicable for making observations over many centuries."[23] It was certainly the only place where he himself had made any observations; and if there were any reliable tide tables accessible to him at that time from other shores, I do not know where they are to be found.

But let us suppose that Galileo's theory did entail only a single daily cycle of tides and that he failed to note this or to offer any explanation of the discrepancy between this consequence and the most elementary observations of the phenomena at Venice. Suppose further that Galileo read and pondered over Kepler's theory as set forth in the preface to the *Astronomia Nova* (as I believe he did).[24] Now, on what grounds might one ask him to abandon his own theory and accept that of Kepler? How many daily cycles of tides would Kepler's moon-attraction theory produce? Not quite one. Kepler's theory, instead of accounting for two tides a day in the Adriatic, would account for but one tide anywhere in nearly twenty-five hours, so he would be an hour farther from the truth than adverse critics assert that Galileo was (neglecting all but the primary causes in his theory). In short, Kepler made no effort whatever to square his theory with the observed facts, which is perhaps fortunate when we consider that one of his forerunners had accounted for a double tide under the moon's attraction by endowing the moon with power to confer upon the opposite sign of the zodiac its attractive influence—a theory which Galileo also duly noted and rejected, in terms much less complimentary than those which he applied to Kepler when he reproached him for lending his ear to the doctrine of occult properties.[25]

An amusing aspect of the whole affair is that, in a quite literal sense, Galileo was correct in his fundamental postulate, which was that without invoking the miraculous, one cannot explain the tides on the assumption of a truly immovable earth. For the double period of the tides is now attributed to a literal motion of the earth away from the waters on the side opposite the attracting body. In place of criticizing either Kepler or Galileo, one might well say that both were correct in their physical intuitions, the one seeking an explanatory motion of the earth, and the other seeking an explanatory attraction of the moon. Neither found precisely what was required; yet to anyone who might have accepted Galileo's postulate and Kepler's attractive force, allowing the earth then a motion in response to that force, the essential cause of the basic tidal movement should have become apparent. Only prejudice leads men to see profound insight in one approach and blind recalcitrance in the other.

Fundamentally, Galileo's objection to all rival tidal theories was that they invoked nonphysical causes. In the case of Kepler's theory, the cause was an attraction, which to Galileo's mind was the invoking of an occult quality, the dominion of the moon over the waters, a specific kind of influence that had no application except to the phenomenon it was created to explain. Now, that kind of criticism was valid and was necessary for the origin of modern physics. But it seems not to have been really fair when applied to Kepler's theory as set forth in the preface to the *Astronomia Nova,* because Kepler advanced the idea that the attraction applied to all bodies, and not just to water. He thought that if the earth and the moon were free to move toward each other, they would meet, and that the distance each would travel would be inversely proportional to its size. The fact that only the water was disturbed, he attributed to its fluid character and its loose connection with the earth. This view seems quite modern to us, because we know the right answer. But to Galileo it need not have looked any different from the ancient occult dominion of the moon over the waters. Certainly that would be the case if he had heard of Kepler's view only by hearsay and had not read the more general view of attraction expounded in the *Astronomia Nova*. But assuming that he had read that, it might well have seemed to Galileo that Kepler made the attraction specific to water with regard to tides. For if the attraction were general and the water rose two or three feet on the side where the moon was situated, why should not the earth rise the same two or three feet and cancel the effect, on Kepler's own theory? Kepler did not distinguish (as we do) the strength of the moon's attraction at the earth's nearer surface, at its center, and at its opposite surface. Hence the motion of the water was related by Kepler only to its character as water, and not to some other physical factor such as distance from the moon. And on that basis, Galileo's rejection of it as an occult quality was not entirely unfair to Kepler.

Notes to Essay 10

1. *Opere,* X, 58.
2. Galileo's early relations with Kepler, which have been the subject of much controversy, are discussed in essay 6.
3. *Dialog über die beiden hauptsächlichen Weltsysteme,* trans. E. Strauss (Leipzig, 1891), p. xvii.
4. *Opere,* X, 72, and J. Kepler, *Opera Omnia,* ed. C. Frisch, II, 61; *Gesammelte Werke,* ed. M. Caspar, XIII (Munich, 1945), 178.
5. Theories attributing the tides in general to some sort of terrestrial motion were not new. Galileo mentions the ancient opinion of Seleucus, and such a theory was advanced by A. Cesalpinus at Pisa in Galileo's own student days.
6. *Dialogue,* pp. 445, 462.
7. Paragraphs 569, 570, and 571 are published in Paoli Sarpi, *Scritti Filosofici e Teologici,* ed. R. Amerio (Bari, 1951), p. 115. Paragraph 568 is taken from a microfilm of the manuscript through the courtesy of the Biblioteca Marciana at Venice.

8. Sarpi, *Scritti,* paragraphs 29 and 104; paragraph 85.

9. [F. Micanzio] *Vita del Padre Paolo* (Leyden, 1646), p. 105.

10. Ibid., p. 211.

11. Ibid., pp. 43–44.

12. E. J. Aiton, "Galileo's Theory of the Tides," *Annals of Science,* 10, no. 1, p. 48.

13. [J. E. Drinkwater-Bethune], *The Life of Galileo* (London, 1829), pp. 71, 73.

14. *Dialog,* trans. E. Strauss, p. 566.

15. E. Mach, *The Science of Mechanics,* trans. Thomas J. McCormack (La Salle, 1942), p. 263.

16. E. Wohlwill, *Galilei und sein Kampf,* vol. I (Hamburg, 1909), p. 600, note 2.

17. Aiton, *op. cit.,* p. 46; Arthur Koestler, *The Sleepwalkers* (London, 1959), pp. 453–54, 464–66. H. Burstyn, who rejected Galileo's argument in a paper read to the History of Science Society, later gave qualified support to it; see his "Galileo's Attempt to Prove that the Earth Moves," *Isis,* 53 (1962), 161–85, contending (pp. 171–72) that Galileo did not have in mind any illustrative model involving two circular motions.

18. ". . . secondary causes are partly variable and not subject to observations (the changes due to winds, for example) and partly, though determinate and fixed, are not observed because of their complexity. Such are the lengths of the sea basins, their varied orientations . . . and the various depths of the waters. Who could possibly formulate a complete account of these except after very long observations and reliable reports? Without this, what could serve as a sound basis for . . . anyone who . . . wished to furnish adequate reasons for all the phenomena?" *Dialogue,* p. 460; compare the article "Tides" in the eleventh edition of the *Encyclopaedia Britannica:* ". . . the irregular distribution of land and water and the various depths of the ocean in various places produces irregularities in the oscillations of the sea of such complexity that the rigorous solution of the problem [of representing theoretically the actual tides at any port] is altogether beyond the power of analysis."

19. Galileo remarked that it was not possible to impart different speeds to the ends of an actual vessel of size practicable for experimentation; yet on the following page, he claimed to have a mechanical model that would exhibit the effects of such compounding of motion as he had described; see *Dialogue,* pp. 429–31.

20. For example, one might cut a segment from the rim of the grindstone, fill the equivalent space with water, and hold this in place by means of a flexible membrane which, when at rest, would conform to the shape of the portion removed. Rotation would then produce a bulge. When revolution about another center was added, the bulge would change its shape and position cyclically.

Whether the tide was high or low at "noon" would depend on whether the observer (say an ant) stood at the leading edge of the "sea" in the direction of rotation, or at the opposite edge, or on an island provided centrally and rigidly fixed to the grindstone.

21. Koestler, *The Sleepwalkers*, p. 454.
22. *Opere*, XIII, 450.
23. *Dialogue*, pp. 432–33.
24. This was probably the source for Galileo's knowledge of Kepler's tidal theory.
25. *Dialogue*, p. 419; the theory was given by Marcantonio de Dominis in *Euripus* (Rome, 1624).

Free Fall and Uniform Acceleration

Second only to the law of inertia in its importance to the origin of modern physics is the discovery of the law that governs the speed of bodies falling freely to the earth. This law, which relates the speed at any moment to the time elapsed from rest, and the spaces traversed from rest to the squares of the elapsed times, was first set forth in Galileo's *Dialogue* of 1632. Its consequences were developed in many ways in his *Two New Sciences* of 1638, particularly with respect to the motions of projectiles. The parabolic shape of ideal projectile trajectories, utilizing both ideas, was first disclosed by his disciple Bonaventura Cavalieri in 1632. Cavalieri had studied mathematics under Benedetto Castelli, Galileo's most able pupil at Padua.

The development of Galileo's law of falling bodies has been the subject of many studies and much debate. In modern times, those studies have been guided primarily by considerations of the history of ideas; that is to say, by reconstruction of Galileo's line of thought as continuing that of his predecessors. A highly plausible picture has thus been built up, and is widely accepted, in which Galileo is seen as the heir of a well-defined medieval tradition in the mathematical analysis of the problems of motion. Many of Galileo's writings, both published and manuscript, have been used to support that picture. At the same time, some lingering problems have kept this historical portrayal from being regarded as certain, however plausible it has been shown to be.

An approach to the problem from the other side—that is, by a study of all the surviving papers of Galileo and an attempt to put them into reasonable chronological order as a means of retracing his steps—has received less attention. The task is not a simple one, because many fragments were jotted on undated sheets kept by Galileo, sometimes mixed with notes on quite different topics. Antonio Favaro first attempted to arrange these in tentative order of composition when he published them in Galileo's collected works. A close study of the manuscripts, with attention to the watermarks of the papers, the ink, and the handwriting, will be necessary before any final conclusions can be reached. Meanwhile, however, working from the published manuscripts and correlating them with stages of thought discernible in Galileo's published books and in his correspondence, I have arrived at a reconstruction that differs profoundly from the prevailing view. If it is substantially correct, as I believe it is, it will ultimately have some notable consequences for studies of Galileo's relations to his predecessors and for our conceptions of continuity in the history of physics. It is with this reconstruction that the present study is concerned; for corroborative details, the reader is referred to two papers on which it is based.[1]

Galileo's unpublished treatises on motion and on mechanics, composed before 1600, show that in those early years he believed that acceleration in free fall was not an essential and continuing phenomenon, but an evanescent event at the beginning of fall that was swiftly replaced by a constant speed, which in turn depended on the excess of weight of the body over the weight of a like volume of the medium through which it fell. Accordingly he linked the speed of motion with the effective weight of the falling body, just as Aristotle had taught, but according to a radically different rule. For fall along inclined planes, Galileo's rule departed widely from the observed events.

The year in which Galileo first began to make careful observations on the motions of pendulums is not known, but there is good evidence that he had done so by 1602, when he corresponded with Guido Ubaldo del Monte on the subject. His earlier derivation of the rule for equilibrium on inclined planes implicitly related motions thereon to pendulum motions and to descent along circular arcs.[2] Guido Ubaldo disputed a rule Galileo had given him concerning the latter, saying that experiments made along the rim of a sieve did not bear it out. Galileo defended the rule and attributed the discrepancy with experience to the crudeness of observations made.[3]

Careful observations of pendulums would suffice to call into question the assumption that acceleration is a temporary rather than a continuing effect, especially in a long pendulum swinging through a considerable arc. The same observations would suggest also the symmetry of descent and ascent, and Galileo had noted long before that a body thrown upward cannot remain for any time at a constant speed.[4] Now, by 1604 we find him in possession of a rule for the spaces traversed in successive equal times by a freely falling body. It is apparent that he had abandoned his previous assumption that acceleration was evanescent, and was seeking the rule that governed increase of speed in actual falling bodies.

What he had found was in fact the right rule for the relation of spaces traversed and times elapsed, but not the correct assumption for increase of speed. He appears to have been quite certain of the former, as if he had found some independent evidence for it, while he described his assumption about the latter as merely probable and not as itself demonstrated. The same assumption— that the increase of speed is proportional to the space traversed from rest—is to be found in nearly every author before Galileo who concerned himself with actual acceleration in free fall. Medieval authors who had dealt with the question of uniform acceleration as such, apart from falling bodies, made quite a different assumption; namely, that the increase of speed is proportional to the time elapsed. It took Galileo a long time to see that this was also the correct assumption for actual falling bodies, as had been suggested earlier by but one writer, Domingo de Soto. It took him still longer to see also that his former assumption was incorrect. To us it seems obvious that both could not be correct at the same time, but that was not obvious to Galileo or to any of his predecessors; at least, no evidence has yet been presented that anyone, even Soto, had so much as raised the question. Ultimately it became obvious to Galileo, but that fact and its consequences (some of which are quite curious) come much later in our story.

In the autumn of 1604, Galileo conversed with his Venetian friend, Fra Paolo Sarpi, concerning accelerated motion. From surviving letters it appears that Galileo had asserted that in free fall, the successive spaces passed over in equal times were as the odd numbers starting from unity; that a body thrown upward and one falling through the same height would move with the same degrees of speed in reverse order; and that the distances fallen from rest were in the ratio of the squares of the times of fall. Sarpi wished to see a proof of these relationships, which were in fact correct.

Thinking over the whole matter again at Padua, Galileo wrote that he had been unable to find any truly unquestionable principle to assume for his proofs, but had adopted one that he thought to be physically reasonable, and for which he had hoped eventually to find a demonstration; this was the common assumption that the speed increased with the distance fallen. In support of the assumption he adduced the observational evidence of pile-drivers, which show that force, and hence speed, increase with height of fall. These thoughts he sent to Sarpi in Venice, saying that on the above assumption he could demonstrate the conclusions in question. He asked Sarpi to think over this assumption prior to a visit to Venice that Galileo planned for the end of October 1604.[5]

An attempted demonstration was duly written out by Galileo and is preserved among his papers. Whether he discussed it with Sarpi is not known. At precisely this time the nova of 1604 was first observed, and Galileo's attention was diverted for a while from problems of physics. Galileo's demonstration was fallacious, and various attempts have been made to analyze the reasons that prevented him from perceiving its lack of rigor. Here it suffices to say that the concept of a mean speed did not appear in it, nor was the fundamental assumption of Galileo the same as that of medieval writers on uniform acceleration.[6] My own view is that the attempted demonstration was entirely ad hoc; that Galileo was perfectly certain of the truth of the conclusion, and was therefore less critical of the steps in the proof than he would have been had he not had independent reasons for believing in the result proved. One of those steps invoked a "contrary ratio" of speed and time, neither defined nor explained, that enabled him immediately to produce the desired conclusion.

But the real interest at this point is the source of Galileo's certainty as to the correctness of the conclusions; especially the correctness of the rather complicated notion that spaces traversed are as the squares of the times. Had he relied on the medieval

Merton School writers or on Soto, the correct assumption would have been explicitly in front of him and the conclusions would follow directly. But if he had relied on them, he would logically have shown greater faith in the assumption than in the conclusions. Hence we should look for other possible approaches. And there are two ways that he might have been led to his rule without having relied on the speculations of any of his predecessors.

One of these is by means of observation. I hasten to add that I do not mean by elaborate experiments such as those he later described as having performed in order to corroborate the rules. It would be grossly anachronistic, both with respect to the history of experimental physics and with respect to the known procedures of Galileo, to assume that he reached the mathematical law of fall by carefully controlled measurements of falling bodies. That he confirmed the law in that way is virtually certain.[7] But he could have arrived at it indirectly in a much simpler and more plausible way.

The times-squared law follows immediately from the odd-number rule for successive spaces in equal times. It has already been noted that in 1602 Galileo was making observations that led him to recognize the continuing character of acceleration. A crude and hence plausible way in which he could have confirmed that would be to allow a heavy ball to roll a considerable distance over any convenient smooth slope, such as a paved ramp. In order to find out whether the ball continued to accelerate, he would have only to mark its place after equal times—say pulse-beats—and compare the distances between marks. In that way the approximate 1–3–5–7 relationship between marks might have been noted, from which the square law would be evident to any mathematician of the time.[8]

A purely logical approach was also accessible to Galileo. If the spaces traversed in free fall grow uniformly, they form an arithmetic progression. It would, however, be a special kind of progression, in which the sum of the first two terms must be in the same ratio to the sum of the second two terms as the first term is to the second, and the sum of the first three must be in this same ratio to the second three, and so on, since we could have taken the double or triple (and so on) of whatever we took for the first arbitrary space. If one then asks whether such a progression exists, one finds it almost immediately. It is not 1–2–3–4, because 3 plus 4 is not double 1 plus 2. But it is 1–3–5–7, the very next progression to be tried, because 5 plus 7 is three times 1 plus 3. Moreover, no other arithmetic progression will fulfill the condition.[9]

Thus we need not assume that Galileo found the law of falling bodies by reasoning from the conclusions of previous philosophical or physical writers; he might have found it by rough observation, or by mathematical reasoning of his own; perhaps by a combination of both, or in some other way that has not occurred to me. Whether or not he hit on the rule by the above reasoning, he certainly was in possession of that reasoning by 1615, when he conversed with one of his correspondents who later wrote of ". . . a proposition that Sig. Galileo told me as true but without adducing the demonstration for me; and it is that bodies in natural motion go increasing their [successive] velocities in the ratios of 1, 3, 5, 7 etc. and so on *ad infinitum;* but he did adduce a probable reason for this, [namely] that only in this proportion [do] more or fewer spaces preserve always the same ratio. . . ."[10] It seems to me very likely that Galileo would be willing to give out to his acquaintance only the initial reasoning that he himself had used to establish this law, keeping its correct derivation to himself for later publication. If so, it is an interesting clue to his procedure in 1604 and to the source of his faith in the conclusions he gave to Sarpi.

In 1604 Galileo was forty years old and had been a professor of mathematics for fifteen years. Much of that time he had devoted to studies of motion and mechanics. It is highly unlikely that after he was in possession of the correct law of falling bodies, in 1604, but before he modified his initial attempt to derive it from a false principle, about 1609, he turned back to the study of medieval writings for assistance. But did these writings assist in leading him to the correct law *before* 1604? The prevailing view is that long before that time, Galileo was already familiar with the Merton Rule (or mean-degree theorem) and that he used it repeatedly throughout his career.

This view has its basis in three grounds. First, there is the general continuity principle in the history of ideas: it is said that the doctrine of the latitude of forms, developed in the Middle

Ages, had become an integral part of university education before Galileo entered Pisa. Second, there exists a philosophical treatise in Galileo's own hand, dating from his student days (1584, to be precise), that mentions the doctrine and the names of several medieval authors who discussed it. Third, there is a formal resemblance between the diagram used in the 1604 fragment and diagrams employed previously in unpublished discussions of the Merton Rule. Taken together, these grounds seem very convincing in favor of the prevailing view, particularly when it is added that the Merton Rule seems to lie at the very basis of Galileo's ultimate presentation of his law of falling bodies in 1638. When these grounds are taken separately, however, it will be seen that each alone is highly provisional and may ultimately be rejected.

As to the first, there is no question that the doctrine of the latitude of forms, as developed in the fourteenth century, had a deep and continuing interest to philosophers up to the beginning of the sixteenth century. The mean-speed theorem was printed and reprinted several times between 1490 and 1515. After that time, however, it was not reprinted again during the sixteenth century in Italy. After 1530 there was in Italy a general drift of interest away from medieval writings toward those of classical antiquity on the one hand, and toward contemporary authors on the other. During the half-century that elapsed between the last printing of the Merton Rule in Italy and Galileo's matriculation at Pisa, mere lip service to great medieval writers may have replaced the serious study of their works.

As to the second point, there is good reason to believe that the 1584 treatise in Galileo's hand was not his own production, but was either a set of dictated lectures or his copy of a manuscript treatise composed by a professor. The virtual absence of changes and the nature of the relatively few corrections, coupled with the vast number of authorities cited, suggest such an origin. In any event, the treatise is by no means conclusive proof that Galileo himself had read the works of all the authorities mentioned in it, who number more than one hundred.

As to the formal resemblance in diagrams, this is not matched by any resemblance in the demonstrations based on them, nor does any representation of mean speed, essential to Merton Rule diagrams, appear in Galileo's works. Diagrams virtually identical with those of the letter to Sarpi and the 1604 fragment will be found in Michael Varro's *De motu tractatus* of 1584, a work devoid of any connection with the Merton Rule. The use of a line to represent distances and of triangles to represent proportionality is not in itself sufficient evidence on which to base a case for a common source. Differences in aim and viewpoint militate against such a source.

Essential to the ideas of the Merton School writers was the concept that in uniform acceleration, "the motion as a whole will be as fast, categorematically, as some uniform motion according to some degree of velocity contained in the latitude being acquired, and likewise, it will be as slow."[11] The determination of such a degree—a single value by means of which an overall uniform change might be represented—constituted the Merton Rule, or mean-degree theorem, which stated that to the midpoint in time corresponded the mean degree in uniformly difform change. To represent a set of changing velocities, medieval writers took a single velocity, chosen from within that set, and the same in kind with every member of that set.

It is evident to us now that the comparison of two uniformly accelerated motions, or of two segments of a single such motion, could have been most simply carried out by utilizing the ratio of two means, each representing one of the motions and each being by definition the same kind of entity, capable thereby of forming a ratio. But that was not the procedure adopted by Galileo in 1604, after he had become convinced that acceleration was an essential and continuing phenomenon of actual falling bodies. The Merton Rule directly related instantaneous velocities, mean velocities, and times elapsed. Galileo related instantaneous velocities to spaces traversed, spaces traversed to sets of such velocities, elapsed times to such sets by their "contrary" relation to spaces traversed, and thereby, finally, times elapsed to spaces traversed. He did not assume the existence of a mean speed within the set, or attribute any property to a midpoint, temporal or spatial.

Even if we assume that as early as 1584 Galileo was familiar with the Merton Rule sufficiently to know that it applied to uniform acceleration, in which velocity increased proportionally to time, and that it made the mean speed correspond to the midpoint in time, we cannot reasonably maintain that he still remembered that rule in 1604. At that time he was convinced that the spaces traversed in equal times from rest were as the odd numbers commencing from unity, and that the successive distances from rest were as the squares of the times of fall. In attempting a mathematical proof of those convictions, he appears not to have tried the Merton Rule. Had he done so, the desired proof would have emerged at once. He told Sarpi that he had been unable to find an unquestionable principle on which to base a proof, and therefore had recourse to one that was merely physically probable; namely, that velocities increase in proportion to spaces traversed. This sounds as if he had tried to think of others, and makes it unlikely that among them he had remembered the Merton Rule and tried in vain to apply it, or to put the increase in velocity proportional to time.

The central role of the mean-speed concept for medieval mathematicians of motion and its total absence in the 1604 fragment are highly significant for the history of science. We merely miss the point when we attempt to make the Merton Rule the historical, as well as the logical, predecessor of the law of falling bodies. It is here as with impetus and inertia; medieval studies had prepared the way for recognition and acceptance of Galileo's physics, but they did not put it in his hands. It is a mistake to suppose that we can divine a man's ideas without paying attention to his precise words. I am not sure that Galileo ever used the expression "mean speed" (or "mean degree") in his life, though every medieval writer on the Merton Rule did. Nevertheless, English translators of the *Two New Sciences* put the expression in his mouth when he did not use it. For example, in Galileo's crucial first theorem on accelerated motion, they have him say ". . . a uniform speed whose value is the mean of the highest speed and the speed just before acceleration began," whereas Galileo said only, ". . . by a uniform motion whose degree of speed is as one-half to the highest and last degree of speed . . ." (*motu aequabili . . . cuius velocitatis gradus subduplus sit ad summum et ultimum gradum velocitatis*). The distinction may not be as trivial as it appears. What Galileo consistently presents only as a ratio, the medieval writers (and Galileo's translators) presented also as some kind of entity. There are reasons for the difference.

Generally, medieval writers were concerned with a specific

change from a definite *terminus a quo* to a definite *terminus ad quem,* in accordance with the Aristotelian concept of change. Philosophically, the determination of a single measure of overall change was the solution of their problem. The Merton Rule accomplished such a determination. It solved the problem not only for uniform acceleration from rest (change from its beginning), but also for change from any subsequent point to a definite *terminus ad quem.* It should be noted, however, that medieval writers solved this latter problem as a separate one, noting that such intermediate motions had their own means, but disclaiming the possibility of a general rule of proportionality. For like reasons they did not seek rules of proportionality for any change that had no *terminus ad quem.* Such a change was for Aristotelians a contradiction in terms; in the case of accelerated motion, it would lead to infinite speed. Proportionality was used by medieval writers to determine relations within a finite change; hence it tended to be confined by them to converging series.

Galileo cared little or nothing for the determination of a mean value as such, but he was deeply interested in proportionality in every form. It was his key to the discovery of physical relationships. (The mean proportional, not the arithmetic mean, became his specialty.) When he became convinced that the spaces in free fall progressed as 1, 3, 5, 7 . . . ad infinitum, he sought a general relationship of velocities, spaces, and times. It is perfectly true that the Merton Rule would have afforded a simple and direct path to the solution of that problem; it is also true that Galileo's ultimate solution at a later date coincided with that way and embraced that rule. Yet it is neither necessary nor even probable that he achieved either his first (incorrect) or his ultimate solution by means of applying the Merton Rule, in the sense of his having relied upon a past tradition for either solution. It is not necessary because there is more than one way to arrive at the same truth. It is not probable because of the chronological order in which his physical conclusions first appear, as well as because of fundamental differences in concepts and methods between mean-speed and velocity-ratio determinations as outlined above.

To sum up the stages of Galileo's thought on falling bodies to the end of 1604: He had begun, about 1590, with a causal explanation of speed of descent that related speed to the ratio of densities of the falling body and the medium. That ratio being constant, he supposed the speed to be essentially constant, and treated acceleration as a mere temporary event at the beginning of motion. Around 1602 he became aware of the fact that acceleration persisted throughout free fall and had to be taken into account. By 1604 he was convinced that the spaces fallen from rest were as the squares of the times, but assumed that the speeds increased in proportion to the distances fallen from rest, believing that he had proved the correct relationship from that assumption. He had not yet considered the growth of speed with time as a separate possibility since he was satisfied with his first attempted demonstration. He had just completed it when the nova of 1604 appeared, and for a time he was taken up with the controversies that arose over this celestial phenomenon. During the following summer he gave instruction to the young heir of the Medici family, later Cosimo II. He then composed his first book, dedicated to Cosimo, which dealt with the proportional compass. The plagiarism of this book led him into a legal action and the composition of another book against a pirating of his work, published in 1607. It is not surprising that nothing identifiable was done by Galileo concerning motion during this period.

It was probably during 1608 that Galileo turned his attention once again to problems of motion: at any rate, during the first half of 1609, he announced to the Roman mathematician, Luca Valerio, his intention of founding the science of motion on two propositions. From this it appears that he had been engaged in organizing his previous work, extending it, and preparing a systematic treatment of it for a book. A series of undated fragments regarding motion, preserved in Codex A of the Galilean manuscripts at Florence, may therefore be ascribed principally to the period beginning about 1608 and continuing, at broken intervals, up to 1635 or thereabouts. The problem of establishing a chronological order for these fragments, in order to retrace Galileo's steps, is simplified by the fact that the great bulk of them are fairly sophisticated and show a clear understanding of uniform acceleration, whereas we are concerned only with the smaller number that belong to the period before that understanding was completely achieved. Again, among the latter are some that are evidently associated with work done before 1602, and these do not bear on questions of acceleration at all. It is with the intermediate group that we are concerned.

First comes a proof, written in Latin, that is essentially identical with the fallacious demonstration composed in Italian in 1604.[12] This Latin version is not in Galileo's handwriting and is canceled by two crossed lines. The hand is that of Mario Guiducci, who did not meet Galileo until 1614, so the copy cannot be earlier than that year. The demonstration, however, is almost certainly one composed by Galileo in 1608–9 when he was preparing his book on the science of motion.

Another fragment of great importance begins with the words *Cum enim assumptum sit . . .* , and from its content it is evident that the words refer to the asumption contained in the demonstration copied by Guiducci.[13] This fragment is in Galileo's hand, and deals with a proof that the times of motion along the vertical and along an inclined plane of the same height are in the ratio of those lengths. This document is of considerable importance in reconstructing and dating the development of Galileo's ideas.

Galileo had believed at first, when his attack on problems of motion was still based on the idea of cause, that the speeds (not the times) of motion on vertical and inclined planes must be in the above proportion. This notion was set forth in his unpublished *De motu* of 1590, with the rueful remark that the ratios were not observed in actual bodies.[14] After his recognition that acceleration must be considered, he was in a position to obtain the correct result embodied in the fragment under discussion. This he did by an analysis in terms of one-to-one correspondence between points on lines of differing length, and between intercepted segments of such lines. On the verso of the same sheet he undertook to prove the corollary that the speeds from rest to two different points in the vertical were as the squares of the distances fallen. But here the diagram is only partly lettered, and the attempted proof is abruptly broken off. Over it, as the document is preserved today, are pasted two slips of paper bearing in Galileo's hand two propositions of an entirely different nature, referring to the "moments of gravity" (a phrase related to Galileo's earliest work on motion) of bodies along the vertical and along inclined planes of the same height.

Now, on 5 June 1609 Galileo wrote to Luca Valerio to secure his opinion on the validity of introducing two propositions relating effective weight to speed as a basis for a new science of motion. Galileo's letter is lost, but Valerio's reply, dated 18 July 1609, makes possible the identification of the two propositions with those pasted over the abandoned demonstration mentioned above. Thus it is safe to date the fragment with the pasted slips as belonging to the early months of 1609, and to identify that fragment (and the demonstration later copied by Guiducci that must originally have immediately preceded it) with the systematic treatment of accelerated motion that Galileo was preparing in 1609.

The same fragment further affords strong evidence that it was during the early months of 1609 that Galileo first detected something seriously wrong in his attempted demonstration of 1604, and still did not abandon the false assumption on which he had based it. What he did instead was to substitute, for the corollary he had attempted to prove, two propositions of a dynamic character as a basis for reasoning about speeds in fall. It was concerning the validity of this maneuver that he wrote to Valerio.

The manner in which Galileo discovered the inapplicability of his previous reasoning to the speeds over different vertical spaces, without seeing instantly that he must abandon the idea of having (instantaneous) speeds proportional to those spaces, is extremely interesting in its bearing on his use of diagrams to represent physical variables. I have reconstructed the process in some detail elsewhere.[15] It appears to me that by mid-1609 Galileo had grasped the essential nature of an acceleration proportional to space traversed; namely, that it cannot allow continuous growth from rest, but that if we grant the slightest discontinuity at the very beginning of motion, it is in no way self-contradictory. All that one must give up is the concept of such acceleration as *uniform;* and it is of interest that in all the fragments under consideration, there is no mention of uniform acceleration, but only of "natural acceleration" or of "accelerated motion." Quite possibly Galileo entertained the view for a time that natural acceleration is not quite mathematically uniform, in the above sense. Such a view would explain the fact of Guiducci's having copied, as late as 1614 (and his copy may be of even later date), a demonstration of Galileo's that still assumed increase of speed proportional to space traversed.

In any case, astronomy once more intervened at a crucial moment to interrupt Galileo's investigation of motion. Just as the nova of 1604 had appeared on the very day that Galileo sent the earlier letter to Sarpi, so the news of the newly invented Dutch telescope reached Galileo's ears in the very same month that he was awaiting a reply from Valerio. From July 1609 to an undetermined later date Galileo was occupied with the duplication and improvement of the new instrument, with astronomical observations, with a change of position from Padua to Florence, and with controversies over floating bodies, sunspots, and other matters unconnected with the mathematics of motion. Hence the most that can be done with the ensuing fragments is to put them in a plausible order, without attempting to give them any precise dating.

The next development appears to have been the derivation of the double-distance rule for uniform motion following accelerated motion from rest.[16] The fragment containing this derivation proceeds also to apply it to the proposition that Galileo had already proved before he wrote to Valerio; namely, that the times of motion along inclined planes are as their lengths. Here it is of interest that Galileo makes no assumption concerning a mean speed, nor does he draw completely the triangular diagram associated with the medieval mean-speed theorem.

The long delay in any reference by Galileo to the double-distance rule is significant. That rule is not to be found in the 1604 letter or demonstration, nor in the Latin version of his similar demonstration of 1608–9. Yet it is a very simple rule to state, and it is even more comprehensible and impressive to the nonmathematician than the times-squared rule sent to Sarpi and embodied in those documents. I can only surmise that Galileo was not yet aware of the double-distance rule by 1609, and consequently that he was still oblivious to the medieval corpus of works in which that very rule was given for uniform change.

In the fragment just discussed, we find also a new proof of the proportionality of times along vertical and inclined planes (of equal height) to their lengths. This proof utilizes the mean-proportional relation for times of fall from rest to different points, embodied in the Latin version of the 1604 demonstration. The mean-proportional relation is of course a direct consequence of the times-squared relation; it has no direct and evident relation to the mean-speed concept.

Another fragment that seems to be of about the same date is

the first to state, in flat contradiction with the demonstration of 1609, that the overall speeds of falling bodies are as the square roots, and not as the squares, of the distances fallen.[17] But no proof is offered, nor is there any notation to indicate either Galileo's joy at a new discovery or his recognition at last of the proportionality of increase of speed to elapsed time. The accompanying diagram suggests the manner in which the proposition first occurred to Galileo, because it represents accelerated motions separated from any consideration of instantaneous velocities, but associated with times of fall. It is probable that Galileo himself did not at once perceive the full import of this proposition, which, coupled with his long-standing knowledge of the times-squared rule, would at last put the speeds directly proportional to the times. At the same time it would clearly contradict any lingering idea that an accelera-tion could exist in which proportionality both to space and to time could be indifferently applied.

Finally there is a fragment containing a memorandum that I am inclined to date as belonging to 1615, though hesitantly. It reads as follows:

> The spaces [covered] in accelerated motion from rest and the spaces in uniform motion following accelerated motions, and made in the same times, maintain the same ratio between them; the latter spaces are doubles of the former. The times, however, and the velocities acquired, have the same ratio between them; this ratio is the square root of the ratio of the said spaces.[18]

This at last summarizes all the correct ideas. It embodies a concept that Galileo imparted orally to G. B. Baliani in 1615, and it has the appearance not of the record of some new development, but of a summary of earlier results, such as one often jots down upon resuming a previous inquiry that was left unfinished. Quite possibly it belongs to 1616, after Galileo had been silenced by the Church on astronomy; this would be a reasonable time for him to have returned to his studies of motion. It is also possible that the Guiducci copy mentioned earlier belongs to the years 1616–20; if so, the fragment cited above would be of still later date. But I doubt this, largely because of the Baliani communication.

In any event, this fragment ends the intermediate period and opens that of the more sophisticated notes, most of which appeared in some form in Galileo's *Two New Sciences.* In the whole process up to this point I find no trace of any use of the concept of a mean speed, but only of ratios and of one-to-one correspondences. Galileo's ultimate discovery of the essential difference between putting speeds in acceleration proportional to space and relating them to time emerged as a result of conclusions that Galileo could not doubt and therefore felt obliged to reconcile; not as a result of his having explored first one alternative and then the other. It is my considered opinion that during all this time, they never appeared to him as truly alternatives at all; as we shall see, he ultimately admitted candidly that he long thought them to be equivalent and mutually compatible.

Galileo's ultimate published rejection of the proportionality of speed in actual fall to the spaces traversed from rest has been widely misunderstood for two reasons. First, it has generally been discussed apart from the context that precedes it; and second, the context in which it has been discussed in modern times is that of a knowledge of physics and a theory of history so deeply rooted as to induce us to alter Galileo's own words inadvertently. For we shall see translators into different languages agreeing in a mistranslation, from which it is clear that strong prepossessions are at work.

Alexandre Koyré, seeking the true meaning of Newton's *Hypotheses non fingo,* had occasion to remark of its English and French translators: "As the Italian proverb has it, *traduttore-traditore* (translators are traitors). . . . They did not limit themselves to translating; they made an 'interpretation,' and in so doing gave to Newton's assertion a sense that was not Newton's sense."[19]

Koyré was perhaps too severe with the offenders. Real difficulties exist in translation; not only the translator's prepossessions, but what he regards as common knowledge, will enter into the product. A striking illustration is provided by Koyré's own rendition of a passage from Galileo's *Two New Sciences*—a passage of considerable historical significance and one that has been the subject of dispute from the time of its original publication in 1638 down to the present. Koyré's translation in 1939 was even more defective than the English of 1914 or the German of 1891. It read:

> *Lorsque la vitesse à la même proportion que les espaces franchis ou à franchir, ces espaces seront franchis en temps*

égaux. Car si la vitesse avec laquelle le grave franchit l'espace de quatre coudées était double de la vitesse avec laquelle il a franchi les deux premiers, etc.[20]

The English translation of a quarter-century earlier at least preserved the initial plural noun, in accordance with Galileo's invariable treatment of all such measures as ratios:

> If the velocities are in proportion to the spaces traversed, or to be traversed, then those spaces are traversed in equal intervals of time; if, therefore, the velocity with which the falling body traverses a space of eight feet were double that with which it covered the first four feet (just as the one distance is double the other) then the time-intervals required for these passages would be equal. But for one and the same body to fall eight feet and four feet in the same time is possible only in the case of instantaneous [discontinuous] motion; but observation shows us that the motion of a falling body occupies time, and less of it in covering a distance of four feet than of eight feet; therefore it is not true that its velocity increases in proportion to the space.[21]

The German translation, two decades earlier still, was virtually identical with the English:

> *Wenn die Geschwindigkeiten proportional den Fallstrecken wären, die zurückgelegt worden sind oder zurückgelegt werden sollen, so werden solche Strecken in gleichen Zeiten zurückgelegt; wenn also die Geschwindigkeit, mit welcher der Körper vier Ellen überwand, das doppelte der Geschwindigkeit sein solle, mit welcher die zwei ersten Ellen. . . .*[22]

Thus all modern readers of this text, except perhaps some who have used the original Italian, are likely to have received the impression that pervades all recent discussions of it. Even those using the Italian may have had the same prepossessions as the three translators cited, and hence the same impression. That impression is that Galileo, in his published argument against proportionality of velocity to space traversed in uniform acceleration, relied on some concept of *average* speed in free fall, and made the naïve assumption that such *average* speed would obey the rule applying to uniform motion. Under that impression, many historians have advanced reconstructions of Galileo's thought in which he is supposed to have known and misapplied the Merton Rule.[23] This in turn has strengthened the widespread conviction that the historical inspiration behind Galileo's law of falling bodies was his study of certain medieval writings.

But the original wording shows that whatever the reasoning was that Galileo relied on in this argument, it had nothing to do with a mean-speed comparison, nor did it rely on the application of any theorem derived from the analysis of uniform motion. Galileo's own words were:

> *Quando le velocità hanno la medesima proporzione che gli spazii passati o da passarsi, tali spazii vengon passati in tempi eguali: se dunque le velocità con le quali il cadente passò lo spazio di quattro braccia, furon doppie delle velocità con le quali passò le due prime (si come lo spazio è doppio dello spazio)....*[24]

That is to say:

> If the velocities have the same ratio as the spaces passed or to be passed, those spaces come to be passed in equal times: thus if the velocities with which the falling body passed the space of four *braccia* were doubles of the velocities with which it passed the first two (as the space is double the space)....

Although the word *velocità* remains the same in Italian whether singular or plural, the definite articles, verb forms, and relative pronouns here leave no doubt that Galileo meant the plural. The first use of "doubles" is also plural (*doppie*), unlike the second "double" (*doppio*).Very early English translations by Salusbury (1665) and Weston (1730) correctly gave the plural "velocities," but for *doppie* reverted to a singular. The anonymous Latin translator of 1699, however, preserved *all* the plurals of Galileo's Italian.

It is hardly a mere coincidence that all three early translators were almost perfectly faithful to Galileo's precise wording, while their three modern counterparts agreed almost completely in ignoring that wording. The modern translators were so well informed about the truths of physics that Galileo's strange syntax did not attract their attention. In the case of Koyré, scientific knowledge was reinforced by a philosophical prepossession that is of no small importance to the present state of opinion regarding Galileo's thought. What Galileo said was trivial to Koyré; the important thing was what he must have meant. But Koyré's treason to Galileo was loyalty to a higher cause; it was at worst a feat of legerdemain, of *traduttore-tragitore*. His fault was that of excessive knowledge, even greater than that of his German and English counterparts. The virtue of the early translators was that of scientific and historical ignorance, a state in which it was best to let Galileo speak for himself.

As previously remarked, the disputed passage has customarily been examined not only in mistranslation, but also out of context. It lent itself to the latter treatment because the rejection of space-proportionality was presented by Galileo as a "clear proof" in a single long sentence. It is easy to jump to a conclusion about what it is that was to be proved, something that may much better be determined by reading carefully the discussions that precede and follow the passage in question. Here I shall merely summarize that context, but the reader is urged to examine it carefully for himself.

Salviati has begun by reading, from a Latin treatise of Galileo's, the definition of uniform acceleration as "that in which equal increments of velocity are added in equal times." There follows a lengthy discussion of another matter, the relevance of which will be pointed out below. Returning to the definition, Sagredo suggests that its fundamental idea will remain unchanged, but will be made clearer, by substituting "equal spaces" for "equal times." To this he adds an assertion that in actual fall, velocity grows with space traversed. Salviati replies that he once held the same view, and that Galileo himself had formerly subscribed to it, but that he had found both propositions to be false and impossible.

Now, it is universally believed that Salviati was here asserting that the *definition* of uniform acceleration in terms of equal space-increments was false and impossible, implying in it an internal contradiction. His words, however, do not support such a view. Sagredo's two propositions are (*a*) that there is no fundamental difference between relating velocity in uniform acceleration to time and relating it to space, and (*b*) that in actual fall, speed is in fact proportional to space traversed from rest. Salviati is thus obliged to show Sagredo that those two propositions are false and impossible.

But at this point, Simplicio intervenes to assert *his* belief that (*c*) an actual falling body does acquire velocity in proportion to space traversed, and that (*d*) double velocity is acquired by an actual body in fall from a doubled height. Nothing is said by Simplicio about the definition of uniform acceleration, nor does he overtly deny that doubled time of fall would equally produce doubled velocity. Both of Simplicio's assertions are restricted to material falling bodies; he asserts first that their speeds are proportional to distances traversed, and second that this is a simple geometric proportionality.

It is to Simplicio, not Sagredo, that Salviati replies with the disputed argument, which he prefaces with the words, "and yet [your two propositions] are as false and impossible as that motion should be completed instantaneously, and here is a very clear proof of it." Thus if we pay attention to the logical structure of Galileo's book, the proof in question relates only to actual falling bodies, and that is why it invokes observation as a step. Salviati's answer to Sagredo is by no means completed after that proof. In order to satisfy Sagredo, Salviati still must show that there is a difference in the consequences that flow from time-proportionality, and that those consequences *are* compatible with the observed phenomena of actual falling bodies. That Galileo is perfectly aware of all this is shown by the fact that the additional steps are carried out, in an orderly manner, in his ensuing pages. That part of the discussion, however, does not concern us here.

Let us instead examine Galileo's argument, correctly translated, in the hope of discovering his line of thought.

> If the velocities [passed through] have the same ratio as the spaces passed or to be passed, those spaces come to be passed in equal times: thus if [all] the [instantaneous] velocities with which the falling body passed the space of four *braccia* were [respectively the] doubles of those with which it passed the first two *braccia* (as one distance is double the other), then the times required for these passages [over the spaces named] would be equal.

No diagram accompanies this statement, and none has preceded it. Galileo expects his readers (indeed, his imaginary auditors) to grasp his meaning without a diagram. If he wanted them to conceive of and compare mean speeds, he would have had to introduce and to illustrate that concept. Instead, he called their attention to all the varying velocities with which the falling body moved, not to any uniform velocity that might represent this totality. If the plural "velocities" leaves any doubt on that score, the plural "doubles" removes it. Salviati did not slip inadvertently into the unusual and rather awkward plurals; they were essential to his argument, and he stressed them. If each conceivable velocity passed through in the whole descent is the double of some velocity passed through in the first half of the descent, then there is no way of accounting for any change in the time required for one descent as against the other. That is all there is to his argument. The first statement does not invoke a rule for comparing uniform motions, as is generally believed; the phrase "or to be passed" can only refer to continuing acceleration from rest. The opening words simply state in general terms what the balance of the passage applies to Simplicio's numerical exemplification.

But how many velocities are meant in each case by the deliberate plurals? The answer to that question had been given in the long discussion that intervenes between the definition of uniform acceleration and the argument with which we have been concerned. The relevance of that discussion becomes apparent only when the above argument is correctly understood; I, at any rate, regarded it as one of Galileo's habitual digressions, made to keep things interesting, as long as I accepted the general view that Galileo had erred in his "clear proof." Let us review that discussion.

Sagredo and Simplicio had at once objected to Galileo's definition on the grounds that it could not apply to real bodies, for it would require them to pass through an infinite number of speeds in a finite time. Salviati pointed out that this is in fact possible, because the body need not (indeed, cannot) remain at any one velocity for a finite time. He satisfied them that there could thus be infinitely many velocities in any uniformly accelerated motion, however small. That concept was fresh in the minds of Galileo's hearers when he spoke to them of the doubles of all the velocities in the whole motion as compared with those in its first half. No diagram was necessary for them, nor was any diagram appropriate to Galileo's meaning. The conception he desired was inescapable— or so Galileo thought. Removed from its context, it nevertheless seems to have escaped nearly everyone who analyzed the passage.

The single exception known to me is J. A. Tenneur, who in 1649 intervened in a dispute over this very point. His conception of Galileo's argument was this:

> If possible, let the heavy body fall [from rest] through two equal spaces AB and BC so that its speed at C has become double that which it had at B. Certainly, under the hypothesis, there is no point in the line AC at which its speed is not double that at the homologous point in the line AB. . . . Therefore the speed through all AC was double the speed through all AB, just as the space AC is double the space AB: therefore AC and AB are traversed in equal times.[25]

Tenneur had grasped the essential clue from Galileo's plurals, as shown in the second sentence above. If in the final sentence Tenneur reverted to the singular for each overall speed, instead of comparing the spaces and times for the infinite assemblages directly, as Galileo did, it was not a fault in this case, for he did not substitute any particular value, or assume any particular rule of "compounding," for it. That he understood Galileo's reasoning exactly is shown by his further argument, omitted here, based (like Galileo's) on the idea of one-to-one correspondence.

The absence of a diagram is also characteristic of the medieval writers, but their arguments began with the assumption of a representative single value within the set of speeds. Galileo's argument in the *Two New Sciences* needed only the notion of one-to-one correspondence between two infinite aggregates. That concept had already been developed earlier in the same book.[26] Thus Salviati's reply to Simplicio refers to no single speed and may be properly paraphrased thus:

> If all the infinite instantaneous velocities occurring in actual accelerated fall from rest over any finite space, say one of four *braccia*, were the respective doubles of all the infinite velocities occurring over the first half, or two *braccia*, of the same fall, then no difference in the times of fall could be accounted for. But we observe a difference in the times; hence proportionality of speed to space traversed from rest cannot govern the fall of actual bodies.

In this there is no appeal to the correct definition of uniform acceleration, or to any of its consequences; neither is any contradiction asserted to exist within the correct law for falling bodies, which is merely shown to be in conflict with experience. Nor is there any illicit use of a rule restricted to uniform motion, as suggested by writers from the time of Tenneur's opponent to our own day.

Sagredo's opinion that it is a matter of indifference whether time or space be taken as the measure of velocity-increments in uniform acceleration has important historical implications. One might suppose it to have been introduced merely to enliven the dialogue. In that case, however, it would scarcely have been necessary to have Salviati admit that he had once accepted the notion, and still less so for Galileo to acknowledge publicly his own former misapprehension. The purpose of diversion would be as well served by having Simplicio offer the incorrect definition as a rival to the correct one, and state that one must be false if the other was true. Instead we have Sagredo, who is never the spokesman for foolish positions, asserting that he believes the two to be equivalent. Salviati's admission that he had once believed this, to say nothing of Galileo's similar admission in print, show that the view was widely held and needed refutation. What is important about Galileo's admission is that it concerns not just the idea of space-proportionality, but also the idea of its equivalence to time-proportionality.

Inability to believe that the two could ever have been considered equivalent is so natural to us that we tend to impute one view or the other to Galileo's predecessors. We note that the Merton School writers (and Oresme) put velocity in uniform acceleration proportional to time, while many Peripatetics (and Tartaglia) put speed in free fall proportional to space. Soto gave free fall as a case of uniform acceleration. All these things are true, but they do not imply (as we are likely to think) that any one of these views was regarded as contradicting another.

Sagredo's assumption seems to have been universally adopted up to the time of Galileo. It reflects this kind of reasoning: "Space and time are both measures of velocity, so they must be proportional to each other with respect to velocity. Acceleration is merely increase of velocity, and if uniform acceleration is proportional either to spaces traversed or times elapsed, it must thereby be proportional also to the other. Since it is easier to think of equal spaces than equal times, it is more sensible to say that in uniform acceleration increases in proportion to spaces traversed. But if anyone prefers to relate it to times, there is no reason he should not do so." No one worked out the "proportion" for space, and only the "average" had been worked out for time.

The Merton Rule writers, who were quite specific in using time as the measure of uniform difform motion, were in fact discussing change in general, of which local motion was only a special case. The Merton Rule is really a general mean-degree theorem, not just a mean-speed theorem. Looked at in that way, it is clear that the existence of that rule did not automatically call attention to a problem of changing speed any more than to a problem of changing heat, or redness, or any other variable quality. Thus Albert of Saxony could remark that in free fall the speed grew with the growing spaces traversed, and at the same time he could know that the Merton Rule was valid for all changes with respect to time, without his perceiving any contradiction.

Had the possibility of a contradiction been perceived, one would expect it to have been raised as a question in at least some of the many commentaries on Aristotle's *Physics* written in *quaestio-dubitatio-responsio* form. At least some writers of such commentaries may be presumed to have been familiar with both views and to have been fond of disputation; yet they did not pose the question "Whether velocity increases in a falling body in proportion to distance or to time." The right answer to that question first appeared in 1545, when Domingo de Soto linked free fall to the Merton Rule, but in producing the answer he did not ask the question. In using free fall to exemplify the Merton Rule, it is likely that he also considered this linkage compatible with space-proportionality in free fall, since he did not contradict that popular opinion.

The first person known to have both asked and answered the question was Galileo. To clarify the previous confusion was precisely his purpose when he introduced the question in the *Two New Sciences,* where he also candidly confessed that it had long escaped his attention.

Notes to Essay 11

1. "Galileo's 1604 Fragment on Falling Bodies," *British Journal for the History of Science*, IV, 4 (December, 1969), 340–58; "Uniform Acceleration, Space, and Time," *BJHS*, V, 1 (June, 1970), 21–43.
2. See essay 5.
3. *Opere*, X, 97–100.
4. I. E. Drabkin and S. Drake, *Galileo on Motion and on Mechanics* (Madison, 1960), p. 85; *Opere*, I, 315.
5. *Opere*, X, 115. Full translations of the letters mentioned and of Galileo's attempted demonstration are contained in the first paper cited in note 1 above.
6. Galileo assumed increase of speed proportional to distance; they assumed increase proportional to time.
7. Contrary to the opinion of Alexandre Koyré, the experiments Galileo described in his *Two New Sciences* were quite adequate to verify the law; see Thomas Settle, "An Experiment in the History of Science," *Science*, 133 (1961), 19–23.
8. It is natural to object that such an observation, even if carefully prepared and carried out, would never accurately give 1–3–5–7. This is true, but beside the point. The question here being one of discovery, and not of verification, it is sufficient to describe some means by which the 1–3–5–7 law might have been suggested. A casual, even a careless measurement, using a string to represent the first interval as a unit, would here be an advantage to discovery. If careful measurement in some conventional unit gave the values 1.6, 5.4, 8.2, 11.3 for distances moved by a cannonball down a marble slab, no numerical relation would automatically suggest itself to a person interested only in the continuance of increase; but a string of length 1.7 would promptly answer 1–3–5–7 as a probable rule. With any rule once in mind, refinements for its verification would quickly suggest themselves.
9. Many progressions can be found that will fill the condition, such as 1–7–19–37–61 . . . , but not other uniform (arithmetic) progressions. Christian Huygens, as a young man, used similar reasoning to derive the odd-number rule for uniform acceleration and to exclude all geometrical progressions.
10. G. B. Baliani to B. Castelli, *Opere*, XIII, 348. The letter was written in 1627, but Baliani's only conversations with Galileo had occurred in 1615.

11. M. Clagett, *Science of Mechanics in the Middle Ages* (Madison, 1959), p. 271. The passage cited is from Heytesbury.

12. *Opere*, VIII, 383.

13. *Opere*, VIII, 388.

14. Drabkin and Drake, *op. cit.*, pp. 68–69; *Opere*, I, 301–2.

15. In the second paper cited in note 1 above.

16. *Opere*, VIII, 383–84.

17. *Opere*, VIII, 380.

18. *Opere*, VIII, 387.

19. A. Koyré, *Newtonian Studies* (Cambridge, Mass., 1965), p. 36.

20. A. Koyré, *Etudes Galiléennes* (Paris, 1939), II, 98, note 2. A new French translation of Galileo's book, published in 1970, repeats Koyré's mistake in this passage.

21. *Two New Sciences*, trans. H. Crew and A. De Salvio (New York, 1914, and later eds.), p. 168.

22. *Unterredungen und mathematische Demonstrationen*, trans. A. von Oettingen (Leipzig, 1891, and later eds.), II, 16–17.

23. See, for example, A. Koyré, *Etudes Galiléennes*, II, 95–99; I. B. Cohen, "Galileo's Rejection of the Possibility of Velocity Changing Uniformly with Respect to Distance," *Isis*, 47 (1956), 231–35; A. R. Hall, "Galileo's Fallacy," *Isis*, 49 (1958), 342–46; *Discorsi*, ed. A. Carugo and L. Geymonat (Torino, 1958), pp. 776–78.

24. *Opere*, VIII, 203.

25. J. A. Tenneur, *De motu accelerato* (Paris, 1649), p. 8. Tenneur employed a diagram designed to refute his opponent, but for the purpose of this argument a single vertical line AC, bisected at B, suffices. The deduction of Huygens (note 9 above), was first published in Tenneur's book.

26. *Two New Sciences*, pp. 31–33.

I 2

Galileo and
the Concept of Inertia

The origin of the law of inertia, and Galileo's role in it, involve questions more intricate than is generally supposed, being still subjects of study and debate today. And there are few questions more fascinating in the whole history of physics. One need only try to conceive of a science of physics without the concept of inertia in order to perceive that the introduction of this fundamental notion must have produced a revolution in physical thought as profound as any that have occurred since. One can then hardly fail to wonder who it was that introduced this idea, and how it came to occur to him. I shall try to indicate roughly the part that Galileo played in this great revolution in physical thought.

Newton implied in his *Principia* that Galileo, being in possession of the first two laws of motion, thereby discovered that the descent of falling bodies varied as the square of the elapsed time.[1] Historically, and biographically with regard to Galileo, this remark leaves much to be desired, though it is interesting autobiographically; that is, as a clue to Newton's own source of the concept of inertia and to his method of thought. Because Newton easily perceived that the law of free fall followed directly from a correct understanding of his first two laws together with the assumption that gravity exerted a constant force, it was natural for him to assume that his great Italian predecessor had actually made these discoveries in that orderly fashion. In point of fact, however, Galileo arrived at the law of free fall long before he gave any explicit statement of his restricted law of inertia, and though he was first to recognize the true physical significance of acceleration, he never did formulate the force law. With Galileo's law of free fall, as with Kepler's laws of planetary motion, Newton was able to produce mathematical derivations and demonstrations of results that his predecessors had derived only from long study of sometimes chaotic observational data, assisted by flashes of insight rather than by mathematical or even logical deduction. It is interesting that Galileo had already perceived this to be the normal order of events in science; in reference to one of Aristotle's ideas and its proof, he wrote:

> I think it certain that he first obtained this by means of his senses, by experiments and observations . . . and afterwards sought means of proving it. This is what is usually done in the demonstrative sciences. . . . You may be sure that Pythagoras, long before he discovered the proof for which he sacrificed a hecatomb, was sure that in a right triangle the square on the hypotenuse was equal to the squares on the other two sides. The certainty of a conclusion assists not a little in the discovery of its proof.[2]

The historical question is whether and to what extent Galileo is entitled to credit for the anticipation of Newton's first law of motion. Technical priority for the first complete statement of the law of inertia belongs to Descartes, who published it in 1644, two years after Galileo's death, supported by a philosophical argument. But if Galileo never stated the law in its general form, it was implicit in his derivation of the parabolic trajectory of a projectile, and it was clearly stated in a restricted form (for motion in the horizontal plane) many times in his works. A modern physicist reading Galileo's writings would share the puzzlement—I might say the frustration—experienced by Ernst Mach a century ago, when he searched those works in vain for the general statement that (he felt) ought to be found there. It would become evident to him, as it did to Newton and Mach, that Galileo was in possession of the law of inertia, but he would not then be able to satisfy those historians who demand a clear and complete statement, preferably in print, as a condition of priority.

To physicists, if not to historians, it is ironical that this particular law should be credited to Descartes, whose physics on the whole operated to impede the line of scientific progress begun by Galileo and continued by Newton. They both possessed in a high degree one special faculty that Descartes lacked; that is, the faculty of thinking correctly about physical problems as such, and not always confusing them with related mathematical or philosophical

problems. It is a faculty rare enough still, though much more frequently encountered today than it was in Galileo's time, if only
because nowadays we all cope with mechanical devices from childhood on. In Galileo's day, thinking was not continually brought to
bear in this (or any other) way on mere physical processes. There
were of course skilled technicians, craftsmen, and engineers, but
their impressive achievements had been derived rather from the
accumulation of practice and tradition than by the deductive solution of physical problems. Thinkers as a class, then comprising
roughly the university population, were concerned mainly with
medicine, law, theology, and philosophy. Formal instruction in
physics consisted largely in the exposition of Aristotle.

A cardinal tenet of Aristotle's physics was that any moving
body must have a mover other than itself, and since this notion also
appeals to experience and common sense, it stood as a formidable
obstacle to the discovery of the principle of inertia. It was difficult,
of course, to explain under Aristotle's rule the continuance of motion in objects pushed or thrown. The first man to override that
rule and to suggest that a force might be impressed on a body, and
endure in it for some time without an outside mover, was probably
Hipparchus. This idea was developed and advocated by Johannes
Philoponus, a brilliant sixth-century commentator on Aristotle.
During the Middle Ages a few daring philosophers developed this
thesis further into the concept of *impetus,* largely in opposition to
antiperistasis, an idea mentioned (though not clearly accepted) in
two forms by Aristotle. This was the view that the separate mover
for a projectile is the medium through which it travels. Aristotle
preferred the form in which it is supposed that the mover of the
object imparts to the medium the power of continuing its motion.
In the other form, the argument was this: As a body moves, it
tends to create a vacuum in its wake; since nature abhors a vacuum,
the surrounding medium rushes in, striking the object from behind
and thus impelling it further. It is easy to see why the theory of
impetus gained ground against that of antiperistasis—which was
ridiculed by Galileo, incidentally, in virtually the same manner as
that which we should employ today. After his time little more was
heard of it, or of the medieval impetus theories that had never
entirely succeeded in displacing it.

From the end of the nineteenth century until recent years,

historians of science tended to regard Galileo's inertial concept as a natural and logical outgrowth of medieval impetus theory. That view is now undergoing review and modification, thanks to a more careful analysis of the actual writings of medieval philosophers, as well as to the complete accessibility of Galileo's own papers, including his long unpublished early studies on motion and mechanics. Indeed, if inertia were nothing more than a simple and logical outgrowth of impetus theory, developed and debated over a period of several centuries by astute philosophers, then this outgrowth might be expected to have developed much earlier in the game as a way out of various difficulties inherent in impetus theory that conservative Aristotelians had always been quick to point out. The belief that inertia grew naturally out of an earlier theory was plausible, as we shall see, but turns out to have been historically unsound. It is at best a half-truth, and as Mark Twain said, a half-truth is like a half-brick; it is more effective than the whole thing because it carries further. I shall try to put matters in a new perspective by explaining the sense in which impetus theory opened a road for acceptance of the law of inertia, though it did not thereby suggest that law, and by indicating the steps that Galileo actually took in arriving at his concept of inertia, which went along a quite different road.

Aristotle's idea that every motion requires a moving force, and ceases when that force stops acting, appeals to common sense because it is roughly borne out by experience. In most cases the relatively short persistence of motion in an object after the propelling action has ceased is not nearly so impressive as the effort required to set or even to keep the object in motion. Perhaps that is why many philosophers did not feel the need of any stronger force to account for it than some fanciful action of the medium. But there were other continued motions which could not be explained in that way at all; for example, that of a grindstone. This not only persisted in free rotation for a long time, but strongly resisted efforts to stop it, and in such cases no explanation in terms of a push from air rushing into any vacated space could apply. That in turn suggested that circular motions might be exceptions to Aristotle's dictum, an idea that fitted in rather well with his general scheme of things in which perfection and a variety of special physical properties were attributed to circles and circular motions of various kinds. This scheme had helped Aristotle to explain the motion of the heavenly bodies. For him, the earth was at absolute rest in the center of the universe, and the only motions appropriate to earthly bodies were straight motions up and down. Circular motion, being perfect, belonged naturally to the perfect heavenly bodies. To the fixed stars, Aristotle assigned a special source of motion called the Prime Mover. In later times some attempt was made to explain their regular rotation by analogy to the grindstone, since the stars had then come to be considered as embedded in a solid transparent crystalline sphere. Thus, without great violence to Aristotelian orthodoxy, the conservation of angular momentum could be conceived as a natural phenomenon in which Aristotle's outside mover might be replaced by an impressed force, which normally wasted away with time or through external resistance. In the special case of the stars, loss of motion could still be offset by action of the Prime Mover, or eliminated by postulating the absence of resistance to motion in the heavens, as was done by several philosophers.

While the strictest Aristotelians continued to oppose any postulation of impressed forces, more enterprising philosophers went on to extend this concept to the case of projectile motion under the general name of *impetus*. Loss of impetus by projectiles was likened to other familiar phenomena requiring no special explanation, such as the diminution of sound in a bell after it is struck, or of heat in a kettle after it is removed from the fire, and this accorded with a further important rule of Aristotle's that nothing violent can be perpetual. Hence to the extent that impetus theory paved the way for eventual acceptance of the idea that motion might be perpetually conserved, it rested on a philosophical basis that inhibited the taking of that ultimate step. Not only was an indefinitely enduring impressed force unnecessary to experience, but it was ruled out in theory by Aristotle; and to reconcile a theory with Aristotle's opinions was at that time just as important as to reconcile it with experience. Thus impetus theory, given its philosophical context, did not lead on to inertial physics; rather, it precluded the need for that so long as physical judgments remained qualitative and were not replaced by quantitative measurements. And that brings us to the time of Galileo.[3]

It should be remarked in passing that no fundamental revolution in science takes place until the way has been paved, usually by vague or incorrect notions, for the acceptance of a radically new idea. Hence the new idea, when it comes, is very likely to have the appearance of a natural extension of the old ones. That is why it was perfectly plausible for historians of science to suppose, when medieval impetus theory was first brought to their attention, that the inertial concept had originally arisen as a natural outgrowth of that theory. And indeed, it might have arisen so, in a different philosophical context. But the actual road to the first announcement of the inertial principle, through its first physical application, was not the same road at all as the one which had led people to a point at which they would be able to accept the new idea of indelibly impressed motion as the limiting case of lingering impressed motion.

The most objective summary of the relation of medieval impetus theory to inertia in the sense of modern physics has been given by Miss Annaliese Maier, as follows:

> Thus the situation around 1600 was that impetus theory was taken over by the official scholastic philosophy as such. That of course does not mean that there were not isolated supporters of the Aristotelian theory; nor, on the other hand, does it mean that orthodox philosophy on its part stood against impetus theory and forbade it. And here it was expressly contrasted with the Aristotelian view and exhibited in the earlier way. Among those who still clung thus to impetus theory in the sixteenth century, and who for the rest opposed those who bore the Aristotelian stamp, belong Telesio, . . . Bruno, . . . Benedetti, . . . and finally Galileo. For them, impetus theory was mainly a polemic point against Aristotelianism. It was this group alone that Duhem took into consideration, and those who follow his view. The result was naturally a not entirely accurate picture of the factual historical situation. Impetus theory at the end of the sixteenth century was seen as a resumption of the great revolution in thought of the fourteenth century, that was just having its full weight and full influence against Aristotelianism; and it was further thought that the new mechanics had developed in a straight line out of that impetus theory. But that is not how things happened.[4]

Miss Maier goes on to say that whereas in impetus theory each motion impresses an inhering moving force on the body moved,

the inertial concept sees in uniform motion, as in rest, a state that
is conserved so long as it is undisturbed; whereas according to
impetus theory the moved body has an inclination to return to rest
and thus opposes the inhering force, according to the inertial concept the inclination in the case of uniform motion is to continue
with no resistance on the part of the body; and whereas impetus
theory would allow for an acting force in circular as well as
straight motion, the inertial concept postulates only a continuance
of the latter. This last point, she says, is of secondary importance;
the essential differences between the concepts of impetus and inertia
are the two first named, for these are in direct conflict with the
Aristotelian principle that everything moved requires some mover;
"and this contradiction is so sharp that the new thought could
develop not *out of* the old, but only *against* it."[5]

We may safely take Miss Maier's summary as definitive with
respect to the historical aspect of the relation between impetus
theory and the inertial concept. Grounded as it is on the most
thorough analysis of the writings of the scholastics and of modern
students of this problem, it comes as a welcome conclusion to a
series of controversies that related rather to the theory of history
than to the ostensible subject matter, and it is unlikely to be seriously modified by further investigations. But as to Miss Maier's
comments on the conceptual or philosophical aspects of the matter,
though I thoroughly agree with them, it must be admitted that they
are by their nature less apt to receive universal acceptance. The late
Professor Alexandre Koyré, for instance, took quite a different position; and though his main writings on the subject preceded those
of Miss Maier, I do not believe that he was inclined to modify them
after hers appeared. Here, for example, is an indication of his fundamental difference of opinion:

> Now, . . . if Galileo's dynamics is, at its deepest base,
> Archimedean and founded entirely on the notion of weight, it
> follows that Galileo could not formulate the principle of inertia.
> And he never did. In fact, in order to be able to do so—that is,
> in order to be able to affirm the eternal persistence not at all
> of movement in general, but of *rectilinear* movement; in order
> to be able to consider a body left to itself and *devoid of all
> support* as remaining at rest or continuing to move *in a straight
> line* and not *in a curved line*—he would have had to be able to

conceive the motion of fall not as natural motion at all, but on the contrary . . . as caused by an external force.

Thus, throughout the *Dialogue,* impetus is found identified with *moment,* with movement, with speed . . . successive glides [of meaning] that insensibly lead the reader to conceive of the paradox of motion conserving itself all alone in the moving body; of a speed "indelibly" impressed on the body in motion.

In principle, the privileged situation of circular movement is destroyed; it is movement as such that is conserved, and not circular motion. In principle; but, in fact, the *Dialogue* never goes so far. And as was said, we never glide, nor ever will, to the principle of inertia. Never; no more in the *Two New Sciences* than in the *Dialogue,* does Galileo affirm the eternal conservation of rectilinear motion.[6]

Clearly, to Professor Koyré it would by no means be acceptable to say that the third of Miss Maier's distinctions between impetus theory and the inertial concept is of secondary importance; for him, the limitation of the inertial concept to uniform rectilinear motions was every bit as important as the recognition of continuance in a state of rest or motion by a body otherwise undisturbed. Now, opinions will always differ concerning the aspects of any concept which are to be considered essential and those which are secondary or subordinate. My opinion, like Miss Maier's, is that the essential aspect of the concept of inertia is that of motion and rest as states of a body which are indifferently conserved. If the disagreement ended there, all would be well. But Professor Koyré went on to argue at length that because Galileo asserted that truly straight motions are impossible in nature, *only* circular motions could for him be really perpetuated, and hence that the inertial concept was inextricably linked in Galileo's own mind with privileged circular motions. The prevalence of this view is illustrated by the following passage from a work by Professor E. J. Dijksterhuis:

> The situation is thus as follows: according to the Galilean law of inertia proper, a particle that is free from external influences (note that gravity is not included among them) perseveres in a circular motion having the centre of the earth for its centre. Over short distances this motion is considered rectilinear; subsequently the limitation to short distances is forgotten,

and it is said that the particle would continue its rectilinear motion indefinitely on a horizontal plane surface if no external factors interfered. Thus what might be called the circular view of inertia of Galileo gradually developed into the conception that was formulated in the first law of Newton.[7]

The imputation to Galileo of a view in which all inertial motions are essentially circular, rather than one in which some cases of inertial motion are illustrated by bodies supported on a smooth sphere concentric with the earth, seems to me wrong; this aspect of the question is discussed in the final essay. The present problem is that of reconstructing the steps taken by Galileo in arriving at the views he held concerning conservation of motion by an examination of all his writings. If my reconstruction is correct, it has very different implications for the history of science than the prevailing opinion as expressed by Professors Koyré and Dijksterhuis. For the first clue to conservation of motion in Galileo's thought had nothing to do with the question of projectile motion, and circularity entered into it because of angular momentum rather than translatory motion.

During his first years as professor at the University of Pisa, Galileo wrote a treatise on motion that he intended to publish. In that treatise, which survives in manuscript, he attacked Aristotle boldly, often in favor of ideas originated by medieval philosophers. He opposed various Aristotelian notions about the role of the medium, including that of antiperistasis, but at the outset he adopted the Aristotelian division of all motions into "natural" and "violent" motions. This concept was, however, somewhat modified from Aristotle's in the definition adopted by Galileo for the dichotomy; he said, "There is natural motion when bodies, as they move, approach their natural places, and forced or violent motion when they recede from their natural places."[8]

Without going into detail, Aristotle's physics may be described as a theory of natural places, high for light bodies (fire and air), low for heavy bodies (earth and water). Bodies were supposed to seek these natural places by an occult property inherent in them. Galileo dissented from this view; for him, all bodies were heavy bodies and differed only in density, so all tended to approach the center of the universe, which at that time was for him the center of the earth.

But as he pursued this idea in his treatise on motion, he came to question whether all motions *were* either natural or violent. He perceived that a body might be moving, and yet be neither approaching nor receding from the center of the earth; and he reasoned that any body rotating on that center itself would be moving neither naturally nor violently—in contradiction of Aristotle, who allowed no third possibility except "mixed" motion. Galileo went on to show that any rotating homogeneous sphere, wherever situated, would also have this un–Aristotelian kind of motion (assuming no friction of its axis with its support), since for every part of that sphere which was approaching the center of the earth at a given moment, an equal part would be receding from it; thus the sphere as a whole would be moving, but neither naturally nor violently. Others before Galileo had pursued similar reasoning. But Galileo arrived in this way at the idea that there was a third kind of motion which was not a mere mixture of the other kinds, as his predecessors had supposed.

This recognition of a special kind of motion was Galileo's first essential step toward the concept of inertia. For in the same treatise, analyzing the force required to maintain a body in equilibrium on an inclined plane, Galileo concluded that horizontal motion of a body on the earth's surface would similarly be neither natural nor violent, in the sense of Aristotle, and in a note added to this section he said that this should be called a *neutral* motion. He then went on to prove that, in theory at least, any heavy body could be moved on a horizontal plane by a force smaller than that required to move any body upward on any other plane, however gently inclined, but he was careful to add that:

> Our proofs, as we said before, must be understood of bodies freed from all external resistance. But since it is perhaps impossible to find such bodies in the realm of matter, one who performs an experiment on the subject should not be surprised if it fails; that is, if a massive sphere, even on a horizontal plane, cannot be moved by a minimum force. For in addition to the causes already mentioned, there is the fact that no plane can be actually parallel to the horizon, since the surface of the earth is spherical. . . . And since a plane touches a sphere in only one point, if we move away from that point, we shall have to be moving upward. So there is good reason why it will not be pos-

sible to move a (massive) sphere from that point with an arbitrarily small force.[9]

The manuscript treatise from which this is quoted was written about 1590, but Galileo did not publish it. He was dissatisfied with it for various reasons; principally, in my opinion, because he had tried in this treatise to account for the observed speeds of bodies along inclined planes by a formula for their equilibrium conditions, and in this he had not succeeded, by reason of a misconception of accelerated motion which is irrelevant to the subject of the present study. But in the process he had found a new approach to physics in his concept of a "neutral" motion. It is important to note that the origin of this concept was in no way related to impetus theory, with which Galileo was perfectly satisfied at the time, as shown in his chapter on projectiles.

In 1592 Galileo moved to the University of Padua, where he continued or resumed his observations of motion on inclined planes and in the pendulum. Here he wrote a little treatise on mechanics for his private pupils, which he also left unpublished. Dealing with the inclined plane in this new work, he wrote:

> On a perfectly horizontal surface, a ball would remain indifferent and questioning between motion and rest, so that any the least force would be sufficient to move it, just as any little resistance, even that of the surrounding air, would be capable of holding it still. From this we may take the following conclusion as an indubitable axiom: That heavy bodies, all external and accidental impediments being removed, can be moved in the horizontal plane by any minimal force.[10]

From these two propositions, written not later than 1600, Galileo can hardly have failed to deduce the corollary that horizontal motion would continue perpetually if unimpeded. This second essential step in his progress toward the principle of inertia was not explicitly stated until several years later. Yet Galileo must have been teaching it in his private classes, for one of his pupils, Benedetto Castelli, who had left Padua some time before, wrote to Galileo in 1607 mentioning "your doctrine that although to start motion a mover is necessary, yet to continue it the absence of opposition is sufficient."[11]

Galileo's ideas on these matters were probably not widely

known until 1613. In that year he published a book on sunspots, in which he argued (among other things) for the sun's axial rotation, and as a preliminary to that argument he wrote:

> I have observed that physical bodies have an inclination toward some motion, as heavy bodies downward, which motion is exercised by them through an intrinsic property and without need of a special external mover, whenever they are not impeded by some obstacle. And to some other motion they have a repugnance, as the same heavy bodies to motion upward, wherefore they never move in that manner unless thrown violently upward by an external mover. Finally, to some movements they are indifferent, as are heavy bodies to horizontal motion, to which they have neither inclination . . . nor repugnance. And therefore, all external impediments being removed, a heavy body on a spherical surface concentric with the earth will be indifferent to rest or to movement toward any part of the horizon. And it will remain in that state in which it has once been placed; that is, if placed in a state of rest, it will conserve that; and if placed in movement toward the west, for example, it will maintain itself in that movement. Thus a ship . . . having once received some impetus through the tranquil sea, would move continually around our globe without ever stopping . . . if . . . all extrinsic impediments could be removed.[12]

In my opinion the essential core of the inertial concept lies in the ideas, explicitly stated above, of a body's indifference to motion or to rest and its continuance in the state it is once given. This idea is, to the best of my knowledge, original with Galileo. It is not derived from, or even compatible with, impetus theory, which assumed a natural tendency of every body to come to rest.[13] It is noteworthy that this first published statement of a true conservation principle was used by Galileo to support an argument for the conservation of angular momentum, in this case by the sun, as described previously. He seems always to have continued to associate the phenomena of inertia and of conservation of rotatory motion, which has led most historians to believe that Galileo's inertia had a circular quality. In my opinion, the association had quite another basis; namely, the linkage in Galileo's mind of these two phenomena by the unifying concept of a "neutral" motion which had first led him to an inertial principle.

Statements relating to inertia in Galileo's later books, the *Dialogue* of 1632 and the *Two New Sciences* of 1638, are more elaborate than the above but are essentially repetitions of it. His argument always proceeds from a consideration of motion on inclined planes to the limiting case of the horizontal plane, where motion once imparted would be perpetual, barring external obstacles or forces. The *Dialogue* is of particular interest for a long section dealing with the motion of a projectile, in which it is made clear that this motion would be rectilinear if it were not for the immediate commencement of the action of the body's weight, drawing it downward as soon as it is left without support. But Galileo never gave a statement of the law of inertia in the form and generality which we accept today. That was done by Descartes shortly after Galileo's death.

Because of the fundamental significance of the inertial concept to the later development of celestial mechanics, I should like to stress its importance in Galileo's arguments in favor of the Copernican theory and to mention some implications that have been drawn from that use of it. A strong objection to Copernicus in those days was that if the earth rotated at the rate of a thousand miles an hour, then any body separated from the earth, such as a bird or a cannonball or an object falling freely from a high place, would be rapidly displaced westward from an observer stationed on the earth. Copernicus had offered as a possible explanation for the absence of such effects some natural tendency of terrestrial bodies to share in the earth's motion wherever they were. But this was not widely accepted, and to Galileo it was no better than those "occult properties" invoked as explanations by the very philosophers against whom he contended. In the *Dialogue* he replaced this explanation by giving numerous examples of inertial motion, such as that of a ball dropped by a rider on horseback, and he refuted the idea that an object dropped from the mast of a moving ship would strike the deck farther astern than on a ship at rest. These arguments, based on observations that anyone could duplicate and supported by correct physical reasoning, did much to gain a fair hearing for the Copernican system from his contemporaries.

But here arises the problem in assigning Galileo's precise role in the discovery of the inertial principle. In the *Dialogue* Galileo sometimes spoke as though the inertial motions of bodies leaving the earth's surface were itself circular, causing historians to question whether he himself fully understood the rectilinear character of translatory motion. Some have gone so far as to say that Galileo believed the planetary motions to be perpetuated by a sort of circular inertia. Leaving those views for the final essay, I wish here to point out the primarily strategic character of the passages from which they derive their only support.

Passages on projectile motion in the *Dialogue*[14] and the derivation of the parabolic trajectory in the *Two New Sciences*[15] show that Galileo as a physicist treated inertial motions as rectilinear. Nevertheless, Galileo as a propagandist, when writing the *Dialogue,* stated that rectilinear motion cannot be perpetual, though circular motion may be. In the same book he ascribed some special properties almost metaphysically to circles and circular motions.

The passages in question occur mainly in the opening section of the book entitled *Dialogue on the Two Chief World Systems, Ptolemaic and Copernican,* and they should be construed in the light of the purpose for which that book was written. It was not written to teach physics or astronomy, but to weaken resistance to the Copernican theory, and it was very effective in doing so. For Galileo was not only an outstanding scientist, but also a first-rate polemicist and a writer of exceptional literary skill and psychological insight. He knew when he wrote the *Dialogue* that strong opposition could be expected from the professors of philosophy, most of them convinced Aristotelians. It was for that reason, I believe, that in the opening section of his book he deliberately conceded (or appeared to concede) to the philosophers everything he possibly could without compromising his one objective. This is still the best way to proceed if you wish to espouse an unpopular view. Accordingly, when I read the metaphysical praise of circles in the *Dialogue,* I do not conclude with most historians that its author was unable to break the spell of ancient traditions; rather, I strongly suspect an ulterior purpose in those passages. This suspicion is confirmed when I read his other books and his voluminous surviving correspondence and find nowhere else any trace of metaphysics about circles. On the contrary, Galileo often scoffs at such ideas; thus in his *Assayer,* published in 1623, he expressly denied that any geometrical form is prior or superior to any other, let alone that any shape is perfect, as Aristotle had claimed for the circle.[16] It is not likely that he had changed that opinion by 1632, as he was nearly sixty years of age before he published it in 1623.

All that Galileo wanted to accomplish in the *Dialogue* was to induce his readers to accept the ideas set forth by Copernicus, and Copernicus had placed the planets, including the earth, in circular orbits around the sun. Galileo probably knew better, having read at least the preface of Kepler's *Astronomia Nova,* from which he gained acquaintance with Kepler's tidal theory. But it was hard enough for him to get acceptance in Italy of any motion for the earth, and for his immediate purpose it would have been fatal to argue for an elliptical orbit. It was far better strategy for him to ennoble the circle, using arguments extracted from Aristotle himself, and to argue that circular motion was as suitable to the earth as to the heavens, if he wanted to win over or even neutralize any philosophers. And I can see in my mind's eye some of them starting to read the *Dialogue* for no other purpose than to find and answer hostile arguments against Aristotle, and then in the first forty or fifty pages finding themselves so much at home as to wonder whether there might not be some merit in the other ideas of so sound a writer.

That, in my opinion, is precisely what Galileo was up to when he composed those opening pages, balancing his adverse criticisms of Aristotle's physics with approving extracts from his metaphysics about circles. Galileo certainly did not state or believe that the celestial motions would perpetuate themselves merely by being circular in form, but this does not mean that he was averse from letting the philosophers believe that if they wished to. If Galileo had held such an opinion, he would not have hesitated to declare it; I see little point in looking for hidden beliefs behind the words of a man who spent his last years under arrest for disdaining to conceal his convictions. And the fact is that in the *Dialogue* itself, Galileo declared that he had no opinion about the cause of the planetary motions, but went on to say that if anyone could tell him the cause of gravitation, he could then give a cause for those motions.[17]

The amusing thing is that in saying that no rectilinear motion can be perpetual, Galileo was on sounder ground than are many of those who now criticize his having said it. Galileo's modern critics seem still blissfully unaware that in the last fifty years a question has arisen about the meaning, the nature, and even the existence of straight lines in the physical universe. Perhaps the general law of inertia is tautological; perhaps it is our only definition of "straight motion." Certainly it has lost the absolute physical character with which those critics still invest it. Nor do Galileo's critics seem to realize that physicists now question the infinite extent of the universe, an attribute which would be a necessary condition of "perpetual straight motion" in the sense in which Galileo denied its possibility. For Galileo has been criticized both for his failure to declare the universe to be infinite, and for his denial of the possibility of perpetual straight motion—as if such views destroyed the modernity of his physics.

Galileo formulated at most a restricted law of inertia, applicable only to terrestrial bodies. Perhaps this too is a tribute to his modernity as a physicist, for there is an advantage in refusing to generalize beyond the reach of your available experimental evidence. That advantage is that four hundred years later, your restricted statement will still be true, while the speculations of your more daring colleagues may have gone out of date. Galileo's restricted law of inertia, applying only to heavy bodies near the surface of the earth, was in a sense all that was needed or justified in physics up to the time of Newton's discovery of the law of universal gravitation. Any speculation by Galileo about the behavior of bodies in interstellar space would at his time have been essentially meaningless metaphysics—the very sort of philosophizing that he had undertaken to replace with a science of physics. With the advent of Newtonian gravitation, inertia was freed from the terrestrial bonds imposed on it by Galileo and purged of the speculative character given to it by Descartes; for the first time, inertia became a universal law of physics.

Notes to Essay 12

1. Cf. Newton, *Principia,* ed. F. Cajori (Berkeley, 1947), p. 21.
2. *Dialogue,* p. 51.
3. Differences between Buridan's suggestion that conservation of angular momentum might persist forever in the absence of resistance,

and the more widespread conception that impetus always wasted away, may be neglected here for reasons that will presently appear.

4. A. Maier, *Zwei Grundprobleme der scholastischen Naturphilosophie* (Rome, 1951), pp. 304–5.

5. Ibid., p. 306.

6. A. Koyré, *Etudes Galiléennes* (Paris, 1939), pp. 246–47. Emphasis Koyré's.

7. E. J. Dijksterhuis, *The Mechanization of the World Picture*, trans. C. Dikshoorn (Oxford, 1961), p. 352.

8. I. E. Drabkin and S. Drake, *Galileo on Motion and on Mechanics* (Madison, 1960), p. 72.

9. Ibid., p. 68.

10. Ibid., p. 171.

11. Ibid., p. 171 n.

12. *Discoveries,* pp. 113–14. The passage is continued in essay 5 above.

13. Kepler, contemporarily with Galileo, in fact used the word *inertia* to denote the supposed tendency of all bodies to come to rest upon the removal of force.

14. *Dialogue,* pp. 174–95 passim.

15. *Two New Sciences,* pp. 244–57.

16. *Discoveries,* p. 263.

17. *Dialogue,* p. 234. The grounds for attributing to Galileo a belief in "circular inertia" are examined at length in essay 13.

The Case against
"Circular Inertia"

Nearly all scholars presently hold that Galileo attributed to inertial motions an essentially circular form. This view was developed in a particularly interesting way by Alexandre Koyré.[1] It has wide implications both with regard to Galileo's physical conceptions and their supposed medieval roots.

Over the years, largely in the course of reconsidering the relevant passages in Galileo's *Dialogue* when revising the notes to successive editions of that work in English translation, I greatly modified my original support for the prevailing view. After arriving at a new view as to the origins of Galileo's inertial ideas, set forth in the previous study, I would have withdrawn my support entirely from the general belief, had it not been for the existence of one passage in which Galileo appeared to have unequivocally assumed the persistence of uniform circular motion in an unsupported body moving near the earth. Despite the fact that Galileo styled that passage a *bizzarria* and stated clearly that he did not believe it to hold precisely for actual bodies, its presence deterred me from going against the almost universal opinion of other students of Galileo.

Now, however, I believe that the passage represents a purely geometrical speculation, unconnected with projectile motions of any kind. It therefore seems to me time to reexamine the whole basis on which Galileo is believed to have seen circularity as an essential component in inertial motions. Before proceeding to that examination, I shall set forth briefly my interpretation of the *bizzarria* and explain why others have so long looked at it differently.[2]

In the *Dialogue* Galileo introduced a discussion concerning the probable shape of the path of a body falling from the top of a tower to its base as seen by an imaginary observer who did not share in the earth's diurnal rotation. He believed that the body would move nearly along a semicircle, of which the diameter would be the line from the top of the tower to the center of the earth.[3] This opinion was opposed by Marin Mersenne five years later in his *Harmonie Universelle.* Mersenne was struck by an absurdity that seemed to be implied. Assuming a diurnal rotation every twenty-four hours, the body would reach the center of the earth in exactly six hours. Yet Galileo had argued elsewhere in the *Dialogue* that a body would fall from the moon to the earth in less than four hours.[4] How, then, could he believe that a stone would require six hours to reach the center of the earth from a point close to its surface?

Mersenne's argument was based on a certain plausible interpretation of Galileo's diagram without close attention to the accompanying text. The diagram is simple and striking; a glance at it strongly tempts one to think of a heavy body descending from the top of the tower to the center of the earth, rather than just to its surface. Mersenne, and later critics, have accordingly been concerned with the question: "What would be the path of a body falling from a tower situated on a rotating and transparent earth, tunneled to its center from the base of the tower, as seen by a distant motionless observer who could watch the whole descent?" This was not Galileo's question, although the interpretation was not unreasonable, considering only Galileo's diagram, which was this:

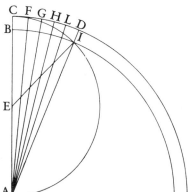

Fig. 11. Diagram shown in Galileo's *Dialogue.* The center of the earth is at A.

The question Galileo was discussing was stated thus: "What may one believe with regard to the line described by a heavy body falling from the top of a tower to its base?"[5] In his reply, Galileo first introduced the concept of uniform acceleration, but postponed discussion of the law of falling bodies to a later section of the *Dialogue*. Returning to the question, he again phrased it in the same way: "In the meantime, let us get back to the line described by the body falling from the top of the tower to its base."[6] The words, "to its base," show that no further generalization was intended.

Admitting that the diagram strongly suggests fall to the center, the manner of its construction as described in his text shows that Galileo considered the fall to be over when the body reached the base of the tower. The semicircle CIA was first constructed. Then successive positions of the tower were marked off and joined to the center of the earth. Finally, the positions of the falling body were identified with these intersections, which stop at the point I. It was only the arc CI that the text discussed. Using dotted lines for construction lines, the diagram would normally be drawn today in this manner:

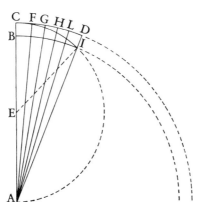

Fig. 12. Galileo's diagram redrawn to distinguish construction lines from lines referred to in his demonstration.

Albert Einstein pointed out to me many years ago another puzzle implied in the usual interpretation of this passage which seems to have escaped discussion. Why did Galileo make the falling body stop at the center of the earth, when by his own law of acceleration it should be going most swiftly? Elsewhere in the *Dialogue,* Galileo himself had discussed the continuation of motion past the center if a body were dropped through a tunneled earth.[7]

Clearly, if Galileo never intended to discuss any motion of the stone beyond that which it would have from the top of the tower to its base, the puzzles mentioned by both Mersenne and Einstein simply vanish. Neither the six-hour descent nor the sudden stoppage at the center have any basis in Galileo's text. This did say that the body "tends to end at the center," that its path "must tend to terminate at the center," and that "such motion tends eventually to terminate at the center," but there is no simple indicative, present or future, to suggest that the center is supposed to be reached.[8] Reference to the center was necessary in order to determine the path of the body above the earth's surface, but played no further role in the discussion.

The specific assignment of a uniform circular component in the short descent of this unsupported body (greatly exaggerated in any diagram) served only the necessities of a geometric speculation about an apparent path. It was based not on a physical assumption, but on the observed fact that a body falling from a tower grazes its side. It had to do not with any physical account of a projectile trajectory, but only with the analysis of an optical appearance from a point separated from the earth.

Let us now turn to the analysis of circularity in Galileo's idea of inertia, as set forth by Alexandre Koyré in the third of his *Etudes,* called *Galilée e la loi d'inertie.*[9] The first forty-four pages of that study are devoted to a statement of physical problems introduced by the Copernican theory, the proposed solutions to them offered by Copernicus, Bruno, Brahe, and Kepler, and the arguments that were brought against these solutions. Then, before examining Galileo's *Dialogue* and its anti-Aristotelian polemic, Koyré devotes four or five pages to a statement of his thesis. There follow some eighty pages of interpretation and comment on selected passages of the *Dialogue,* by which the thesis is ably supported. The balance of the monograph, except for two paradoxes presented immediately after the above sections, will not concern us here.

Now, in a work of the above structure, it is important to be clear about the basis on which the thesis is put forward, for the appearance of invincible solidity of the whole structure is largely achieved by the interpretation of passages chosen to illustrate the thesis. Koyré's general position is stated in these words, which will be translated sentence by sentence as each point is examined in this study.

> *Le problème central qui préoccupe Galilée à Pise est celui de la persistance du mouvement. Or, il est clair que lorsqu'il étudie le cas du mouvement (de rotation) d'une sphère placée au centre du monde, ainsi que celui d'une sphère placée en dehors de ce centre, il a en vue la situation créée par la doctrine copernicienne; la sphère marmoréenne dont il analyse les mouvements représente, sans nul doute la terre; et ses mouvements sont ceux de la terre.*
>
> *Mais le résultat auquel il aboutit—en contradiction, d'ailleurs, avec les prémisses essentielles de la physique de l'*impetus*— nous révèle d'une manière éclatante les difficultés, et la source des difficultés, que recontraient sur leur chemin la physique et l'astronomie nouvelles.*
>
> *En effet, le résultat auquel aboutit l'analyse galiléenne, c'est la persistance naturelle, ou, plus exactment, la situation privilégiée du mouvement* circulaire.[10]

"The central problem with which Galileo was preoccupied at Pisa is that of the persistence of movement."

We can judge Galileo's interests at Pisa objectively only by his own writings while he was there—theorems on centers of gravity, the *Bilancetta,* and *De motu.* In the first two, his preoccupation was with the extension of the work of Archimedes beyond the two books written by the Greek mathematician that relate to mechanics. The first half of *De motu* concerns the application of the principle of Archimedes to a refutation of Aristotle's laws of falling bodies. That constitutes the most important part of *De motu.* Chapters 8, 10, 11, 12, and 13 all contain in their titles the phrase "in opposition to Aristotle," or words to that effect. Chapter 14 comprises the important section on motion on inclined planes; chapter 15 resumes the proofs in opposition to Aristotle. In none of these is the question of persistence of motion discussed; not even in chapter 14, where it is proved that motion on the horizontal plane can be produced by a minimal force. In chapter 16 the question is raised whether the rotation of a sphere situated at the center of the universe would be perpetual or not, but the answer is postponed and never taken up again. At the end of the same chapter it is intimated that a nonhomogeneous sphere situated outside the center of the universe cannot rotate perpetually, but again a promise of future explanation is not carried out. It is only in chapter 17, when Galileo comes to the subject of projectiles, that persistence of motion becomes a topic of discussion. Here Galileo adopts the accepted theory of a wasting impressed force in refutation of Aristotle. Circular motion is not a central question; in a single brief reference to rotatory motion, Galileo says only that it would last a long time, not that it is inherently perpetual. The rest of *De motu* has nothing to say about persistence of motion as such.

What preoccupied Galileo at Pisa was not the persistence of motion, as Koyré asserted. Even at Padua that is not a question on which Galileo left anything written. His *Mechanics,* composed there, contains a passage that implies persistence of motion on the horizontal plane, but only in an aside and only by implication. There is evidence that Galileo had developed that implication in lectures or conversations before 1607, but it was only in 1613, after he had returned to Florence, that he clearly stated an opinion on persistence of motion. What really preoccupied Galileo at Pisa was not the persistence of motion, but the refutation of Aristotle's physics. All this is evident from the structure of *De motu,* its chapter headings, its textual criticisms of Aristotle, and its general polemic tone.

"Now, it is clear that when he studies the case of movement (rotation) of a sphere placed at the center of the universe, as of that of a sphere placed outside that center, he has in view the situation created by the Copernican doctrine; the marble sphere whose movements he analyses represents, without any doubt, the earth; its movements are those of the earth."

Not only is this not clear; it is in a way self-contradictory. If Galileo had been a Copernican at the time he wrote *De motu,* he would not have placed the earth at the center of the universe, even metaphorically. What is clear is that in his anti-Aristotelian *De motu,* he wished to destroy even Aristotle's fundamental division of all motions into natural and violent motions. To do this, he showed that certain bodies might be in movement without their motion being either natural or violent. It is possible that Galileo, while still at Pisa, was already interested in the Copernican implications, but it is by no means clear that he was. In *De motu* there is no reference, even in passing, to any astronomical topic except to the argument of some philosophers that the addition of a single star to the heavens would slow down or stop them. Answering this, Galileo treated the fixed stars as in daily circular rotation, without even a parenthetical remark to indicate that others (or he himself) believed that the fixed stars might not be in motion at all.

"But the result at which he arrived—in contradiction, more-over, with the essential premises of the physics of impetus—reveals to us in a striking way the difficulties, and the source of the diffi-culties, in the path of the new physics and the new astronomy."

The result to which Koyré here alludes is made clear in his next sentence, discussed below. It is, as will be shown, at least partly not Galileo's result at all. Whether it, or Galileo's own result, was in contradiction with the premises of impetus physics, Galileo certainly did not see any contradiction between the two at the time he wrote *De motu*. For in that work, Galileo not only adopted impetus physics for projectiles, but also gave a proof that impetus must waste away, and used this in his explanation of the phenomenon of an initial temporary acceleration in free fall. He saw no contradiction between a wasting impetus and his logical analysis of rotations, set forth in the same book, nor is there evidence that he saw any connection between that analysis and astronomy. For such a connection we have only Koyré's conjecture.

"In fact, the result to which the Galilean analysis led is the natural persistence, or more precisely the privileged character, of circular movement."

This is the thesis put forth by Koyré and adopted by most historians of science after him. Koyré appears to consider the result attributed to Galileo as one already reached at Pisa (though *about it* may refer to some later time). The passages of *De motu* cited by Koyré in his footnote here do not assert anything about the persistence of circular motion, nor do they deal with real physical spheres; still less do they assert that circular movements have any privileged character. In the same footnote, Koyré invites us to compare a passage in Galileo's *Mechanics,* a work composed at Padua after the Pisan period. It is the passage already mentioned above, which still did not assert, though it did imply, the persistence of motion on horizontal planes.

Koyré next reviews Galileo's analysis of the motion of a hypothetical sphere located at the center of the universe, as a motion neither natural nor violent, adding: "But the case of the sphere located at the center of the world is far from being unique; in truth, all circular movement (about the center) is such a movement that is neither natural nor violent."[11] This is where trouble truly begins. Galileo made no such assertion, which would include the case of circulation around the center of the universe, as well as the case of the rotation of a sphere located there. No circulations, and not even all rotations, are said by Galileo to be "neither natural or violent." Yet it is upon circulations (not mere rotations) that the whole question of "circular inertia" has been made to hinge. I shall return to this point shortly. First, however, it is important to note that Koyré's thesis attributes to Galileo a lifelong constancy to this principle: *"Circular movement occupies in physical reality an absolutely privileged position. . . . That is the Galilean situation. It is almost the same at Pisa, at Padua, and at Florence."*[12]

Now in fact, circular motion of any kind occupies only a small part of *De motu.* One chapter is dedicated to it, and that chapter deals hardly at all with physical reality; it is principally concerned with imaginary marble spheres, introduced for the purpose of showing that instances of motion can be adduced that will not fit into Aristotle's classifications of natural and violent. Part of one paragraph, discussing homogenous spheres rotating elsewhere than at the center of the universe, remarks that such spheres must be supported and will therefore be subjected to frictional resistance. That is the only case in which physical reality appears, and such circular motion is most certainly not given a privileged position there. Heterogenous spheres, moving just as circularly, would not continue to move forever according to Galileo. In another chapter, discussing projectiles, antiperistasis is refuted by a paragraph concerning grindstones. These are the sole discussions of circular motion, which is not given a privileged position in *De motu* at all; it is merely seen to require separate discussion.

That Galileo held any single unifying view, virtually the same at Pisa, at Padua, and at Florence, is an inference for which no factual evidence exists. Growth and change characterized his thought; witness the evolution of his view of acceleration. As to circular motion, it is not a principal topic in any of Galileo's published books before 1632, nor in any of his letters. (The persistence of motion is not a principal topic either, though it was discussed in one paragraph of the *Letters on Sunspots.*) In *The Assayer,* Galileo denied circular orbits to comets and ridiculed the idea that any shape (particularly the circle) had any priority over any other; none, said Galileo, had patents of nobility, and none were absolutely perfect; perfection had to do with the intended use, and not the form.[13] So it is gratuitous, if not hazardous, to assume that when Galileo composed the *Dialogue* he had spent a lifetime ruminating over the persistence and absolute privilege of circular motion in the world of physical reality.

The underlying philosophical preoccupation attributed to Galileo by Koyré is equally unsupported by surviving correspondence. Galileo's letters are as devoid of metaphysical discussions as they are of encomiums on the marvels of the circle. Only after he was blind and had published his last book do we find him debating (with Fortunio Liceti) on any abstract principles. Since in that debate he sided with Aristotle, his final position can hardly be called a lifelong unifying philosophical view.

With the philosophical interpretation of passages from the *Dialogue,* conducted in the light of Koyré's thesis, we are not here concerned. Quite different interpretations are capable of being made on other assumptions, and Koyré's interpretation does not easily apply to certain other passages. Let us therefore pass on to the problem with which Koyré was left as he turned to discuss the successors of Galileo. He asks:

> If, as we believe has been shown, Galileo did not formulate the principle of inertia, how is it that his successors and pupils could think they found it in his works? And another [problem]: if, as we believe we have equally shown, Galileo not only did not conceive, but even could not conceive inertial movement

in a straight line, how did it come about—or better, how was it brought about—that this concept, before which the mind of a Galileo was halted, could appear easy, obvious, and self-evident to his pupils and successors?[14]

Let us try to resolve the paradoxes seen by Koyré. And first, let us remove from them the exaggeration inherent in the statement above; that is, that these things have been shown. If it were indeed shown, in the sense of being demonstrated, that Galileo did not conceive or formulate, and could not have conceived or formulated the idea of continued and undiminished rectilinear motion, then Koyré's paradoxes would have to be admitted. As things stand, however, we may for the present take Koyré's position not as something demonstrated, but only as one of several plausible hypotheses. In that case the paradoxes named give way to ordinary questions, questions that may serve as the basis for further fruitful research. These questions would be, for example:

"If Galileo could and did conceive of the possibility of continued and undiminished rectilinear motion, why did he not formulate that conception as a physical law in unequivocal terms? And since he did not so formulate it, whatever his reasons, how did it come about that his pupils and successors not only adopted it as a matter of course, but treated it as something derived from Galileo's own work?"

An answer to these questions should be sought in Galileo's own works, not in general philosophical and historical principles such as those to which Koyré appealed in support of his attempted demonstrations—demonstrations which led him only to paradoxes. Charming as paradoxes are to the philosopher, they are dead ends to the historian, who deals rather in real problems.

That Galileo could and did conceive of the *possibility* of continued uniform rectilinear motion is made evident at various places in the *Dialogue* and the *Two New Sciences*. The treatment of these in Koyré's monograph is unsatisfactory; he neglects to mention certain relevant passages in the *Dialogue,* and he explains away others in the *Two New Sciences* by an argument that proves only Galileo's denial of the *fact,* and not any denial of (or failure to recognize) the *possibility,* of rectilinear inertia. Thus Koyré correctly says, of the celebrated passage in the *Two New Sciences* deriving the parabolic trajectory, that continued uniform motion in the horizontal plane is not, for Galileo, rectilinear motion at all; fundamentally it is circular motion, for the horizontal plane is not a mathematical plane, but the surface of a sphere concentric with the earth. This argument shows, not that Galileo overlooked the possibility of rectilinear inertia, but merely that he avoided any assertion of its existence in fact. Since it does not exist experimentally, that is quite correct. The *possibility* is here neither affirmed nor denied; for its recognition, we must look elsewhere.

A single instance will suffice to show that Galileo recognized the *possibility* of rectilinear inertia. The clearest and best example, as well as the most important, is the existence of the discussion in the Second Day of the *Dialogue* in which Galileo replies to the argument that rotation of the earth would cast off objects resting on its surface. In preparation for his argument, Galileo established this physical proposition:

"The circular motion of the projector impresses an impetus upon the projectile to move, when they separate, along the straight line tangent to the circle of motion at the point of separation . . . and the projectile would continue to move along that line if it were not inclined downward by its own weight, from which fact the line of motion derives its curvature."[15] Thus there would be no curving of the line in the absence of gravity. The ensuing discussion assumes that the rectilinear motion, if it could continue, would be uniform, and this conception is confirmed by Galileo's diagram, in which equal times are laid off along the tangent. The case of a projectile impelled by a cannon had been previously discussed and summed up in a postil: "Projectiles continue their motion along a straight line which follows the direction of the motion that they had together with the thing projecting them while they were connected with it."[16] Here, as elsewhere, Galileo does not assert that an actual cannon ever *is* at rest, or that the absolute path of the ball would ever actually be straight, but the *possibility* of a straight path is pointed out by the statement.

On the other hand, the real existence of "circular inertia," in the sense of an indelibly impressed impetus to follow the diurnal rotation of the earth, is excluded for Galileo by his argument against extrusion.[17] Serious consideration of such an impetus is in effect denied by Galileo's casual treatment of the Copernican suggestion that terrestrial rotation is natural for the earthly objects.[18] Had Galileo considered it a fact that every body resting on the earth is indelibly impressed with a circular motion identical with that rotation, his entire complicated mathematical argument could have been avoided, and in its place we should have had merely a reiteration of the Copernican position. The highly technical demonstration that Galileo attempted in explanation of the quiescence of detached bodies resting on a rotating earth could serve little purpose for himself, and still less for his readers, if he believed literally in "circular inertia." It is therefore significant that Galileo did not repeat and endorse the Copernican "circular inertia" argument, but put his analysis of tangential and central forces in place of it. There is simply no reason that Galileo should ever have worked out this demonstration in the first place if his own conviction was carried by "circular inertia."

Here, however, an interesting point arises. At several places in the *Dialogue,* particularly in connection with the fall of a weight from a tower or a ship's mast, the body is said by Galileo to follow in its descent the circle swept out by the tower in consequence of its diurnal motion, or of the ship in consequence of its own motion. This is indeed "circular inertia," and it is utilized in several places; for example: "Now as to that stone which is on top of the mast; does it not move, carried by the ship, both of them going along the circumference of a circle about its center? And consequently is there not in it an ineradicable motion, all external impediments being removed? And is this motion not as fast as that of the ship?"[19]

If we had to decide which of the two different conceptions Galileo himself held as an inner conviction—that is, whether the ineradicable motion impressed on a heavy body is the uniform rectilinear motion of which he spoke in connection with cannonballs and stones flung from whirling slings, or the circular motion about the earth shared with the ship's mast from which a stone is dropped—there is at least one strong hint to be gained from the discussions in which those two different ideas occur in the *Dialogue.* In the first-named case, whether the original motion is rectilinear (cannon shot) or circular (whirled object), Galileo always adds a comment to the effect that the object would continue along the straight line if it were not immediately drawn down by its own weight, as in the passage cited above. But in the ship-mast or related examples, in which a circular motion is shared by the object with the whole earth, or is imparted to it solely because of the earth's spherical shape, Galileo never adds an analogous statement that the body would continue along that (circular) line if it were free of weight.

In short, Galileo does not say positively anywhere that a heavy body near the earth would continue in circular motion if deprived of support, in any circumstances, whether dropped from a ship's mast or rolled off the end of a level place; but he does say positively in several places that such a body would continue any rectilinear motion imparted to it were it not for the downward action of its weight.

Wherever it appears that Galileo asserts the continuance of a circular motion for terrestrial bodies, the motion is of a character that is indistinguishable from rectilinear motion by reason of the huge size of the earth. It has become customary to suppose him to have been thinking: "and yet, of course, the motion really *is* circular, though we can't see that it is." If that were the case, one would expect him to have made this specific qualification for the cannonball and for missiles flung from slings; but that is the exact reverse of what he did do. We may equally well suppose him to have been thinking, "but the circular character of the ship-mast motion or of the actual horizontal plane is merely accidental, resulting only from the fact that the earth happens to be round"; and then all his statements concerning terrestrial inertia would be consistent and rather easy to explain. The prevailing preference among historians of science for believing Galileo inconsistent and paradoxical on this matter is guided not so much by necessity as by a belief that the history of science receives more light thereby.

The discussion of semicircular fall in the *Dialogue* does not include any consideration of inertia in its physical aspect. The continuation of motion there is introduced as a mathematical assumption rather than an observed fact and is used for the purpose of a geometrical speculation about an apparent path rather than for a physical analysis of any projectile motion. Granting for the sake of argument that it involves inertia, this case corresponds to the ship-mast type of circular motion and hence to a path indistinguishable by observation from a straight line for the amount of arc under consideration. To justify the treatment of such arcs as straight lines, Galileo appealed throughout his life— from the unpublished *De motu* of 1590 to the final *Two New Sciences* of 1638—to the treatment by Archimedes of the pans of balance as hanging by parallel lines, though in fact they converge toward the center of the earth. That is why, in my opinion, it is wrong to suppose that Galileo considered the curvature of the earth as introducing an *essential* circular property into all imparted motions near that surface. Rather, his consistent lifelong statements show that he took Archimedes as his model in the treatment of physical problems, ignoring inconsequential discrepancies in the choice of physical postulates for his mathematical deductions.

There are also other grounds for believing that Galileo's references in the *Dialogue* to an ineradicable circular impetus or ineradicable rectilinear inertia give rise to merely apparent, and not real, inconsistencies. Considering the order in which the references occur, and their relative simplicity and complexity, there is some reason to suppose that Galileo used the less involved (Copernican) assumption of natural rotation earlier in the *Dialogue,* to lead his readers easily along, and the more refined assumption of tangential motion when the argument became more precise. That view is supported by the many instances in which he treated the earth's spherical surface as an approximation to the horizontal plane. It is also supported by considerations of style, since a precise statement of the tangential character of conserved motion would necessarily have been clumsy in his early illustrations as compared with the expressions used. On the whole, it is more plausible that Galileo personally considered rectilinear motion as essentially true for terrestrial bodies.

But we do not really have to decide for one view or the other; if anything, we should avoid a final decision. What we must recognize is that Galileo's discussion leaves open the *possibility* of either circular or rectilinear continuation of uniform motion in the case of free fall (a "natural" motion), whereas he unambiguously specifies *rectilinear* continuation for the "violent" component in the motion of cannonballs and terrestrial objects released from slings or flung from rapidly rotating wheels.

This point becomes still more significant when we turn from

the behavior of heavy bodies on or near the earth's surface (terrestrial physics) to Galileo's cosmological speculations (celestial physics). I paraphrase Galileo's thought thus: "For terrestrial physics (the physics of heavy bodies), the ineradicable *tendency* of terrestrial projectiles is to follow the line of the cannon, or the tangent to the circle of the sling, but the actual *motion* cannot be rectilinear because the body has weight. The *essential* motion of a terrestrial body is one thing; its accidental path is another. Where we cannot distinguish them, we do not have to decide between them as in the case of point-blank shots or of falling bodies sharing the earth's diurnal motion, where the straight tangent and the circular arc do not differ by an inch in a thousand yards." But where the distinction is clear, the *essential* rectilinearity is easily recognizable: "When the stone escapes from the stick, what is its motion? Does it continue to follow its previous circle, or does it go along some other line?—It certainly does not go on moving around. . . . It is necessarily along a straight line, so far as the adventitious impulse is concerned."[20]

These and similar passages answer the question whether Galileo could perceive the possibility of continued uniform rectilinear motion for terrestrial (heavy) bodies, and explain why his pupils and successors treated the principle of inertia as a part of his work, even though he did not formulate it clearly and unambiguously. For a possible answer to the question why he did not do so, we must look also at his cosmological speculations. It is evident that his failure to formulate the inertial law cannot have been, as Koyré supposed, an inherent incapability of perceiving its possibility. Something else made Galileo reluctant to generalize it for the entire universe. Our principal (if not our only) source of knowledge concerning Galileo's cosmological speculations is the First Day of the *Dialogue,* and particularly its opening section. Having begun with Aristotle's position, Galileo has his spokesman (Salviati) agree with Aristotle, supplying additional arguments in favor of the Aristotelian position up to a certain crucial point. But where Aristotle deduces the motions of the heavens from the perfection of the circle, Salviati introduces instead the postulate that the universe is perfectly *orderly.* From this he deduces that it is impossible for integral world-bodies (the planets and their satellites) to move in straight lines: for in that way the cosmic order would perpetually change. This postulate does not commit Galileo with respect to terrestrial objects. Cosmic order, on the other hand, can be preserved only if the heavenly bodies are at rest or in circular motion. Only that motion, he says, is capable of true uniformity; straight motion is either accelerated, decelerated, or infinite, the first two being nonuniform and the last being inadmissible in an *ordered* universe.

It is here that Galileo introduces his "Platonic concept" of cosmogony: the planets, having been created at a certain place, were moved with straight accelerated motion until each had received its assigned speed, at which point its motion was converted from a straight to a circular path by God, who willed that the planet keep that same velocity perpetually thereafter.[21] On the basis of this cosmogony and its attendant arguments, it is widely held today that Galileo attributed the motions of the planets in their orbits to "circular inertia." That, however, contradicts several clear statements by Galileo himself; moreover, it implies certain beliefs on his part that he cannot have held if he was even a competent, let alone a gifted physicist and astronomer.

First, we must note that in this passage Galileo attributes the continuance of the planets in their orbits to the will of God, and not to any physical principle whatever. Much later in the *Dialogue,* he expressly denies that he (or anyone else) knows by what principle the planets are moved.[22] Equally important is his refusal to grant that the universe has a center: "We do not know where that may be, or whether it exists at all. Even if it exists, it is but an imaginary point; a nothing without any quality."[23] Now, Galileo's entire understanding of perpetual uniform movement, wherever it is expressed in his writings, consists always in the body's path being such as not to approach or to recede from some center toward which it has a natural tendency to move. For ordinary heavy bodies, this is the center of the earth. Only by the most tenuous arguments, and in contradiction of Galileo's own words, can a case be made that he believed the planetary circulations to be analogous to such motions. For it cannot be seriously argued that Galileo believed the actual planetary motions to be literally perfectly circular around the sun as a common center. No competent astronomer since Aristotle had believed in homocentric orbits, with the possible exception of Fracastoro. Certainly no

Ptolemaic or Tychonian, let alone Copernican, believed in mathematically concentric paths for the planetary bodies themselves. Galileo was no great theoretical astronomer, but he certainly was aware of the classic problems of planetary orbits, variously solved by eccentrics, epicycles, ovals, and ultimately by ellipses.

If anyone wishes to contend that Galileo was actually so ill-informed as to believe that some set of perfect concentric circles—centered, moreover, about an occupied point—would fit the actual observed motions of planets, and that the "Platonic concept" of the *Dialogue* presents us with his mature astronomical convictions, then "circular inertia" demands further that Galileo must have believed those circular motions to be absolutely uniform. But in the Fourth Day of the *Dialogue,* Galileo argued that the circuits of the sun, the earth, and the moon are not uniform in speed.[24] Hence the attribution to Galileo of a belief in planetary motion by reason of "circular inertia," meaning by that absolutely uniform motion in perfect circles, can be maintained only at the price of rejecting his own words and his astronomical competence, or supposing him to have been so devout a Platonist as to hold to a cosmology refuted by his own perceptions.

We have now reviewed some of the factual weaknesses behind Koyré's thesis, and some of the needless difficulties to which it gives rise. If we abandon his interpretation of "circular inertia" as the unifying principle of Galileo's physics and his astronomy—as the unchanging core of his work at Pisa, Padua, and Florence—what interpretation shall we put in its place? To this question I wish to reply only tentatively, putting forth possibilities rather than conclusions.

The contradictions (or seeming contradictions) in the *Dialogue* are better resolved by paying very close attention to Galileo's exact words than by postulating some unifying conception behind them in Galileo's own mind and then saying in effect: "When he said this, he really meant thus-and-so." Perhaps he did not attempt to explain everything by one principle. Let me give an example.

When Galileo had occasion to speak of a supported body moving along a terrestrial horizontal plane, he usually went to the trouble of pointing out that since no true geometrical plane existed on a spherical surface, the so-called horizontal plane of our experience is really a portion of the sphere. Yet when he argued that a projectile released from a whirling sling tended to move along the straight line tangent at the point of separation, he did not add that the line was not really straight, but must share in the circularity of its previous path, or in that of the diurnal rotation, or anything of the sort. This hardly supports the view that he thought always of circularity and could not conceive of uniform rectilinear inertial movements. The fact that such movements are made nonuniform by air resistance and are curved by downward action of weight has nothing to do with their essential character, and Galileo was perfectly clear about that.

On the other hand, when he spoke of free fall along a tower or the mast of a ship, he plainly said on several occasions that the true path was a compounding of the straight motion toward the earth's center and the general circular terrestrial motion shared by the object before the commencement of its descent. This equally destroys any claim that Galileo really always had in mind a straight tangential motion. It may be that he had such an idea in mind, though he did not adduce it in every case for reasons of style; but there is no more evidence that he always thought of observed terrestrial inertial movements as essentially straight than that he always thought of them as essentially circular. If we pay strict attention to Galileo's own words, we shall have to say that he invoked no unifying principle for all cases of inertial movement.

It does not necessarily follow, however, that Galileo was inconsistent in the matter. If there is some element common to all the cases in which he specified an essentially straight inertial movement, and some other element common to all the cases in which a motion is spoken of as essentially circular, then the apparent inconsistency might vanish as thoroughly as did any supposed unifying principle.

Now it appears to me that Galileo is pretty consistent in applying the idea of essential circularity to instances in which the motion is a "natural" one in his sense; that is, a motion induced by an innate tendency of the body to move when it is set free. The idea of essential rectilinearity, on the other hand, he applied most specifically to instances of "violent" motion—cannonballs and projectiles thrown by slings. One may say that even in this he is not entirely consistent, for his long discussion of bodies that ought to be flung from the earth by its rotation is an apparent exception. Such bodies are not subjected to an external force, yet they are treated as projectiles from slings would be treated; that is, as potentially moving along the tangent in a straight line. Whether the exception is real or apparent may be argued. Galileo's question was how such objects would move if they moved at all, and that question he treated on the analogy of the sling, or wheel, adding that the central tendency, lacking in the latter, prevented detachment from the earth.

In short, I doubt on the one hand that Galileo had a unifying principle in this matter, and on the other hand that he was vague and inconsistent about it. On one point he was quite definite and consistent, though we have made it hard for ourselves to see this. Tangible terrestrial objects subject to observation, to which an external impulse was imparted either by a straight push or by release from whirling, conserved the received impetus in the form of uniform rectilinear motion. Stated several times in the *Dialogue,* usually together with the idea of composition of independent motions, this conception was applied again in the *Two New Sciences,* and it was understood and adopted by Galileo's pupils and successors. He seems to me to be equally consistent in attributing essential circularity to terrestrial objects in "natural" motion only, where it happens that an observer could not actually distinguish the tangential from a very slightly arcal path.

It remains a question whether Galileo had an ulterior purpose if he made the distinction suggested above, and whether it had anything to do with a belief on his part about the planetary orbits. It seems to me not unlikely that he did have a reason, but one that had nothing to do with any cosmology. This reason was that for Galileo, heavy bodies on or near the earth strove by an innate tendency to reach its center (or rather, to reach the common center of gravity of all such bodies); and this they would never reach by the parabolic trajectories implied by rectilinear inertia, though they would reach it along a suitably chosen circular arc.[25] In other words, violent motion could be permitted to disturb natural order, while natural motion could not. If Galileo took such a view, his seeming vacillation between inertia and "circular inertia" in the *Dialogue* would be reasonably explicable without recourse to a unifying principle on the one hand, or the charge of inconsistency on the other.

Galileo's cosmological speculations, which occur almost entirely near the beginning of the *Dialogue,* are usually interpreted as evidence that Galileo believed in an extension of "circular inertia" to the planets. It has already been pointed out that, taken literally, this not only implies an extraordinarily poor knowledge on his part of the actual planetary orbits and the speeds of planets in them, but also contradicts various statements and denials of his own. In the preceding study I have set forth my view concerning the motivation for Galileo's cosmological speculations, giving attention to their polemic value in the *Dialogue* and remarking on the absence of similar passages in Galileo's voluminous correspondence. The fascination with circles that Koyré makes fundamental to the understanding of Galileo's physics is not evidenced by lifelong metaphysical speculations—as is, for example, Kepler's fascination with musical harmonies in the universe.

It is also worth pointing out that in the *Dialogue* itself, Galileo ridicules the Peripatetic insistence on a mathematical perfection of sphericity for the heavenly bodies,[26] and he cheerfully admits that perhaps no perfectly spherical body can be formed of actual matter.[27] This, for Galileo, does not invalidate mathematical reasoning about physics; it merely cautions the calculator to adjust his accounts as necessary.[28] Such things militate against the belief that Galileo was spellbound by circular perfection.

It is in that light, I think, that we should interpret such cosmological statements as: "I therefore conclude that only circular motion can naturally suit bodies which are integral parts of the universe as constituted in the best arrangement."[29] Koyré and his followers (indeed, some of his critics as well) want us to believe that this proves Galileo to have believed in his heart that absolutely perfect uniform circular motions carried the planets around the sun. Taken literally, this would require him to have been alone among all the astronomers after Aristotle to believe that all observed positions of the planets were compatible with a single set of uniform rotations about a fixed center. For in the passage just cited, Galileo does not say "circular motions," as if to allow epicyclic paths made up of combined circular motions; he requires "circular motion" to preserve order.

Against the prevailing view, which would make Galileo ignorant or scornful of actual observation, we may read his phrase "circular motion" as meaning no more than "circulation"; that is, recurrent motion over a closed path. That is perfectly consistent with his manner of arriving at the proposition, which is deduced from the orderliness of the cosmos. It is also consistent with his customary good sense and with his obvious motive in the First Day, which was to prepare a basis for attributing to the earth a circulation about the sun.

The impropriety of Koyré's thesis as a basis for judging Galileo's beliefs about planetary motions seems to me to be conclusively shown by Galileo's mature rejection of the quest for causes in physics—the very attitude for which Descartes most criticized Galileo. To offer "sympathy," "antipathy," or any other occult quality in explanation of a physical effect was repugnant to Galileo. It was this kind of "causation" that he criticized in Kepler's theory of the tides. In the *Dialogue* he reproved Simplicio for offering "gravity" as a cause of the fall of bodies, in a passage that overtly rejected all purely verbal attempts to assign causes to planetary motions.[30] If the phrase "circular inertia" had existed at Galileo's time in the vague sense in which it is offered today as Galileo's own explanation of celestial motions, I cannot doubt that Galileo would have laughingly included it with the "informing spirits" and "guiding intelligences" that he ridiculed as explanations in this very passage.

It is fairly evident to me that Galileo did not offer a complete system of the universe. We need not construct one for him. It is a violation of Galileo's entire approach to physics to represent as his inner thought the completion of a system on the basis of a false principle of circular inertia—or any other unifying principle, true or false. None of his pupils or followers wrote a word to suggest that Galileo ever adhered to or taught such a doctrine; none of his critics noted and condemned "circular inertia" or praised it and condemned those passages in the *Dialogue* that clearly contradict it. If the term "circular inertia" had been presented to him and he had been asked whether that was his explanation of planetary motions, I think he would have replied:

> The introduction of such a phrase is in no way superior to the "influences" and other terms employed by philosophers as a cloak for the correct reply, which would be, "I do not know." That reply is as much more tolerable than the other, as candid honesty is more beautiful than deceitful duplicity.[31]

Notes to Essay 13

1. A. Koyré, *Etudes Galiléennes* (Paris, 1939; reprinted ed., 1966). Citations given below are to original edition; pages in reprint add ten to the number shown.
2. A detailed analysis is set forth in "Galileo Gleanings," XVI; see Bibliography.
3. *Dialogue*, pp. 164–67.
4. *Dialogue*, pp. 223–26.
5. *Dialogue*, p. 162.
6. *Dialogue*, p. 164.
7. *Dialogue*, pp. 22–23, 135–36, 227, 236.
8. Galileo's phrases are *va per terminare, vadia à terminare, andrebbe à terminar;* never *termina* or *terminerà.*
9. See note 1 above.
10. Koyré, *op. cit.,* pp. 195–96. Emphasis Koyré's.
11. Ibid., pp. 197–98.
12. Ibid., pp. 198–99.
13. *Controversy*, pp. 191–97, 279.
14. Koyré, *op. cit.,* p. 282.
15. *Dialogue*, p. 193.
16. *Dialogue*, p. 175.
17. *Dialogue*, pp. 196–203.
18. *Dialogue*, p. 142.
19. *Dialogue*, p. 148.
20. *Dialogue*, p. 191.
21. *Dialogue*, pp. 20–21, 29.
22. *Dialogue*, pp. 234–35.
23. *Dialogue*, pp. 33, 37, 319.
24. *Dialogue*, p. 453; cf. pp. 455–56 for Galileo's comments on the inadequacy of existing planetary theory.
25. *Opere*, XVII, 89–90; *Two New Sciences*, pp. 261–62.
26. *Dialogue*, pp. 80, 94.
27. *Dialogue*, pp. 208–9.
28. *Dialogue*, pp. 207–8.
29. *Dialogue*, p. 32.
30. *Dialogue*, pp. 234–35.
31. *Controversy*, p. 197.

Index